A FOOT IN THE DOOR

A FOOT IN THE DOOR

Dalit Women in Panchayati Raj in
Gujarat and Tamil Nadu

JAYSHREE P MANGUBHAI
ALOYSIUS IRUDAYAM SJ
EMMA SYDENHAM

zubaan

ZUBAAN
128 B Shahpur Jat, 1st Floor
New Delhi 110 049
Email: contact@zubaanbooks.com
Website: www.zubaanbooks.com

First published by Zubaan Publishers Pvt. Ltd. 2020

ISBN 978 93 85932 93 9

Zubaan is an independent feminist publishing house based in New Delhi with a strong academic and general list. It was set up as an imprint of India's first feminist publishing house, Kali for Women, and carries forward Kali's tradition of publishing world-quality books to high editorial and production standards. *Zubaan* means tongue, voice, language, speech in Hindustani. Zubaan publishes in the areas of the humanities, social sciences, as well as in fiction, general non-fiction, and books for children and young adults under its Young Zubaan imprint.

Typeset in Baskerville 11/13 by Jojy Philip
Printed at Raj Press, R-3 Inderpuri, New Delhi 110 012

CONTENTS

GLOSSARY

Adivasi	Tribal or indigenous person in India
Anganwadi	Crèche, nursery for babies and children
Atrocity	A non-legal term that, according to the Ministry of Home Affairs, implies offences under the Indian Penal Code perpetrated against scheduled castes and scheduled tribes by those not belonging to either community, where caste considerations are in fact the root cause of the crime even though caste consciousness may not be the immediate motive.
Backward caste	Caste position below forward castes in the ritualised social hierarchy
Benami	Elected political representative who functions as a proxy representative for another person/s and does not take independent political decisions
Block	Development sub-division of a district
Clerk	Term used unofficially to refer to a secretary of the village panchayat in Tamil Nadu
Commission	The fraudulent act of taking a sum or percentage of public panchayat funds as 'payment' to panchayat members for approving the implementation of a development project.

Dalit	Literally meaning 'broken people', a term employed by rights activists to denote 'untouchables' or scheduled castes, the lowest group in the ritualised social hierarchy of the caste system, facing widespread discrimination on the basis of work and descent.
District collector	Administrative head of a district with quasi-judicial powers
District panchayat	Highest panchayat tier in each state, with jurisdiction over all the panchayats within said district
Dominant caste/s	Those castes, irrespective of any religious affiliation, which are socially, politically and economically dominant from the perspective of Dalits. In most cases, everyone who is not a Dalit or Adivasi in a village or town is dominant vis-à-vis Dalits.
First information report	First report recorded by police of a crime
Forward caste	All 'high' castes that are not classified by the Government of India as backward caste, scheduled caste or scheduled tribe
Goonda	Thug or rowdy
Gram mitra	Village volunteers who are paid to assist in different communities
Gram sabha	Formal assembly of all citizens in a village panchayat jurisdiction
Hindutva	Right-wing ideology promoting Hindu nationalism
Katta panchayat	Traditional village panchayat (Tamil Nadu)
Lakh	1,00,000

Union panchayat	Intermediate panchayat tier, also known as a block panchayat, comprising a group of village panchayats in Tamil Nadu
Panchayati Raj	Formal local self-governance system in India
Patta	Land title
Petty shop	Small goods shop
Poromboke land	Uncultivated government wasteland (in Tamil Nadu)
Purdah	Gender norm prevalent in Gujarat, wherein women are supposed to cover their heads with their saris in public spaces or even at home when in front of male family members
Reservations	Quotas for Dalits allowing for increased representation in education, government jobs and political bodies
Revenue divisional officer	Revenue head of a division within a district with quasi-judicial powers
Safai karamchari	Sweeper or cleaner
Sangha, sangham	Association
Sarpanch	Elected president of a village panchayat in Gujarat
Scheduled caste	Official terminology used to denote communities listed by the Ministry of Social Justice and Empowerment as those castes characterised by extreme social, educational and economic backwardness arising out of the traditional practice of untouchability, for the purposes of accessing special development, protection and affirmative action schemes

Talati	Term used to refer to a secretary of the village panchayat in Gujarat
Taluk, taluka	Revenue sub-division of a district
Taluka panchayat	Intermediate panchayat tier comprising group of village panchayats in Gujarat
Tahsildar	Revenue officer of a taluk/tahsil
Traditional village panchayat	Also known as caste panchayats, referring to the traditional gathering of village elders/leaders of either one caste group, or all dominant caste groups, or all caste groups in a village, to arbitrate on village disputes
Village panchayat	Council of formally elected representatives of a village or group of villages

Note: The report uniformly adopts the term president, vice president and member to denote the head, deputy head and member of a panchayat, regardless of the panchayat tier or state-specific terminology – in Gujarat, the village panchayat head and deputy head are the sarpanch and upa (deputy) sarpanch respectively, and the head and deputy head of the higher level panchayats are the president and vice president respectively; while in Tamil Nadu, the village panchayat head and deputy head are the president and vice president respectively, and the head and deputy head of the higher level panchayats are the chairperson and vice chairperson respectively.

ABBREVIATIONS

BC	Backward caste
BDO	Block development officer
BPL	Below poverty line
CEDAW	*Convention on the Elimination of All Forms of Discrimination against Women 1979*
DDO	District development officer
FC	Forward caste
FIR	First information report
ICCPR	*International Covenant on Civil and Political Rights 1966*
ICERD	*Convention on the Elimination of All Forms of Racial Discrimination 1965*
IC-FR	*Indian Constitution 1949, Fundamental Rights*
IPC	*Indian Penal Code 1860*
MLA	Member of the Legislative Assembly (lower house of Parliament in a state)
MP	Member of Parliament (national government)
NCSCST	National Commission for Scheduled Castes and Scheduled Tribes
NGO	Non-governmental organisation
NHRC	National Human Rights Commission
OBC	Other backward class
PCR Act	*Protection of Civil Rights Act 1955*
RDO	Revenue divisional officer
SC	Scheduled castes, official term used for Dalit communities

SC/ST (PA) Act	*Scheduled Castes/Scheduled Tribes (Prevention of Atrocities) Act 1989*
SC/ST (PA) Rules	*Scheduled Castes/Scheduled Tribes (Prevention of Atrocities) Rules 1995*
SHG	Self-help group
ST	Scheduled tribes, official term used for Adivasi communities
TDO	Taluka development officer
VAO	Village administration officer

1

INTRODUCTION

Societies in which women are excluded from public life and decision-making cannot be described as democratic. The concept of democracy will have real and dynamic meaning and lasting effect only when political decision-making is shared by women and men and takes equal account of the interests of both...
Para 14, CEDAW General Recommendation 23

The government should not stop with saying that the Dalits too have political power and rights; it should help to execute the same. Only then can the hindrances from political parties and the dominant caste system be removed ... The government should keep a watchful eye on whether the elected Dalit women or men are actually ruling. As Dalits are not much educated and have no outside contacts, they have to depend on others. Hence, there should be constant monitoring and political guidance.
Kamachi, village panchayat president,
Coimbatore district, Tamil Nadu

Dalit[1] women are one of the most marginalised communities in India. Historically, Dalits have been excluded from recognition, and the enjoyment of a broad spectrum of social, economic, cultural, civil and political rights. Despite Dalit women (along with their male counterparts) constituting a sizeable social group in India, they continue to experience significant discrimination and 'untouchability' practices arising out of the caste system. This discrimination includes social exclusion and a lack of access to land ownership, meaningful political participation and free employment.

Within the Dalit community, Dalit women suffer greater vulnerability due to the multiple and intersecting factors of their caste, class and gender. "Indian women continue to remain oppressed and struggle over everything from survival to resources…despite the liberal provisions of the Constitution and various laws, serious inequalities remain."[2] When combined with caste, the results manifest in lower education and health levels, lack of political voice, fewer employment opportunities and wages, a denial of access to and control over resources to meet their fundamental needs, and significantly increased experiences of violence and impunity. Dalit women are denied the capacity to exercise control over their lives, the lives of their communities, and their future. As Mukopadhyay states, "Ethnicity [caste] and gender have created a virtual situation of apartheid in which access to justice and to equal citizenship remain unattainable for the majority."[3]

While questions of caste discrimination, untouchability and violence have been discussed and documented in relation to Dalits as a group, there is very little concrete data or research analysing the specific experiences of Dalit women. This book investigates Dalit women's levels of access to and enjoyment of political participation in Panchayati Raj, as protected by internationally and nationally accepted human rights standards, in the two states of Gujarat and Tamil Nadu. It examines the internal and external factors and structures which facilitate or inhibit Dalit women's access to, participation in, and impact on Panchayati Raj, as well as the role of various state institutions in both supporting and limiting the right to political participation. The book further explores whether the political participation of Dalit women has led to increased attention on critical livelihood needs of Dalit women and Dalits in general, and if so, whether this increase in attention leads to improved outcomes. Finally, it examines any impact of Dalit women's political participation on caste and gender relations and its potential as a tool to transform power relationships.

While this research was conducted in 2007–2008, a review of recent studies, and discussions with community leaders across India confirm that little has changed, and that the outcomes of this study remain equally valid and critical to promote. In fact, in some jurisdictions like Rajasthan and Haryana, Bharatiya Janata

Party (BJP) governments have introduced legislative amendments that impose regressive conditions for contesting elections, and effectively deprive an overwhelming majority of citizens of the right to contest an election.[4] The extent of this exclusion in relation to Dalit women is more than 80 per cent. The conditions include things like educational qualifications, a failure to repay loans taken from cooperative societies, electricity bill arrears and not having a *pucca* functional toilet at one's residence.[5] This highlights the ongoing hostility to the inclusion of Dalits within local governance and the need for evidence-informed advocacy to mobilise change.

This chapter introduces the normative framework of the right to political participation and its implementation in India. It briefly sets out the premise that decentralisation has powerful potential as a tool for empowerment and social change for Dalit women, and explores how accessible local political power is for Dalit women. It also outlines the legislative and political context for the right to political participation in India. It then explores the local governance context for the operation of Panchayati Raj in Gujarat and Tamil Nadu, the two states of focus in this research. Finally, it explores the socio-economic context of Dalit women in Gujarat and Tamil Nadu, and considers how the functioning and specific limitations of Panchayati Raj itself factor into Dalit women's ability to access, participate and create impact in panchayat institutions.

What is the Right to Political Participation?

OVERVIEW

Article 21 of the *Universal Declaration of Human Rights* states that everyone has the right to take part in the government of her/his country. The right to political participation is also included in specific human rights treaties, including Article 25 of the *International Covenant on Civil and Political Rights 1966 (ICCPR)*, Article 5(c) of the *International Convention on the Elimination of All Forms of Discrimination 1965 (ICERD)*, and Article 7 of the *Convention on the Elimination of All Forms of Discrimination Against Women 1979*

(CEDAW). Indian national law builds on this to oblige the Indian state to ensure Dalit women's effective enjoyment of the right to political participation[6] without discrimination on the grounds of sex, caste or otherwise.[7] The state is obligated to ensure equality between all women and men in their political participation, as well as equality across caste lines.

The human right to political participation recognises everyone's right to be elected to government through genuine periodic elections and to take direct part in the conduct of public affairs. Political participation is not simply the right to access positions of authority (election to office), but also the assumption of all responsibilities and powers incumbent in that role. It encapsulates the process of standing for election, election to office, the performance of all public functions, and participation in agenda setting and decision-making associated with the elected post. Importantly, for Panchayati Raj institutions this includes active, free and meaningful participation in panchayat meetings and administration as well as influence over local development outcomes.

The human right to political participation also guarantees genuine, free and periodic elections. Persons entitled to vote must be free to vote for any candidate in an election without undue influence or coercion of any kind. This right requires a state to take measures to ensure that elections are conducted in this manner, that those standing for election are genuine representatives, that no coercion is enforced upon citizens in the exercise of their right to vote and that there are effective redressal mechanisms where these rights violations do occur.

This research focuses on one element of the right to political participation: the right to be elected to public office. It does not look at the other two basic entitlements: (a) to participate in public affairs by voting, engagement with elected representatives or independent mobilisation, demonstration or debate; and (b) to have equal access to positions in public service. This is because direct participation in the conduct of public affairs is considered to have the most impact in terms of decision-making and direction over the conduct of public affairs, and focuses attention on the public dimension of representation.

STATE OBLIGATIONS

The right to political participation creates a set of obligations on the state to respect, protect and fulfil this right.

Respect: The state must not take any action that has a negative impact on the ability of a Dalit woman to exercise her right to be elected to local government and to take direct part in the conduct of public affairs at this level. This requires the state to take active steps to protect Dalit women against violations of the right, as well as to provide an enabling environment to ensure that the right can be realised. This occurs through a combination of social, economic, political and legal arrangements, including enacting and enforcing legislation that prescribes that all women and all Dalits are eligible for election to all publicly elected bodies, entitled to hold public office and exercise all public functions, on equal terms with men and other castes without any discrimination.[8]

Protect: The state is required to protect an individual's right to stand for office and to effectively hold office against any prohibited conduct from third parties. This may concern, for example, enforcing appropriate laws to prevent third parties, including powerful employers or local leaders, from violating Dalit women's rights; but also includes taking appropriate measures to ensure that organisations such as political parties do not discriminate against Dalit women, and respect their right to political participation.[9]

Fulfil: The state must take positive steps to cultivate and support an environment conducive to Dalit women's equal access to and enjoyment of their right to political participation. The obligation to fulfil requires measures by the state to identify marginalised and disadvantaged groups and to design, allocate resources to, and implement policies and programmes to ensure their equal access to and enjoyment of the right to stand for elections and freely execute their duties in office. It demands remedial measures to counter prejudice and ensure equal access to and enjoyment of all human rights and fundamental freedoms to all persons. This may include temporary special measures to ensure the equal representation of women in government.[10] Various effective temporary strategies that states have implemented include recruiting, financially assisting and training women candidates, amending electoral procedures, developing campaigns directed at equal participation and setting numerical goals and quotas.[11]

Finally, the state also has an obligation to provide access to an effective remedy for any violation of the right to political participation. This requires ensuring the availability of and subsequent opportunity for Dalit women to access adequate redress for violations of their rights before a court of law, as well as appropriate and accessible administrative mechanisms. They must be able to hold the government accountable for its responsibilities, claim appropriate remedy for breaches, and bring to account other offenders in breach of the law.

RELATED HUMAN RIGHTS

Human rights are indivisible and interrelated. The fulfilment of the right to political participation is dependent on the realisation of a host of other rights; and, conversely, its realisation is a major enabling right for the fulfilment of other human rights. In any discussion of the right to political participation, equality and non-discrimination are clearly central. Participation and accountability are also vital components. Dalit women should be included in the development and implementation of government policies and plans to ensure their equal access to and enjoyment of the right to political participation.

DECENTRALISATION AND THE RIGHT TO POLITICAL PARTICIPATION

It is essential to involve women in public life to take advantage of their contribution, to assure their interests are protected and to fulfil the guarantee that the enjoyment of human rights is for all people regardless of gender. Women's full participation is essential not only for their empowerment but also for the advancement of society as a whole.

Para 17, CEDAW General Recommendation 23

Inclusive democracy, referring to the equitable representation of all social groups and particularly marginalised groups in governance, is intrinsic to strengthening democratic values and politics for more representative, participatory and accountable governance for development. Participation in governance lies at the heart of democracy: all citizens have a basic right and opportunity to contribute to public decision-making, to vote and to be elected. This is critical to the ability to influence decisions that impact our lives and the lives of our families, and to shape the societies we live in. People's political participation is central to effective, efficient and equitable development.[12] Only through such participation can women and men of all backgrounds fully exercise their human rights and achieve substantive equality. From this premise, it is argued that the decentralisation of power in governance, where policy and decision-making move closer to local communities, has the potential to improve access to rights.

This is a primary reason for choosing local governance as the focus of this research on the right to political participation. The introduction of reservations in local governance in India for women and Dalits, and the redevelopment of a stronger system of local governance as a primary means of local development, transparency, responsive and representative democracy is also key. Further, local governance is judged to be the most accessible political space for women, given their current reproductive and productive responsibilities within and outside the household and socially circumscribed freedom of movement in public spaces. It enables women to contribute to important local development decisions and increase their social, economic and political status, potentially also challenging stereotypes concerning their reproductive and productive roles. Local political institutions also are viewed as most likely to encourage women's participation due to their direct role in delivering public services and development programmes that have a day-to-day impact on women's lives. Moreover, there is significant evidence today of the greater orientation of local governance to daily household needs where there is female leadership. These needs include issues of water, sanitation, health and education.[13]

Participation in public decision-making processes is a recognised and powerful tool that helps increase the voice, power and status of the marginalised: essentially "people's power is the only mechanism by which they can articulate, protect and promote their interests".[14] Many argue that the marginalisation of women in the political process, and governance in general, has in fact been both the cause and effect of the slow progress made in the advancement of women.[15] The potential of decentralisation in governance with regard to empowering women has, to varying degrees, been demonstrated worldwide, as well as increasingly in relation to women in Panchayati Raj in India.[16] Tawari, for example, highlights that: "[t]he 73rd amendment [Reservations for local Panchayati Raj]... has been the most effective formal step towards political empowerment of women."[17]

Empowerment is a process whereby the constraints that impede equal participation are reduced so that inequality starts moving towards becoming equality. A focus on empowerment places Dalit women's interests and development needs at the centre, addressing power imbalances in both the public and private spheres. Empowerment emphasises transforming power from a zero-sum relationship of control, or 'power over', as exercised by dominant social actors over the women. Power in relation to women's agency is exercised in more positive, enabling ways: as 'power to', uncovering the potential of every woman to shape her life; and as 'power within', realising women's self-worth and capacities. At a more tangible level, 'power with', or associational activity – organising and engaging in collaborative action with others – is imperative in order to successfully challenge caste and gender hierarchies and engender governance and development at the broader collective level.[18]

The extent to which decentralisation in governance succeeds in achieving increased voice, empowerment and assertion of human rights of the marginalised, however, is not so clear. Constructing a decentralised system of government alone is insufficient: "The basic premise of decentralisation that government is brought closer to people and therefore is more responsive to real peoples' needs and interests is undermined without strategies to mobilise 'voice' of subordinate groups in society, and the forging of institutionalised spaces for participation and accountability".[19]

Another limiting issue concerns the underlying culture of corruption, patronage, patriarchy and non-accountability, which limits the realisation of potential local governance benefits. "Without proper accountability to central government, local councils can slip into bad habits: diversion of funds, corrupt allocation of local contracts, manipulation of elections, biased appointments and other forms of favouritism, all involving discrimination and lack of accountability to their local constituencies. The result will be a further disempowerment of local communities and disadvantaged social groups."[20] This is illustrated by Saxena: "Panchayats are more concerned with consolidating economic and social power with few leaders, often from elite groups. Rather than using the democratic process to change inequitable rural societies, gram panchayats function more or less as "political" bodies, i.e., organisations dealing with power, and development funds are used to consolidate that power."[21]

In this case, rather than investing greater power in communities and more marginalised groups, decentralised governance can in fact elevate traditional local elites historically associated with human rights abuses. These elites can manipulate the situation to seize power again at the expense of marginalised communities. This risk is exacerbated by the fact that the distribution of power and authority is often more hierarchical and embedded in local social structures. It has been shown that traditional or customary panchayats in India act as 'gatekeepers' in controlling nominations to elections in general, with a particularly powerful and damaging influence on women's participation in local governance.[22]

Thus, while instituting local governance holds potential for initiating and supporting change in the power inequalities that exist in society, many factors interrelate to determine whether it in fact meets this potential. The local governance reforms in India and their implementation must be examined to determine the extent to which they have supported and realised their potential to empower Dalit women to claim their legal right to participate in decision-making, and thereby benefit from the allocation of resources, and expand space for the attainment of Dalit rights.

Legal and Political Context for the Right to Political Participation

LEGISLATIVE AND POLICY FRAMEWORK

Community-based management of local affairs has been a common feature throughout India's history. Post-Independence saw a constitutional provision directing state governments to set up local governance institutions or panchayats at the village level. Decentralisation was seen as a means to ensure the basic needs of rural India and achieve distributive justice. India recognised and developed comprehensive laws and policies to guarantee the right to political participation, as well as to redress the discrimination that Dalit women face in accessing and participating in local governance.

Until the early 1990s, the participation of women and Dalits at all levels of governance was merely symbolic. There were female members and state laws prescribing at least one or two seats for women. However, representatives were largely nominated, were from elite dominant castes, and belonged to politically active and wealthy families: "as symbols of tokenism, they rarely took active interest in the functioning of Panchayati Raj institutions."[23]

In 1992, India enacted the *73rd (Rural Panchayats)* and *74th (Urban Nagarpalikas) Constitutional Amendment Acts* to decentralise power, strengthen participation in public decision-making and support those excluded and discriminated against in reclaiming their social, economic and political position in society. These Acts establish a formal three-tiered structure of decentralised governance in India with special affirmative action provisions (reservations) for Scheduled Castes and Tribes, women, and specifically Scheduled Caste and Scheduled Tribe women, "significantly widening the democratic base of the Indian polity".[24]

Democratic elections are to be held every five years for all panchayat members and village panchayat presidents/sarpanchs, while indirect elections apply for president/chairperson positions at the intermediate (taluka/union/block) and district levels. The establishment of State Finance Commissions and State Election Commissions serve to promote financial devolution and regularise democratic elections respectively. Measures to establish the three tiers of panchayats as institutions of self-government include conferring power and authority to prepare and implement plans for economic development and social justice in 29 political, social and economic areas under the Eleventh Schedule in the Indian Constitution: including agriculture, rural housing, drinking water, education, health and sanitation, poverty alleviation, pubic distribution system, women and child development, and the welfare of Scheduled Castes (SCs) and Scheduled Tribes (STs). Further discretionary powers are given to state governments as regards the composition of panchayats, devolution of powers to panchayats to impose taxes and raise funds, and audits of panchayat accounts.

The provision for multiple reserved quotas (affirmative action) in both member and chairperson positions in all panchayat tiers was another critical provision towards an inclusive democracy. Seats are reserved for SCs and STs in proportion to their population in each state, within which a minimum of one-third seats are reserved for SC/ST women;[25] a minimum of one-third of all panchayat seats are reserved for women in general; and provision is made for states to enact legislation reserving seats for 'other backward classes'. At least 20 states now have legislation that requires 50 per cent reservation of their seats in these bodies for women.[26]

The amendments triggered immense change in local governance in India. The response from women was overwhelming and after the first elections women representatives in excess of one million were appointed to rural and urban Panchayati Raj institutions. In Gujarat, at the time of this research, there were 36,400 women and 7,615 Dalits elected at the village level, 1,394 women and 297 Dalits elected at the taluka level and 274 women and 58 Dalits elected at the district level.[27] In Tamil Nadu, at the time of this research, there were 36,824 women and 22,156 Dalits elected at the village level, 2,313 women and 1,358 Dalits at union level, and 227 women and 139 Dalits at the district level.[28] Today there are 43,670 women elected representatives to panchayats in Gujarat, making up 32.9 per cent of all elected representatives. Similarly, in Tamil Nadu the 39,975 women elected representatives to panchayats form 33.5 per cent of all elected representatives.[29] In terms of SC elected representatives, in 2013 there were 8,340 in Gujarat (7.0 per cent of total representatives) and 28,655 in Tamil Nadu (24.0 per cent of total representatives).[30] The Supreme Court in *K. Krishnamurthy (Dr.)* vs. *Union of India* (2010) upheld the constitutional validity of reserved posts for women in panchayats as promoting substantive equality rather than formal equality pertaining to political participation at the grassroots level. Embedded within reservations is the impetus for dominant social groups to slowly begin to accept the principle of an inclusive polity, wherein Dalits and women have a political voice and influence over development decisions.

India has also made legislative efforts to redress discrimination and exclusion against both women and the Dalits in general. The Indian Constitution guarantees non-discrimination on the basis of caste and gender *(Article 15(1))* and the right to life and security of life *(Article 21)*. A constitutional directive specifically enjoins the Indian state to protect Dalits from social injustice and all forms of exploitation *(Article 46)*. There are also a series of laws protecting the rights of Dalits and women that acknowledge the prevalence of discrimination, violence and atrocities against these sections of society, including in the realm of political participation.

In general, India has established a strong legal basis for the full realisation of Dalit women's right to political participation in local governance, with unprecedented affirmative action provisions to redress historical marginalisation. The number of Dalit women elected under the new system is, in effect, a significant development in human rights in itself. This research, however, concerns itself with the extent to which policies at the local governance level have been effective in redressing the caste and gender-based discrimination and exclusion experienced by Dalit women.

PANCHAYATI RAJ INSTITUTIONS IN GUJARAT AND TAMIL NADU

Panchayati Raj in Gujarat: Soon after the formation of the state of Gujarat in 1960, panchayats were statutorily constituted under the *Gujarat Panchayats Act 1961* at the village, taluka and district level. Reservations for SCs and STs were in proportion to their population in the panchayat area, with a minimum guarantee of one seat each, and two to three seats were allotted to women at each panchayat tier. All development programmes were channelled through these bodies initially, with a transfer of resources and the devolution of powers, functions and authority. Out of the three tiers, the village panchayat was given the important functions and powers, while the district panchayat played a significant role with its supervisory and executive powers. After a period of strong growth, the developmental role of panchayats began to decline around 1976. This was closely followed by the introduction of decentralised development planning in Gujarat in 1980 through new District Development Boards that had the resources to implement government development schemes. The trend from this point onward has been towards greater reliance by panchayats on the state government for finances and development schemes.

From the outset, party politics pervaded the Gujarat panchayats, shaped primarily by the Indian National Congress (Congress party), and the Janata Dal which was replaced later by the BJP. The creation of local political party units as support structures for state units aided this process, and has meant that panchayats are dominated by the political party in power.

The *Gujarat Panchayats Act 1993,* enacted in line with the *73rd Constitutional Amendment Act,* sets forth once more a three-tier panchayat system with the *zilla* (district) panchayats holding supervisory and executive powers, the taluka panchayats undertaking supervisory and linking functions, and the *gram* (village) panchayats implementing development schemes. Reservations for SCs and STs in both member and sarpanch/president posts in all three tiers are in proportion to their populations in the panchayat area, with one-third of these seats reserved for SC and ST women. General reservations for women amount to one-third of all panchayat seats, and there are additional reservations on 10 per cent of seats for socio-economically backward classes (SEBCs). Currently, there are 33 district panchayats, 248 taluka panchayats and 14,292 village panchayats in the state.[31]

Reserved seats rotate with every election. This has been criticised on a number of grounds, in particular because many first-time Dalit and women panchayat sarpanchs/presidents need a longer time to build up adequate leadership skills and responsiveness to their constituencies, and the rapid rotation of reserved seats weakens their authority. Other criticisms focus on the fact that the same person is unlikely to be able to contest and win a second term once a seat is de-reserved, and that a single-term quota leaves the reserved seats open to greater manipulation by dominant caste male or family interests.[32]

An important feature of the Gujarat Panchayati Raj system since 1975 is the mandatory creation of Social Justice Committees (SJCs) at all panchayat levels, functioning to secure social justice for the 'weaker sections of society', including SCs and STs. All five committee members, selected by and from the panchayat body, are to be SC and ST members, unless there are insufficient numbers in the panchayat body. Serving a five-year term, the SJCs are charged with, among other things: framing, managing and implementing schemes and providing socio-economic facilities for the weaker sections of the community; investigating cases of injustice to and discrimination against the weaker sections and reporting these to the authorities; and promoting social and moral welfare, including the removal of untouchability practices. Importantly, any failure by the panchayats to improve the conditions of the weaker sections of society or to remove untouchability practices would be penalised by withholding government grants. The decisions of the SJCs are to be treated as panchayat resolutions.

In reality, however, SJC members exercise delegated powers only, and their decisions can be overridden by a panchayat resolution as dominant castes constitute a majority in most panchayats. Many SJC members in practice have no knowledge of the development schemes available, nor of their roles, functions and powers. Hence, while they have the power to decide what schemes, plans and projects should go to the Dalits, this rarely happens in reality. In fact, many of these committees remain on paper only. There is also no coordination between the activities of SJCs at each of the three levels.[33]

Gujarat also has a special system, *Samras Gram Yojana*, where substantial financial incentives and informal priorities for project approvals are given to village panchayats that select consensus candidates rather than hold elections.[34] In 2016, 1,467 (14.3 per cent) of the total 10,279 village panchayats did not conduct elections.[35] There are strong grounds to suggest that this system undermines democracy and leaves power structures unchanged, favouring traditionally powerful communities at the expense of the vulnerable.[36]

The state government also exercises control by appointing its officers – taluka development officers (TDOs) and district development officers (DDOs) – as administrative and executive authorities, and ex-officio secretaries of the taluka and district panchayats respectively, without bringing them under the control of the taluka or district panchayat presidents. By contrast, the *talati*-cum-secretary at the village panchayat level is accountable to the village panchayat sarpanch, who exercises power over the financial and executive administration of the panchayat. It is important to note though that the DDOs have the power to suspend village panchayat sarpanchs, further skewing the balance of power in favour of the state government.

Panchayati Raj in Tamil Nadu: The *Madras Panchayats Act 1958* established a three-tier Panchayati Raj system providing reservations for SCs, and stipulated that one woman be co-opted into each panchayat where none were elected. The panchayat unions at the intermediate level were primarily charged with planning and development, while the district panchayats formed a coordinating and advisory body with district government officials. While significant progress was made by the panchayats in some development areas under a bureaucracy-run governance arrangement, by the mid-1960s progress slowed, and from 1970

to 1986 the state government signalled its unwillingness to devolve
political power by continuously stalling panchayat elections.

Re-establishing the state's three-tier Panchayati Raj system,
the *Tamil Nadu Panchayati Raj Act 1994* complies with all mandatory
73rd Constitutional Amendment Act provisions. Linkages are established
between all three panchayat tiers, with one-fifth of village
panchayat presidents and union panchayat chairpersons within a
district elected as members of the union and district panchayats
respectively. Reservations for women are for half of the panchayat
positions, while reservations for SCs and STs are in proportion
to their population. The reserved seats rotate every two election
periods (i.e. ten years). District Planning Committees, chaired by
the District Collector, are also formed to consolidate development
plans of all lower panchayat tiers into one plan for each district.

The Tamil Nadu government, however, has not fully devolved
funds and administrative functionaries for any of the stipulated
29 development areas under the Eleventh Schedule of the
Constitution. Instead, the government has delegated supervision
and monitoring powers over the 29 areas to the panchayats.
Planning and implementation remains with the government
schemes for rural development.[37]

Autonomy for the panchayats is further reduced by the lack of
panchayat supervision over state development officials – the block
development officers (BDOs) and district development officers
(DDOs, also known as the assistant directors of panchayats).
Thus, a highly bureaucratised panchayat system operates in Tamil
Nadu, with strong control exercised mainly by BDOs and DDOs.
Further, the District Collectors retain discretionary powers to
dissolve village panchayats and remove panchayat presidents/
chairpersons.[38]

In recent election rounds, the majority of panchayats have
been formed along political party lines, with the ruling party
of the time controlling the panchayats. While elections to the
higher two panchayat tiers are held on a political party basis,
party politics are also slowly making their way into the village
panchayats. Caste-based contests and tensions have joined party
politics as a rising factor in panchayat elections. Since 1996, when

the state government identified about 2,250 panchayats in which the post of president would be reserved for SCs, dominant castes have mounted resistance and protests in many parts of the state. Around 120 SC reserved panchayat posts are reported to have been auctioned for large sums of money by dominant castes during the 2001 elections in order to retain political power over these panchayats.[39] Caste tensions were most manifest during the 2001 elections, with 96 SC reserved seats remaining vacant, over half reserved for Dalit women.[40]

Currently there are 31 district panchayats, 385 panchayat unions and 12,523 village panchayats in Tamil Nadu.[41] The village panchayats have several mandatory and discretionary functions related to maintaining basic services, including the provision and maintenance of village roads, lighting, drainage, village sanitation and a supply of drinking water, but these panchayats have insufficient finances and technical or support staff. The village panchayat presidents hold executive powers to decide on development resolutions, carry those resolutions into effect, and sign on all cheques. The panchayat unions likewise have several functions to perform within their administrative areas – the provision and maintenance of public roads, comprehensive water supply schemes, dispensaries, maternity and child welfare centres and elementary schools. However, they find it difficult to fulfil their functions with only State Finance Commission grants, though they have adequate staff. The district panchayats have a purely advisory and monitoring role: they advise the government on all matters of rural development and monitor the progress of the implementation of development schemes by the lower panchayat tiers.[42] The result is that while people have high expectations of efficient service delivery from a local government, the resources mobilised through taxes and other sources of income cannot meet these demands, especially concerning basic amenities.

PANCHAYATI RAJ IN PRACTICE

Effective implementation of reservations within Panchayati Raj institutions requires more than law and policy-based change, but rather, a major overhaul of administrative and social structures[43]

and a great depth of commitment and conviction.[44] The extent
to which this has happened has been highly questioned, and of
course varies across the Indian states. As Teltumbde notes,

> The rhetoric of decentralisation of power or eulogy to panchayati
> raj, without a conscious attempt to dampen the structural
> propensity under which power and domination play out in
> rural India, just amounts to encouraging rural élites to establish
> and maintain control over subordinate groups. A plethora of
> literature on panchayati raj suggests that formal regulations
> stipulating the participation of people like dalits and women have
> had minimal impact on the functioning of the panchayats. There
> is also evidence, albeit in limited cases, that decentralisation has
> helped these groups to make their presence felt in local political
> institutions. This implies that when they are empowered and
> made democratic, panchayats can act as agents of social change.[45]

One common critique of Panchayati Raj institutions has been
the reluctance of both central and state government political elites
to effectively devolve powers, functions, funds and functionaries
to the panchayats, and thereby lose powers of patronage and
influence.[46] The independent annual panchayat reports published
by the Union Ministry of Panchayati Raj have also recognised
this, concluding in 2007 that it was difficult to say that panchayats
had evolved into institutions of self-governance as the control
of functions, functionaries and funds still remained substantially
with state governments.[47] More recently, in 2012, the Ministry
recognised that devolution varied widely among states and, in
a continued attempt to promote devolution, it established an
annual system of evaluation, presenting awards to those who used
devolved authority in an exceptional manner.[48] The Rajiv Gandhi
Panchayat Sashaktikaran Abhiyan was also implemented in the
12th five-year plan (2012–17) to address the major constraints of
an inadequate devolution of power, lack of manpower, inadequate
infrastructure and limited capacity in the effective functioning
of panchayats.[49]

Limited devolution of power has ensured that panchayats remain
apparent development agents of state bureaucracy rather than self-
governing institutions for local development. As Aiyar observes,

The Indian experience of the last six decades would appear to confirm that bureaucratic delivery mechanisms absorb a disproportionately high share of the earmarked expenditure... between 75% and 85% of expenditure on poverty alleviation schemes is absorbed by the delivery mechanism itself. No wonder outcomes are so derisory... In the absence of inclusive governance, the people at the grassroots, that is, the intended beneficiaries of poverty alleviation programmes, are left abjectly dependent on a bureaucratic delivery mechanism over which they have no effective control. The alternative system would be participatory development, or Panchayat Raj, where the people themselves are enabled to build their own future through elected representatives responsible to the local community and, therefore, responsive to their needs.[50]

There is some evidence of a shift, with the BJP government recently accepting the recommendations of the 14th Finance Commission and providing grants to the tune of ₹2,00,292 crore between 2015 and 2020 to gram panchayats directly, and also releasing the allocations to rural local bodies this year. This amount is three times higher than in the period between 2010 and 2015.[51]

The ability of Dalit women to access and use the powers of Panchayati Raj has also been deeply questioned. Implementation struggles arise for both access to and participation in Panchayati Raj. In terms of access, the Committee on the Elimination of Racial Discrimination noted major concerns: "Dalit candidates, especially women, are frequently forcibly prevented from standing for election or, if elected, forced to resign from village councils or other elected bodies or not to exercise their mandate, that many Dalits are not included in electoral rolls or otherwise denied the right to vote, and that public service posts reserved for SCs and STs are almost exclusively filled in the lowest category (e.g. sweepers)."[52]

The main reason for this discord is that *de jure* affirmative action policies run up against huge hurdles in *de facto* implementation. As explored throughout this book, problems arise at the levels of political inclusiveness and responsiveness in Indian society. Specifically, Dalit women experience the outcome of severely imbalanced social, economic and political power equations in the form of numerous obstructions, including pervasive caste-class-gender discrimination and violence, when accessing and participating in local governance. Justice Anand attributes the persistent marginalisation and exploitation of Dalits, as well as the atrocities committed against them, to the indifference of society and refusal on its part to change its mindset, the lopsided implementation of the *SC/ST (Prevention of Atrocities) Act 1989*, and the lack of political will in addressing the historical injustices faced by this section of society.[53] The experiences of Dalit women are at the core of this research, for they are both confirmed and exacerbated by the impunity enjoyed by both state and non-state actors following acts of obstruction, especially discrimination or violence.

Election to power is only the first step – there are three levels of the quality of political participation: passive participation, active participation and decision-making participation.[54] Figures regarding the numbers of political representatives do not reveal how many women actually command decision-making power to influence decisions and outcomes in their elected posts. The Committee on the Elimination of Discrimination against Women has said that, "[w]hile democratic systems have improved women's opportunities for involvement in political life, the many economic, social and cultural barriers they continue to face have seriously limited their participation."[55] In addition to these continual and debilitating struggles against patriarchy, Dalit women experience multiple forms of untouchability and caste discrimination that too often prevent them from effectively carrying out their duties as elected representatives. They are also often pressurised to act as *benamis* or proxy candidates for their male counterparts as well as dominant caste men, and experience physical, verbal and sexual violence and intimidation to prevent them from both accessing and participating in local governance.[56]

The few studies that have been conducted on Dalit women in local governance suggest that while women have assumed formal positions of authority, the power associated with that position has largely not been transferred: formal representation in itself has not led to decision-making power.[57] The *State of Panchayats*

Report 2008–09, an independent assessment done by the Institute of Rural Management Anand, reported that about 59 per cent of elected SC/ST women were proxy representatives.[58] This is a common finding concerning non-Dalit female and Dalit male panchayat representatives as well.[59] Studies of the village panchayats in Orissa found, for example, that women entered politics through a mandatory provision of reservation, due to persuasion by their family or pressure from the village community, and that "[i]n most cases the women representatives are ignored and they are invariably influenced by family members".[60]

A 2012 survey on women's empowerment, commissioned by the Ministry of Panchayati Raj, covered village panchayats in 23 states and a sample of over 20,000 people, with three quarters of the women coming from SC, ST and OBC categories. The survey had some telling results:

- 52.4 per cent of sarpanchs had attended a panchayat meeting during their term.
- 31.9 per cent of sarpanchs had chaired the panchayat meeting.
- 35.3 per cent of sarpanchs had called a meeting during the term.
- 18.5 per cent indicated that they played a significant role in the distribution of development schemes.
- 72 per cent of SC/STs indicated an internal reason for poor participation in the panchayat, including their proxy status, fear, low self-confidence, lack of knowledge, and compliance to traditional caste and gender roles. This was 22.9 per cent for all women.
- 34.2 per cent of SC/ST women indicated that officials promptly acted on their requests or complaints. This was 40.8 per cent for all women.[61]
- 36.8 per cent of SC/STs indicated that officials supported them in implementing schemes. When it came to women in general, this number was 40.8 per cent.

The author of the study concluded that "[i]n many cases because of lack of availability of forums and lack of proper grievance redressal mechanism for gender related issues, most women elected representatives in panchayats have very minor role in decision making and mostly they are dummy".[62] The study did highlight, however, that 58 per cent of women representatives are now taking their own decisions to contest elections. This is a significant achievement. Similarly, the survey highlighted that women are prioritizing developmental needs that seem to be more pressing from their perspective, such as bringing in piped water and building schools.[63]

Another author comments: "The more active role of women in [the] village often contributes to the welfare of the entire community and several important areas which were neglected earlier now get prioritised. Thus, it is in the interests of not just women but the entire village community to encourage the further empowerment of women in village affairs."[64]

Similarly, a 2014 case study of Karimganj district in Assam found that SC and ST women were being pressured to stand for election by their husbands, sons, other male members of the family, village leaders or political parties.[65] Only 16.25 per cent indicated self-motivation behind participation in the panchayat.[66] While 52 per cent did confirm that they speak in gram sabha meetings, only 30 per cent of them make decisions. The author noted that: "[t]he violence of caste war in some regions dominates the participation of women in Panchayati Raj institutions elections. Societal restrictions, traditional concepts on women, women get setback in participation... Women want to work for the society, express and raise their points and views in the panchayat meetings. But very often they fail to do so."[67] As another author concludes: "The stranglehold of the caste structure...has resulted into a paradoxical situation, where, on the one hand, Panchayati Raj Act provides de jure powers to the office of the chairpersons at different levels and, on the other, de facto, they remain bereft of these powers."[68]

Evidence suggests that non-state actors, particularly socio-politically powerful dominant caste men with vested economic and political interests, exert control over Panchayati Raj institutions, thereby preserving the inequitable social, economic and political status quo. These non-state actors often are aided by the district administration and local police's failure to enforce laws that protect Dalit women's right to political participation and to enable their exercise of meaningful political power for the development of their communities. As a result, Dalit women too often remain silent voices in local governance, leaving other more powerful social groups to capture a majority of the development benefits that accrue through local governance institutions.

This element of impunity in fact appears to be one of the key structural issues confronting Dalit women in accessing and participating in local governance. There is much evidence to suggest that India continues to fail in its duty to protect Dalit women from violations of their right to political participation by persons such as dominant caste villagers, local leaders, other panchayat members, husbands and families. Forcing the women into benami positions, evicting women presidents through no confidence motions, and refusing to recognise their authority and thereby precluding them from fulfilling their functions are some prominent examples of practices found through the course of this research. Local political party leaders and cadres, for instance, can also wield a significant influence over and marginalise Dalit women, despite the prohibition on party-based village panchayat elections. Local government officials and police are also directly responsible for violations of Dalit women's right to political participation and their right to redress before the law. The National Human Rights Commission's *Report on Prevention of Atrocities against Scheduled Castes* details in-depth evidence of impunity from an array of sources.[69]

Socio-Economic Context of Dalit Women

> [We must not] be content with mere political democracy. We must make our political democracy a social democracy as well. Political democracy cannot last unless there lies at the base of it social democracy... We must begin by acknowledging the fact that there is complete absence of two things in Indian society. One of these is equality. On the social plane, we have in India a society based on the principle of graded inequality which means elevation for some and degradation for others. On the economic plane, we have a society in which there are some who have immense wealth as against many who live in abject poverty. On [enacting the Constitution], we are going to enter into a life

of contradictions. In politics we will have equality and in social and economic
life we will have inequality... How long shall we continue to live this life of
contradictions? How long shall we continue to deny equality in our social and
economic life? If we continue to deny it for long, we will do so only by putting
our political democracy in peril.
                              Dr B.R. Ambedkar, Third Reading of the Draft
                                                    Indian Constitution, 1949

Any assessment of Dalit women's enjoyment of their right to
political participation in Panchayati Raj cannot be separated from
the socio-economic and political context in which these women
are situated. This is because viewing political participation
as an entitlement, and the corresponding state obligation to
ensure the right to political participation without discrimination,
requires attention to be paid to two things simultaneously: (a)
the legal processes that seek to guarantee rights, and (b) the
social, economic and political processes embodied in formal and
informal institutions.

The context for Dalit women is a power structure that
entrenches gender, caste and class discrimination and poses
significant hurdles to the enjoyment of equal rights in governance
and development. This creates systemic social, economic and
political discrimination and deprivation, as well as the devaluation
of social identity. The result is a circumscription of Dalit women's
rights, freedoms and opportunities, with implications for how they
access and enjoy their right to political participation.

DALIT WOMEN IN GUJARAT AND TAMIL NADU

Gujarat and Tamil Nadu are interesting states to analyse in terms
of their relative development and differing Dalit populations.
While the SC population in Gujarat is merely 6.7 per cent of
the state population, Tamil Nadu has the fifth largest Dalit
population in the country with SCs forming 20.0 per cent of the
state population. Most SC women reside in rural areas in both
states: 56.3 per cent in Gujarat and 65.5 per cent Tamil Nadu.[70]
Despite their relative development, however, a gender disparity
remains: the gender disparity index for Gujarat is 0.624 and for

Tamil Nadu is 0.655.[71] Meanwhile, the sex ratio is much lower in Gujarat (931) as compared to Tamil Nadu (1,004).[72] The socio-economic and political context for Dalit women in Gujarat and Tamil Nadu varies.

Poverty: The development levels in both states are reflected in their lower poverty rates as compared to the national average. However, higher incidences of poverty still persist among SCs as compared to the non-Scheduled Caste/ Scheduled Tribe (non-SC/ST) population within each state. In rural areas, the SC poverty rate is 21.8 for Gujarat and 31.2 for Tamil Nadu, while for non-SCs/STs the rate is 19.1 and 22.9 respectively.[73]

Land ownership: The poor economic status of rural Dalit women is further reflected in their lack of ownership of land combined with their concentration in wage labour. Of the total SC rural households, only 25.2 per cent in Gujarat and 15.5 per cent in Tamil Nadu own any land. These figures can be compared with land ownership for households in general, which stands at 49.4 per cent in Gujarat and 28.2 per cent in Tamil Nadu.[74]

Labour: The additional significance of low levels of land ownership combined with poverty is that the majority of Dalit women eke out their livelihood by engaging in wage-labour occupations in the unorganised sector. This sector is synonymous with low wages, a lack of assets to buffer against risk factors, and economic dependence on dominant castes. SC women's contribution as a significant workforce in each state's economy is revealed through their work participation rates (23.1 per cent for Gujarat and 39.6 per cent for Tamil Nadu) as compared with women in general (23.4 per cent in Gujarat and 31.8 per cent in Tamil Nadu). Most of these SC women are main workers (62.4 per cent in Gujarat and 74.3 per cent in Tamil Nadu), that is, they work for six months or more per year.

Moreover, the overwhelming majority of SC women, both main and marginal (working for less than six months per year) workers, are concentrated in the unorganised sector as agricultural labourers (53.1 per cent in Gujarat and 61.4 per cent in Tamil Nadu), with less than 10 per cent cultivating land (6.4 per cent in Gujarat and 6.4 per cent in Tamil Nadu). An even smaller per cent are household industry workers (2.5 per cent in Gujarat and 3.0 per cent in Tamil Nadu), while the remainder are engaged in other occupations (38.0 per cent in Gujarat and 29.2 per cent in Tamil Nadu). Note that all these official figures do not take into account the numerous other forms of non-remunerative work Dalit women engage in as part of their livelihood, such as cattle rearing, minor produce collection and sales, and so on.

By comparison, main and marginal non-SC female workers in these states are generally less concentrated in the unorganised sector, with fewer women agricultural labourers (47.1 per cent in Gujarat and 41.6 per cent in Tamil Nadu) and more women engaged in the cultivation of their lands (17.8 per cent in Gujarat and 13.2 per cent in Tamil Nadu).[75] This indicates the higher economic status of other caste women in general.

Education: The educational status of Dalit women in these states, measured by their literacy rates (69.9 per cent for Gujarati SC women and 65.6 per cent for Tamil SC women) is also better than the national average for Dalit women (56.5 per cent). However, SC women still lag far behind their male counterparts in literacy: literacy rates for SC men in Gujarat are 87.9 per cent and in Tamil Nadu 80.9 per cent. When it comes to a comparison between Dalit women and women in general, the literacy rate in Gujarat is almost equal (69.7 per cent for women in general), while a significant gap remains in Tamil Nadu (73.4 per cent for women in general).[76]

Health: A combination of poverty and sub-standard living conditions results in Dalit women being prevented from enjoying their right to health on par with the non-SC/ST population. Dalit women's poorer health standards can be seen in their lower nutritional status as compared to non-SC/ST women: 29.2 per cent of SC women in Gujarat and 17.5 per cent in Tamil Nadu have a body mass index of less than 18.5 kg/m^2 as compared to an average of 23.2 per cent for non-SC/ST women in Gujarat and 11.9 per cent in Tamil Nadu. Further, in both states, SC women generally consume less food than non-SC/ST women. Consequently, 57.0 per cent of SC women in Gujarat and 58.0 per cent in Tamil Nadu are moderately to severely anaemic, as compared to an average 53.3 per cent of non-SC/ST women in Gujarat and 54.7 per cent in Tamil Nadu.[77]

Atrocities: In the absence of comprehensive gender-and-caste disaggregated data on violence against Dalit women, crimes against SCs serve as an indication of prevailing trends. This is because, as Indian government representatives acknowledged during the hearing of India's initial report under the *Convention on the Elimination of all Forms of Discrimination against Women 1979*, it is Dalit women who bear the brunt of caste-based atrocities.[78] In 2016, a reported 1,322 crimes were committed against SCs in Gujarat, ranking the state fifth in the country in terms of crimes against SCs. For Tamil Nadu that year, a total of 1,291 reported crimes placed it fifteenth in the country in terms of crimes against SCs.[79] To be noted is the large number of cases of violence against Dalit women which go unreported each year. This suggests that the violence targetting these women may be much more prevalent than official statistics indicate.[80]

The fact that a large percentage of reported cases were investigated and a final report true submitted, or charge sheeted for trial, reveals that the majority of atrocity cases are seen as genuine and requiring referral to courts of law for adjudication. In Gujarat, of the 1,304 crimes against SCs where police completed investigation in 2016, 94.5 per cent of cases saw police charge sheet the cases for trial. Similarly, that year in Tamil Nadu, of the 1,291 crimes against SCs where police completed investigation, they prepared charge sheets for trial in 78.3 per cent of the cases.[81]

However, of the 480 cases of crimes against SCs in Gujarat disposed of by the courts that year, only 4.6 per cent ended in convictions. Likewise, of the 982 cases of crimes against SCs in Tamil Nadu for which trials were completed that year, only 7.7 per cent ended in convictions. Contrast this with the court disposal of cases of crimes committed under the *Indian Penal Code*, where the conviction rate stood at 35.1 per cent in Gujarat and 58.6 per cent in Tamil Nadu, and it becomes clear that the conviction rate for crimes against SCs remains abysmally low in both states.[82]

Political situation: In the absence of disaggregated data on the presence of Dalit women in the state assemblies, an overall picture can be drawn from the proportion of SCs and women in state assemblies. In Gujarat SCs represent 7.1 per cent and in Tamil Nadu 18.7 per cent of the state legislature.[83] However, Gujarati women represent a mere 9 per cent of the state legislature, while Tamil women represent only 7 per cent of that state legislature.[84] Within these categories, the presence of Dalit women is minimal. This is partly because the politics operative in both states, as across the country today, are characterised by fragmentation along caste-class lines and the rise of caste-based parties that grant little political space to Dalits. This is compounded by a similar lack of political space granted to women, who have been traditionally confined to the domestic sphere of the family. The continuing debate over 33 per cent reservations for women in parliament and the languishing of a bill to this effect for many years bears testimony to the political resistance to gender inclusion in governance in the country.

In Gujarat, it is the dominant castes, particularly the forward caste (FC) Patels, Brahmins and Baniyas, who continue to dominate politics in the state. The two main political parties in the state, the Congress party (Cong. (I)) and the BJP, are headed mainly by FC Darbars and Patels. No Dalit political parties have emerged. The previous Congress government from 1975 tried to bring the 'backward castes-classes' together under the KHAM – Kshatriyas, Harijans, Adivasis and Muslims – strategy in order to challenge the power of the traditionally landed rural elites. By contrast, the BJP's entry into Gujarat politics in the 1980s has concentrated on bringing diverse castes together under its Hindutva platform. Local party units have become entrenched at the local level in which Dalits enjoy few leadership positions. The presence of Hindutva forces is strongest in Gujarat. Hindutva forces have engineered several anti-reservation riots in the state, as well as the 2002 mass violence targeting the Muslim community in which Dalits and Adivasis were co-opted into the violence.

By contrast, in Tamil Nadu, local Dravidian political parties – predominantly the Dravida Munnetra Kazhagam (DMK) and the All India Anna Dravida Munnetra Kazhagam (AIADMK) – have alternated power in the state in recent years. Both parties grew out of the rationalist and Dravidian movements in the state around the time of Indian Independence, which were anti-brahmanic and broke the hold of the four-*varna* system in Tamil Nadu. As a result, social groups in the state today can be roughly classified as Brahmin, non-Brahmin and Dalit. However, the *jati* system still prevails, with groups increasingly identifying with their caste groups over the broader category of non-Brahmin. Moreover, the rationalist and Dravidian movements failed over the years to integrate Dalits into the movement, breaking the hold of the landed Brahmin elites only to replace them with dominant backward caste elites and leave Dalits out of the process of land and power redistribution. The dynamics of Dravidian politics has also led to the rise of caste-based politics in which predominantly dominant backward castes jostle for political power by forming changing alliances to oppose specific groups on issues. While dominant castes dominate the two main political parties in the state and control their leadership, Dalit politics have evolved in reaction to the emergence of mass atrocities against Dalits and Dalit movements, increasingly mobilising along political lines from the 1990s. Consequently, today there are two main Dalit political parties in the state, the Viduthalai Chiruthaigal Katchi (Dalit Panthers of India or DPI) and the Puthiya Thamizhagam (PT). Their influence over state politics, however, remains limited.

Hence, the overall picture that emerges for Dalit women in Gujarat and Tamil Nadu reflects the general situation of Dalit women all over India: higher poverty levels than dominant castes, with a reduced enjoyment of rights in most spheres of life including land, labour, education, health, politics and security of life. Their socio-economic status impacts their political situation in terms of exclusion from political positions of power and authority, which means a lowered ability to negotiate for political spaces and resources to achieve socio-economic rights. It is for these reasons that Dalit women's participation in local governance becomes important, as a means of ensuring representative, participatory and accountable governance that will propel the development of these women and their community.

GENDER, CASTE AND CLASS IN GOVERNANCE

The socio-economic and political – including local governance – context of Dalit women in Gujarat and Tamil Nadu indicates the basic hurdles and rights deprivations Dalit women deal with in day-to-day life, and have to work with as elected representatives in the panchayats. Underlying these are the key structural factors of caste, class and gender, which also impact their access to and enjoyment of the right to political participation in local governance. The nature of this impact cannot be comprehended without first understanding the gendered nature of governance, the role of caste and class in governance, and the function of affirmative action via reserved quotas in laying a foundation for equitable political participation and social justice.

Gender in Governance: The gendered nature of governance institutions is characterised by male dominated social and political positions of power, as well as policies that disproportionately distribute resource entitlements and development benefits to men. A number of issues impact women's participation in governance, including the existing socio-political power structures that grant little space to women; women's devalued social identity; their disentitlement to social and material resources and power; and pervasive gender discriminatory norms that inform and are reinforced by political institutions. Women also often lack assets such as education, social capital, information networks and control over productive resources that are inputs into substantive political participation. Unequal participation in decision-making in the private sphere often replicates itself in a lack of familial and community support for women's freedom of voice in the public sphere.[85]

Given these factors, women are often unable to articulate their gender interests and needs in public decision-making fora. They lack control over the decision-making processes that provide opportunities for development. Moreover, the focus of governance discourse on public institutions arguably reinforces the public-private divide that forms the core of gendered power structures: it supports a socio-political construction that distinguishes and prioritises (male) political activities in the 'public sphere', while de-emphasising governance in the 'private sphere' where women are primarily located.[86] Thus, men appropriate the public sphere, while relegating the private sphere to women.

The creation of inclusive governance institutions, therefore, involves examining the process of women's participation as well as the achievement of gender equitable development and policy outcomes. Attention is placed on the legal and political processes that enable participation as well as the informal social institutions that dictate the 'legitimate' behaviour of women in the public domain. The category 'women' also has to be disaggregated in order to examine the extent to which promoting women's participation in governance entrenches or transforms interlinking biases such as caste or class. Inclusive governance further aims to produce policy outputs that will guarantee women's rights in both the public and private spheres, thereby collapsing this distinction in terms of women's right to development.[87] In this regard, institutionalising the participation of women at the local government level is considered the best means of ensuring equal political participation and more targeted development interventions benefiting them, as well as entrenching the rule of law locally.[88] These institutions should enable women to build political skills, motivation and experience in political decision-making, which might precipitate the expansion of their decision-making power in their families as well as aid in transforming discriminatory gender norms.

Caste-Class in Governance: In the Indian context, any discussion of gender in social relations and, by extension, in governance cannot be divorced from the consideration of two other interlinking structural factors: caste and class. Different Indian women are subordinated in different ways, with caste and class being key factors which intersect with gender. Moreover, the convergence of caste and class are commonly acknowledged because of the historically systemic discrimination against 'lower' caste groups, which continues to deny them economic and knowledge resources.[89] In other words, in a hierarchical society where the social structure is itself based on a social exclusion arising from caste inequality, caste becomes a key factor in understanding how marginalisation from economic, social and political spheres leads to poverty. This close class-caste nexus is evidenced in linkages between production relations and the ritual-based arrangement of social relations among caste groups. The brahmanical rationale for structuring society along hierarchical caste lines was to vest economic and political resources, power and social status with so-called 'pure' dominant castes, who appropriated the labour of the so-called 'impure', 'lower' castes in order to advance the former's interests. Hence, a system of graded inequality was created in which dominant castes were traditionally the landowning rural elite and political power holders.[90]

Dalits, in particular, were and continue to be denied rights and any economic and political mobility. The marginalisation of Dalits is manifested in a denial of rights to property, social justice and social protection, education, skills capacitation and healthcare, and participation in agenda setting for development. This ensures that Dalits do not secure basic livelihood needs, vital resources such as land and education and information and social networks that could aid their upward social mobility. Consequently, Dalits today continue to make up a substantial proportion of the poor in India, disproportionate to their population; they remain primarily labourers undertaking menial and 'polluted' tasks for the other castes. Their continued economic dependence on dominant castes allows traditional socio-political power structures to flourish. Moreover, discrimination and violence against Dalits are built into the social system in order to protect dominant caste economic and political interests. 'Untouchability', specifically, serves as a means to deny Dalits any political status, as in the case of panchayat governance, based on the argument that the Dalits' 'impure' status precludes any capacity to govern.[91] This is reinforced by the lack of supportive redressal mechanisms for discrimination and violence against Dalits in governance. Caste-class biases manifest themselves when state actors – government officials or police – collude with dominant caste perpetrators of discrimination and violence, or are themselves active obstructers to Dalits' political participation. The consequences are to frustrate justice and claims for political rights by Dalits.

India's modern democratic system of governance, therefore, rests upon a social system in which caste, kinship and community relationships are given high value; and where the exercise of power on behalf, and for the benefit, of one's caste group is expected.[92] As such, dominant caste political institutions, formal and informal, and caste patronage networks of dependence and power co-exist with a formal governance system based on impartial standards and rules of enforcement. This pattern is further evidenced in political parties, most of which, barring emergent political parties of 'lower' castes, are under dominant caste male leadership. Where elections are run along party lines, as at national and state levels and the higher tiers of the panchayats, candidates are often selected by these political party leaders on the basis of caste factors, patronage networks, political contacts and monetary power.[93] A fundamental contradiction thus arises in the *de jure* intention that all social groups equally participate in governance and reap development benefits, and the *de facto* political power vested in and retained by select groups (dominant castes) over others, including Dalits. In other words, structural changes in political leadership from traditional caste-class-gender based patterns have not yet occurred to any substantial degree.

DEMOCRATISING GOVERNANCE THROUGH AFFIRMATIVE ACTION

Overall, therefore, a starting point to democratise the caste, class and gender bases of governance is to guarantee entry into governance institutions for politically marginalised groups such as Dalits and women. One rights-based tool for this purpose is legal affirmative action quotas or reservations. Reservations are seen as particularly necessary given the rigid functioning of the patriarchal caste system, and allocation of economic and political resources to exclude Dalits and women from political power.[94] The premise is that ensuring the adequate representation of socially marginalised Dalits and women in political institutions such as panchayats will change the nature and functioning of these (dominant caste) male-dominated institutions. This change to a more enabling political environment for these groups should encourage more equitable planning and development policies and processes, thereby bringing Dalits and women from the peripheries of human development to the centre.

Moreover, reservations are said to be a key element in empowerment, improving the political awareness of these groups and creating a stronger perception of their right to a share in decision-making at the local level. Reservations also offer the potential over time for Dalits and women to gain the necessary political skills and self-confidence with which to challenge inequitable socio-economic and political power relations. For women as a group to exercise agency and voice, and to transform policies in male-dominated governance institutions, it is generally recognised that a 'critical mass' of at least one-third women in governance structures is essential.[95] In the case of Dalits, reserved quotas in proportion to their population strength aim to ensure their proportionate representation in governance. Importantly, affirmative action has the potential to catalyse social change by offering opportunities for Dalits and women to mobilise around rights issues.[96]

Entrenching formal political participation through reserved quotas, however, is arguably insufficient to restructure power relations and resources, and achieve substantive equality for marginalised social groups. Most commentators also point to the need for wider state-sponsored structural reforms in social (caste-class-gender) and economic relations to equalise these bases of power. This would build the capacities of marginalised social groups and women to freely access and participate in governance, and influence policy outcomes. For example, land reforms and the restructuring of production relations in rural areas are seen as vital to loosening traditional caste-class patronage networks and allowing political processes led by political parties to take precedence instead. Further action is then required to democratise political parties and political competition in the country, to make parties more broadly representative of the country's diverse social groups and derive their legitimacy or power base from their ability to support the needs of socio-economically marginalised groups such as Dalits and women. This would secure more caste-and-gender equitable policy outcomes.[97]

Complementing legal affirmative action to facilitate the entry of Dalits and women into political institutions, supportive capacitation policies have to ensure their empowered participation and greater voice in political decision-making in order to transform policy decision-making. In addition, Dalits and women entering political institutions should be encouraged to establish and maintain their links to progressive social movements, in order for both internal and external pressures to be applied to ensure responsive development policies and accountable, democratic governance.[98] As a final point, political will, popular awareness and building of equitable traditions and norms underpinned by constitutional and legislative measures are seen as essential for any far reaching changes to be brought about in Indian society.[99]

Conclusion

With regard to Dalit women elected representatives, therefore, three questions arise. First, how can Dalit women's election to reserved political seats and their political participation be ensured without socio-political pressures or coercive caste and patriarchal patronage relationships? Secondly, how do legally created spaces that enable Dalit women's formal political representation lead to these women's empowerment in terms of increased agency and voice in development processes? Thirdly, how are these elected representatives able to generate more caste-and-gender responsive development outcomes and generate wider social change of caste and gender biases?

The reservation system is a major step forward, but is in itself insufficient. As Bryld states, "[t]he problem is that in the current design, reservation is not empowering. This is true not only of the reservation of seats for women, but of the reservations for Scheduled Castes as well."[100] Certain key issues emerge regarding the right to political participation for Dalit women and its implementation in India. While a strong legal and policy context exists, there is much evidence to suggest that political, social and economic realities render empowered political participation largely inaccessible to Dalit women.

The assumption of a reserved panchayat seat does not guarantee a Dalit woman control over resources, participation in decision-making and effective functioning as a leader. The political participation of Dalit women cannot be separated from women's assertion of civil rights: in particular, the right to equal protection under the law and the right to an effective remedy. Central to the struggle to realise the right to political participation is the challenge of overcoming impunity.

The realisation of the right to political participation for Dalit women, then, is indeed complex and taps into the pervasive power inequalities in caste, class and gender that are deeply woven into the fabric of Indian society. This highlights the need for a holistic government response. Such a response should build on the reservation policy with comprehensive policies and practices to surmount the immense social and cultural barriers that Dalit women face in order to participate meaningfully in the functioning of panchayats. The reservation policy, however, provides a useful starting point to realistically explore the potential for Dalit women to exercise political power in local governance and how this can be achieved. This is the focus of this research.

This book shares the results of research conducted with 200 Dalit women across Tamil Nadu and Gujarat on their experience in seeking access to and the ability to participate in Panchayati Raj through reservations. It seeks to better understand the determinants necessary for, or conducive to, effective access to and the enjoyment of political participation in Panchayati Raj. It identifies new trends in panchayat leadership emerging under the current system and explores the extent to which local governance is enabling a change in the stronghold of caste and gender in leadership posts.

This book includes the following chapters:

Chapter 2 describes the methodology adopted in this research.

Chapter 3 introduces the profile of the 200 Dalit women who participated in this study across the states of Gujarat and Tamil Nadu.

Chapter 4 – *Getting A Foot in the Door* explores women's access to political participation. It covers issues around the decision to contest panchayat posts, nominations, canvassing for support, financial costs, voting and entry into the panchayats.

Chapter 5 – *From Representation to Participation* explores women's decision-making powers in the exercise of their roles as elected representatives and any discrimination that they face. It unpacks the different domains of these powers, including meetings and interactions with government officials and other panchayat tiers.

Chapter 6 – *Impacting Development* focuses on Dalit women's ability to further positive development for the Dalit community within their electorate, the obstructions that they face in seeking to further these outcomes and strategies to enable Dalit women to deliver development outcomes.

Chapter 7 – *Impacting Social Relations* explores the extent to which Dalit women elected representatives in the panchayats were able to challenge and transform inequitable caste and gender norms. It examines what changes in caste and gender perceptions, behaviours and norms occurred because of the political participation of the Dalit women elected panchayat representatives that participated in this study.

Chapter 8 – *Addressing Obstructions in the Panchayats* details key aspects of Dalit women's experiences in seeking justice for obstructions faced in obtaining access to and participation in local governance. It assesses the extent to which the Indian state fulfils its duties to both prevent and respond to obstructions against Dalit women in the panchayats.

Notes

1. Note that the terms 'Dalit' and the legal term 'Scheduled Caste' are utilised interchangeably throughout this book.
2. Singh, A.P., *Women's Participation at Grassroot Level: An Analysis*, *Mainstream*, vol. XLVII, no. 12 (2009), p. 1.
3. Mukopadhyay, M., *Decentralisation and Gender Equity in South Asia: An issues paper* (Ottawa: Gender Unit, IDRC, 2005), p. 5.
4. Singh, I. *Haryana's Panchayati Raj. Excluding the Deprived*, Economic & Political Weekly, vol. II, no. 16 (2016), pp. 19-20.
5. Ibid.
6. Articles 325 & 326 *Constitution of India 1949* guarantee an equal right to participation in political activities and right to vote respectively.
7. Articles 14, 15 & 19 *Constitution of India* and the *Representation of the People Act 1951* provide for equal participation of women in the political process.
8. CEDAW Committee *General Recommendation No. 23*, supra note 17, para 41; Articles 2 & 3 *Convention on the Political Rights of Women*.
9. CEDAW Committee *General Recommendation No. 23*, supra note 17, para 42.
10. Articles 7 & 8 *CEDAW*; CEDAW Committee *General Recommendation No. 23*, supra note 17, paras 15 & 43. Articles 15(3) & 16(4A) *Indian Constitution* provide for affirmative action in favour of women and Dalits respectively.
11. Mukopadhyay, M., *Decentralisation and Gender Equity in South Asia: An issues paper* (Ottawa: Gender Unit, IDRC, 2005); Committee on the Elimination of Discrimination against Women, *General Recommendation 23, Political and Public Life* (Sixteenth session, 1997), U.N. Doc. A/52/38/Rev.1 at 61 (1997), para 15.
12. Nazrul Islam, M.D. and Sangita, S.N., "Decentralised governance and people's participation: Lessons from West Bengal", *ISEC Working Paper 131* (Bangalore: Institute for Social and Economic Change, 2003), p. 2.
13. Datta, B. (1998), in Baviskar, B.S., *Impact of Women's Participation in Local Governance in Rural India* (New Delhi: Institute of Social Sciences, South Asia Partnership Canada, International Development Research Centre, 2003), pp. 5-6.
14. Nazrul Islam and Sangita, supra note 12, p. 3.
15. United Nations Development Programme (ed), *Women's Political Participation and Good Governance: 21st Century Challenges* (New York: UNDP, 2000).

16. Baviskar, B.S., *Impact of Women's Participation in Local Governance in Rural India* (New Delhi: Institute of Social Sciences, South Asia Partnership Canada, International Development Research Centre, 2003), pp. 3, 6; Jain, D., "Panchayat Raj: Women Changing Governance", *Gender in Development Monograph Series No. 5* (New York: UNDP, 1996), p. 10.

17. Tiwari, N., *Women's Empowerment Survey: Women and Panchayati Raj*, YOJANA (June 2012), p. 40.

18. VeneKlasen, L. and Miller, V., *Power and Empowerment*, PLA Notes vol. 43 (2002), pp. 39-41, on p. 39.

19. Mukopadhyay, supra note 3, pp. 10-11.

20. International Council on Human Rights Policy, *Enhancing Access to Human Rights: Summary* (Versoix: ICHRP, 2004), p. 44.

21. Saxena, N.C., *Need for More Teeth to Panchayati Raj System*, Kurukshetra (November 2015), p. 1.

22. Ananth Pur, K., "Rivalry or Synergy? Formal and Informal Local Governance in Rural India", *IDS Working Paper No. 226* (Brighton: Institute of Development Studies, 2004).

23. Baviskar, B.S., *Impact of Women's Participation in Local Governance in Rural India*, paper presented at a conference – A Decade of Women's Empowerment through Local Government in India, 20-21 October 2003, New Delhi (New Delhi: Institute of Social Sciences, South Asia Partnership Canada, International Development Research Centre, 2003), p. 3. See also Dhaka, S. and Dhaka, R.S., *Behind the Veil: Dalit Women in Panchayati Raj* (New Delhi: Abhijeet, 2005), p. 148.

24. Mathew, 2002, quoted in International Council on Human Rights Policy, *Local Rule: Decentralisation and Human Rights* (Versoix: ICHRP, 2002), p. 19.

25. While no constitutional stipulation on one-third reservation of SC and ST president/chairperson seats for women exists, all states have legislated this further quota.

26. Nair, S., *NDA states stall 50 per cent quota for women in panchayat elections*, Indian Express, September 23, 2017, available at <<http://indianexpress.com/article/india/nda-states-stall-50-per-cent-quotas-for-women-in-panchayat-elections-4856903/>>, last accessed on 20.06.2018.

27. Ministry of Panchayati Raj, *The Status of Panchayati Raj: State profile – Gujarat, 2006-2007*, available at <<www.panchayat.nic.in/viewContentItem.do?View=viewItem&ptltid=357&itemid=3210&folderid=3185>>, last accessed on 08.12.2007.

28. Ministry of Panchayati Raj, *The Status of Panchayati Raj: State profile –
Tamil Nadu, 2006–2007*, available at <<www.panchayat.nic.in/
viewContentItem.do?View=viewItem&ptltid=357&itemid=3196&
folderid=3185>>, last accessed on 08.12.2007.

29. Ministry of Panchayati Raj, *State of Women in PRIs (2016)*, available
at <<https://www.panchayat.gov.in/documents/10198/384335/
Representation%20of%20Women%20in%20PRIs.pdf>>,
accessed on 21.02.2019.

30. Indian Institute of Public Administration and Ministry of Panchayati
Raj, *Strengthening of Panchayats in India: Comparing Devolution across States,
Empirical Assessment: 2012–13*, available at <<http://www.iipa.org.
in/upload/Panchayat_devolution_Index_Report_2012-13.pdf>>,
accessed on 08.09.2013; Ministry of Panchayati Raj and Indian
Institute of Public Administration, *Devolution to Panchayats in India:
Ranking Functional Environment at Sub-National Level*, (New Delhi:
Government of India, 2012).

31. Local Government Directory As per Consolidated Report of
Panchayats (2018-19), <<https://lgdirectory.gov.in>>, accessed on
24.02.2019.

32. Buch, N., "Panchayats and Women", in Matthew, G. (ed), *Status
of Panchayati Raj in the States and Union Territories of India 2000* (New
Delhi: Institute of Social Sciences & Concept Publishing Company,
2000); Bryld, E., "Increasing Participation in Democratic
Institutions through Decentralisation: Empowering Women and
Scheduled Castes and Tribes through Panchayati Raj in Rural
India", *Democratization* vol. 8, no. 3 (2001), pp. 149-172; Inbanathan,
A., "Affirmative Action and Dalits: Political Participation in
Panchayats", *ISEC Working Paper 138* (Bangalore: Institute for Social
and Economic Change, 2003).

33. Unnati, *Status of Panchayati Raj Institutions in Gujarat 1995–2000*
(Ahmedabad: Unnati, 2000); Sheth, P.N., "Gujarat", in Mathew,
G. (ed), *Status of Panchayati Raj in the States and Union Territories of
India 2000.* (New Delhi: Institute of Social Sciences & Concept
Publishing Company, 2000).

34. Guha, A., *Undermining Panchayati Raj Institutions in Gujarat*, Economic
& Political Weekly, vol. XLIX, no. 22 (2014), pp. 21-22.

35. Indian Express, "Gujarat: 1,467 gram panchayats go Samras, need
no elections", 16 December 2016, <<https://indianexpress.com/
article/cities/ahmedabad/gujarat-1467-gram-panchayats-go-
samras-need-no-elections-4429254/>>, accessed on 28.02.2019.

36. Guha, supra note 34, pp. 21-22; Mathew, G., *Elections in Gujarat: A dismal record of grassroots democracy*, PUCL Bulletin, September 2002.
37. See Aram M. and Palanithurai G., "Tamil Nadu", in Mathew, G. (ed), *Status of Panchayati Raj in the States and Union Territories of India 2000* (New Delhi: Institute of Social Sciences & Concept Publishing Company, 2000).
38. Interviews with Ossie Fernandes and M. Santhi Saraswathi, Human Rights Advocacy and Research Foundation (HRF) (Chennai, 21.03.2007).
39. Satish, K., Tamil Nadu presentation at regional seminar held on 13-14.12.2001, reported in Institute of Social Studies Trust (ISST), *Gender, Governance and Grama Sabha: Regional Seminar Report – Karnataka, Tamil Nadu and Andhra Pradesh* (Bangalore: ISST, 2001); see also Hindustan Times, "Auctioning of Panchayats", 29.09.2001.
40. Tamil Nadu State Election Commission, *2001 Panchayati Raj Election Results* (Chennai: Government of Tamil Nadu, 2001).
41. As per Local Government Directory, *Consolidated Report of Panchayats*, <<https://lgdirectory.gov.in>>, accessed on 24.02.2019.
42. Palanithurai G., *Status of Financial Devolution to Panchayats in Tamil Nadu* (Gandhigram: Rajiv Gandhi Chair for Panchayati Raj Studies, Gandhigram Rural Institute, 2004), p. 16.
43. Tiwari, supra note 17, p. 40; A.P. Singh, Women's Participation at Grassroot Level: An Analysis, Mainstream, vol. XLVII, no. 12, March 7, 2009, p. 1.
44. Venkat Reddy, M., *Has The Panchayati Raj Worked?*, Kurukshetra, January 2014, pp. 20-23.
45. Teltumbde, A. *India's (Jati) Panchayati Raj*, Economic & Political Weekly vol. XLVI, no. 36 (2011), p. 11.
46. Aiyar, Mani Shankar, "Inclusive Government for Inclusive Development: The History, Politics and Economics of Panchayat Raj", in Faguet, J.P. and C. Pöschl, C. (eds.), *Is Decentralization Good for Development? Perspectives from Academics and Policy Makers* (Oxford: Oxford University Press, 2015), p. 2; Saxena, supra note 21; Banerjee, R., *What Ails Panchayati Raj?*, Economic & Political Weekly, vol. XLVIII, no. 30 (2013), pp.173-176, on pp. 173; Ministry of Panchayati Raj, *Roadmap For The Panchayati Raj (2011–17): An All India Perspective*. (Delhi: Government of India, 2011), p. 5.
47. Government of India, "Annual State of the Panchayats Report 2007–2008", in Banerjee, supra note 46.

48. Ministry of Panchayati Raj, *Annual Report 2011–2012* (Delhi: Government of India, 2012), p. 2.
49. Ministry of Panchayati Raj, *Annual Report 2017–2018*. (Delhi: Government of India, 2018), p. 35.
50. Aiyar, supra note 46, p. 15.
51. Venkaiah Naidu, M., "True Panchayati Raj", *The Indian Express*, April 26, 2016, at <<https://indianexpress.com/article/opinion/columns/gram-swaraj-nda-government-panchayati-raj-narendra-modi-2770111/>>, accessed on 28.02. 2019.
52. CERD Committee, *Concluding Observations, Report of India*, UN Doc. CERD/C/IND/CO/19 (2007), para 17.
53. Saxena, K.B., *Report on Prevention of Atrocities against Scheduled Castes: Policy and Performance* (New Delhi: National Human Rights Commission, 2004), foreword by Dr. Justice A.S. Anand, Chairperson of the Commission.
54. Sharma, M., "Women's Participation in Gram Panchayats: A Study in Haryana", in Shiv Raj Singh et al. (eds.), *Public Administration in the New Millennium—Challenges and Prospects* (New Delhi: Anamika, 2003), p. 216.
55. CEDAW Committee *General Recommendation No. 23*, supra note 17, para 14.
56. Baviskar, supra note 16, pp. 6-7; Jayal, N.G., "Engendering Local Democracy: The Impact of Quotas for Women in India's Panchayats", *Democratization* vol. 13, no. 1 (2006), pp. 15-35, on p. 22.
57. Vijayalakshmi V. and Chandrashekar, B.K., "Gender Inequality, Differences and Identities: Women and Local Governance in Karnataka", *ISEC Working Paper 72* (Bangalore: Institute for Social and Economic Change, 2001); Vijayalakshmi V. and Chandrashekar, B.K., "Authority, Powerlessness and Dependence: Women and Political Participation", *ISEC Working Paper 106* (Bangalore: Institute for Social and Economic Change, 2003).
58. Pal, M., *Panchayati Raj in India: Deepening Grassroots democracy*, Kurukshetra, November 2015.
59. *Ibid*; also Vijayalakshmi V., "Gender Accountability and Political Representation in Local Government", *ISEC Working Paper 102* (Bangalore: Institute for Social and Economic Change, 2003).
60. Jaya Bharati, I., "50% Reservation of Women in Panchayats: A Step towards Gender Equity", *The Orissa Review*, Feb-March 2011, pp. 38-40, on pp. 39-30.

61. Tiwari, supra note 17, pp. 37-38.

62. *Ibid*, p. 40.

63. *Ibid*, p. 39.

64. Jaya Bharati, supra note 61, p. 40.

65. Das, S., *Women Participation in Panchayati Raj: A Case Study of Karimganj District of Assam*, International Journal of Humanities & Social Science Studies (IJHSSS) Volume I, Issue I (2014), pp. 52-58, on p. 54.

66. *Ibid*, p. 56.

67. *Ibid*, p. 54.

68. Pal, supra note 59, p. 3.

69. Saxena, supra note 54, p. 111.

70. Office of the Registrar General & Census Commissioner, *Census of India 2011* (New Delhi: Government of India, 2011).

71. Ministry for Women and Children Development, *Gender Human Development Indices: Recasting the Gender Development Index and Gender Empowerment Measure* (New Delhi: Government of India, 2009).

72. Office of the Registrar General & Census Commissioner, supra note 71. The sex ratio is the measure of the number of females per 1000 males.

73. National Planning Commission data 2004-05, reported in Planning Commission, *India Human Development Report 2011: Towards Social Inclusion* (New Delhi: Oxford University Press, 2011). Note that the all-India rural poverty ratio stood at 36.8 for SCs, and 28.3 for non-SC/STs.

74. Government of India, *Rural Labour Inquiry, Report of General Characteristics of Rural Labour Households 2004–05* (New Delhi: Government of India, 2011).

75. Office of the Registrar General & Census Commissioner, supra note 71. The work participation rate (WPR) is the percentage of main and marginal workers to the total population.

76. *Ibid*.

77. International Institute for Population Sciences, *National Family Health Survey (NFHS-4), 2015-16: Gujarat and Tamil Nadu* (Mumbai: IIPS, 2017).

78. Amnesty International, "The Battle against Fear and Discrimination: The Impact of Violence against Women in Uttar Pradesh and Rajasthan", *AI-Index: ASA 20/-10/2001* (London: Amnesty International, 2001), p. 12; see also Saxena, supra note 54, p. 161.

79. National Crimes Records Bureau (NCRB), *Crimes in India 2016 Report* (New Delhi: NCRB, 2017), Table 7A.1.
80. For example, Irudayam, A. et al, *Dalit Women Speak Out: Caste, Class and Gender Violence in India* (New Delhi: Zubaan, 2011), which revealed over two-thirds of incidents of violence against Dalit women did not reach the police.
81. NCRB, supra note 80, Table 7A.6.
82. NCRB, supra note 80, Table 18A.2.
83. Data obtained from <<http://www.gujaratassembly.gov.in/members/PDF%20Files/emembers14.pdf>>, accessed on 07.03.2019; <<http://www.assembly.tn.gov.in/15thassembly/members/201_234.html>>, accessed on 07.03.2019.
84. Association for Democratic Reforms, Women Representation among All MPs and MLAs (2012), available at <<https://adrindia.org/research-and-report/election-watch/combined-reports/2012/women-representation-among-all-mps-and-mlas>>, accessed 24.02.2019.
85. See Hamadeh-Banerjee, L., "Women's Agency in Governance", in United Nations Development Programme, *Women's Political Participation and Good Governance: 21st Century Challenge* (New York: UNDP, 2000).
86. Jayal, N.G., "Locating Gender in the Governance Discourse", in Human Development Resource Centre, *Essays on Gender and Governance* (New Delhi: UNDP, 2003).
87. Tambiah, Y., "The Impact of Gender Inequality on Governance", in Human Development Resource Centre, *Essays on Gender and Governance* (New Delhi: UNDP, 2003).
88. Webster, N., "Democracy, Development and the Institutionalised Participation of the Poor for Poverty Reduction", in Collins, P. (ed), *Applying Public Administration in Development: Guideposts to the Future* (Chichester: John Wiley & Sons Ltd, 2000).
89. J.V. Meenakshi et al, "Estimates of Poverty for SC, ST and Female-Headed Households", *Economic and Political Weekly* (29 July 2000), pp. 2748-2754; Verma, B.M., *Social Justice and Panchayati Raj* (New Delhi: Mittal Publications, 2002), pp. 216-17.
90. Irudayam, A. et al, Supra note 81, Chapter 1.
91. *Ibid.*
92. Kumar, N. and Rai, M., *Dalit Leadership in Panchayats: A Comparative Study of Four States* (New Delhi: Indian Institute of Dalit Studies & Rawat Publications, 2006).

93. Inbanathan, supra note 32.
94. *Ibid*, p. 23.
95. Hamadeh-Banerjee, supra note 86.
96. Manor, J., "Democratisation with Inclusion: Political Reforms and People's Empowerment at the Grassroots", *Background Paper for Human Development Report 2003* (New York: UNDP, 2002), p. 25.
97. Crook, R.C. and Sverrisson, A.S., "Decentralisation and Poverty-Alleviation in Developing Countries: A Comparative Analysis, or is West Bengal Unique?", *IDS Working Paper 130* (Brighton: Institute of Development Studies, 2001).
98. Basu, A., "Gender and Governance: Concepts and Contexts", in Human Development Resource Centre, *Essays on Gender and Governance* (New Delhi: UNDP, 2003).
99. Mathew, G. and Mathew, A., "India: Decentralisation and Local Governance – How Clientelism and Accountability Work", in Hadenius, A. (ed), *Decentralisation and Democratic Governance: Experiences from India, Bolivia and South Africa* (Stockholm: Almqvist and Wiksell International, 2003), p. 16.
100. Bryld, supra note 32, p. 162.

2

METHODOLOGY

This research aimed to provide specific data and case studies on Dalit women's participation in Panchayati Raj for all those working on issues of local governance in India and all those interested in empowering Dalit women to secure their rights. It sought to promote and strengthen advocacy at the local, state and national level to highlight the situation of Dalit women vis-à-vis their enjoyment of the right to political participation and interrelated rights, and to demand state accountability and appropriate state action to respect, protect and fulfil these rights. At the same time, given the dearth of research on the political rights of Dalit women, this research aimed to stimulate further academic and social activist research on Dalit women as a separate category within both the Dalit and women's social groupings.

This chapter sets out the objectives of the research, its scope, as well as the methodology adopted for data collection and analysis.

Research Objectives

The objectives of this research were to:

i. Generate systematic and reliable data on Dalit women's access to and enjoyment of their right to political participation in Panchayati Raj, and on the responsiveness of Dalit women elected panchayat representatives in addressing Dalit and/ or women's development needs and changing caste, class and gender power relations.

ii. Examine the internal and external factors which facilitate or inhibit Dalit women's access, participation and impact in Panchayati Raj.

iii. Assess the role of state institutions in both preventing and responding to cases of obstructions (including discrimination and violence) against Dalit women in Panchayati Raj, as per nationally and internationally accepted human rights standards.

Scope of Research

The research adopted a *human rights perspective* and focussed on Dalit women's access to and enjoyment of their right to political participation, and the impact of the enjoyment of political participation on socio-economic rights for Dalits and women. Accordingly, the three aspects focused on were: direct political participation as a core human right; the human rights needed to realise this right; and the rights that are accessible through the right to political participation.

This was *action research* examining the level to which Dalit women enjoyed their right to political participation, how this right had been violated, and what interventions should be made with appropriate state and civil society institutions to guarantee these women's right to political participation. The research report, therefore, was tailored towards this purpose, by providing an analysis of key aspects of access, participation and impact, and also highlighting both gaps and opportunities.

In terms of approach, the research drew out *Dalit women's experiences and perspectives* on participation in Panchayati Raj. It was, therefore, based primarily on data gathered from quantitative questionnaires, and qualitative case studies on and interviews with Dalit women.

Dalits are defined in this research by the criterion of the social practice of 'untouchability'. Thus, while the vast majority of the Dalit women who participated were Scheduled Caste (SC) in their legal identity, there were also a few Dalit Christians who are not legally SC. Nonetheless, Dalit Christians are very much 'untouchable', and therefore Dalit in their social identity, as defined by the communities in which they live.

The research was conducted in the two Indian states of Gujarat and Tamil Nadu. The choice of states was based on the following criteria:

i.   Broad geographical coverage of India: one state in the south (Tamil Nadu), one state in the north (Gujarat).

ii.   Duration and recent stability of Panchayati Raj in the state: both states established statutory Panchayati Raj institutions in the 1950s–60s, and have had regular panchayat elections since the *73rd* and *74th Constitutional Amendment Acts* in 1992 and the consequent enactment of their respective *Panchayati Raj Acts*.

iii. As both Gujarat and Tamil Nadu had held panchayat elections at the end of 2006, Dalit women's recent experiences of political participation could be recorded.

iv.   Dynamics of differing SC populations: while SC in Tamil Nadu comprise almost one-fifth of the state's population, making it one of the most Dalit populated states, in Gujarat SC comprise less than 10 per cent of the state's population.

v.   Both states have relatively high development levels, though development disparities remain between Dalit women and others. Furthermore, in both states Dalit women's literacy is higher than the national average for Dalit women. Both these factors are consistently mentioned in much of the panchayat literature as having an impact on participation levels.

vi.   Diverse political party leadership in the state: Tamil Nadu is governed by Dravidian parties, while Gujarat is governed by national parties.

vii. Lack of data generated on the research topic to date: both states have not produced any substantial research on Dalit women's experiences in Panchayati Raj.

viii. Contacts of the Indian coordinating researchers with Dalit organisations working with Dalit women in these states.

The research focused on *rural panchayats* at all three tiers – gram/ village, taluka/union and district, and within that, *constituencies reserved for women, scheduled castes and scheduled caste women* – all of which are available quotas for Dalit women. Rural panchayats were chosen because 80 per cent of Dalit women live in rural India. Moreover, untouchability practices, discrimination and violence are more prevalent and openly practised in rural India. The focus on only reserved seats, and not general seats, resulted from the need to interrogate two common assumptions regarding representation through quotas as institutionalised under the *73rd Constitutional Amendment Act*: that quotas will enhance the participation and development of marginalised social groups such as Dalit women and their community; and that their social, economic and political mobility and the empowerment arising from their new political status in the panchayats will decrease the discrimination and violence against them.

Data collection on Dalit women's experiences in Panchayati Raj was limited to the *two panchayat elections* of 2000/2001 and 2006 for both states. The limited timeframe helped Dalit women to more accurately recall experiences of accessing and/or enjoying their right to political participation in the panchayats, and to gauge the impact of their participation in the panchayats.

Research Team

The research was a collaboration between the Institute of Development Education, Action and Studies (IDEAS) in Madurai, South India and Equalinrights in The Hague, The Netherlands, and was part of the Dalit Research Programme of Justitia et Pax, The Netherlands. Jayshree Mangubhai, Human Rights Research Associate at IDEAS, Aloysius Irudayam SJ, Director, Department of Advocacy, Research and Human Rights Education at IDEAS, and Emma Sydenham, Coordinator of Equalinrights, coordinated the research at the national level (referred to herein as the coordinating researchers).

At the state level, two social activists from established Dalit organisations coordinated the fieldwork in their respective states:

Manjula Pradeep, Executive Director of Navsarjan Trust in
Gujarat and R. Thilagam, Programme Director at Evidence in
Tamil Nadu. Both organisations and coordinators were chosen
based on their work with Dalit communities across their respective
states and their working knowledge and experience of Panchayati
Raj functioning. This meant a capacity to translate the research
into concrete advocacy outcomes. Two junior researchers in each
state who were linked to or employed by these organisations, as
well as research associate Satyendra Kumar in Gujarat, aided the
state coordinators in operationalising the fieldwork.

Methodology

The research was conducted in the following stages from January
2007 to October 2008.

PREPARATORY PLANNING

Preparatory planning commenced with meetings between the
national and state-level coordinating researchers. Two-day
participatory planning consultations were then organised in
Gujarat and Tamil Nadu. The coordinating researchers, state
coordinators, junior researchers, some Dalit women panchayat
representatives, and members of civil society organisations working
on Panchayati Raj issues attended these consultations. Participants
discussed, clarified and finalised the research objectives, scope,
purpose, methodology and sampling, as well as issues related to
Dalit women's access to and participation in Panchayati Raj in
each state. Dalit women panchayat representatives also worked with
the researchers to suggest questions for the structured questionnaire.
   Following the consultations, the coordinating researchers
developed the questionnaires on political participation, one
for women who had attempted but failed to access panchayat
institutions, and another for women elected panchayat
representatives. Initial work on developing the indicators for
access, participation and development/social impact drew on
UN conventions, reports and general comments on the right to
political participation, as well as other literature on governance

and participation indicators. The questionnaires were formulated attempting to combine questions arising from these indicators with the questions drafted at the planning consultations.

SAMPLING CRITERIA

Fixed, non-probability sampling was used rather than random sampling because of the research focus on traditionally excluded Dalit women, its sensitive area of inquiry, local caste-class-gender power dynamics and consequent local logistical support requirements. Women were first approached to confirm their consent to discuss their political participation in the panchayats. In cases where women declined, other women were identified. Sampling criteria, therefore, was fixed so that within each state five districts were chosen: Ahmedabad, Anand, Kheda, Surendranagar and Vadodara districts in Gujarat, and Coimbatore, Cuddalore, Madurai, Nagapattinam and Thirunelveli districts in Tamil Nadu. The choice of districts was based on the following criteria, as ascertained through secondary sources and field experience:

i.   High Dalit population;
ii.   Low socio-economic development among Dalits;
iii. Dalit and gender atrocity-prone area;
iv.   High incidence of untouchability practices;
v.   High incidences of Dalit assertions; and
vi.   Areas where state coordinator's organisation or networks are working.

Within these districts, sampling objectivity and the representation of differences within Dalit women, as well as their diverse experiences of political participation, was sought through a sample of 100 Dalit women per state. This sample was based on the following interlinking criteria:

i.   Rural panchayats at all three levels: village (80 per cent), taluka/panchayat union (15 per cent) and district (5 per cent);
ii.   SC women (80 per cent), women (10 per cent) and SC (10 per cent) reserved constituencies;

iii. Dalit women sarpanchs/presidents/chairpersons (45 per
     cent) and panchayat members (25 per cent), as well as those
     women who have tried but not succeeded in accessing
     panchayat posts (30 per cent);

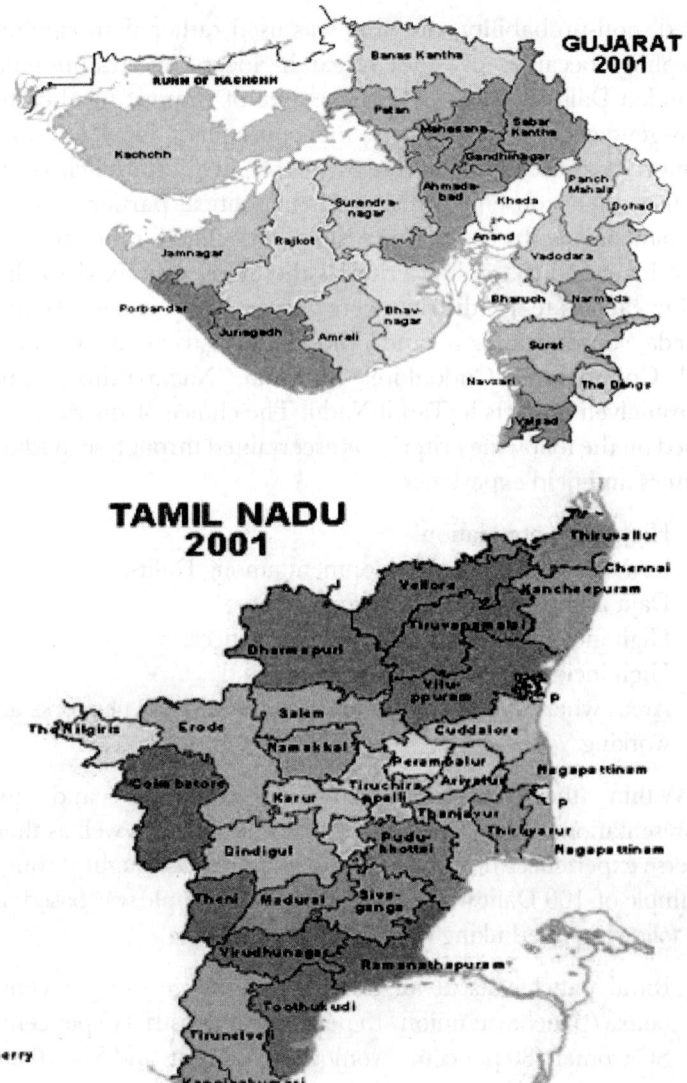

iv. Dalit women representatives elected in 2000–01 (70 per cent) and in 2006 (30 per cent);

v. Range of representation on social development indicators such as sub-caste, class/social status including leadership roles in community, educational attainment and land ownership;

vi. Differing positive and negative experiences in the panchayats, to be able to examine both the enabling and hindering factors for Dalit women's political participation.

DATA COLLECTION TOOLS

Secondary Data: Secondary data was collected on the functioning of Panchayati Raj in general, as well as the participation of women, Dalits and Dalit women in the panchayats of the focus states and across the country. This was sourced from state statistics, articles and books from academic institutes and universities. However, very little disaggregated information is available on the status of Dalit women's participation in the panchayats. At most, the information is either on the functioning of women or Dalits in the panchayats. Moreover, much of the aforementioned information is presented from a development and not human rights perspective, with little analysis of the caste-class-gender power relations that surround local governance.

Structured Questionnaire: A general survey with objective, close-ended questions was administered to 100 Dalit women per state. Two questionnaires were drafted. One was for women who had attempted but failed to access panchayat institutions because they were either forced not to nominate themselves for positions or to withdraw their nominations, or they lost the elections. A second was for women elected panchayat representatives, either members or presidents. The survey tool was chosen because it would provide representative and quantitative data about Dalit women who have sought access to the panchayats. Draft questionnaires, once translated into Gujarati and Tamil, were tested with a group of Dalit women elected representatives in each state. The aim was to remove ambiguities, misunderstandings and confusion over the questions, ensuring precise wording, an easy-to-read format and a logical ordering of questions.

Focus Group and Individual Interviews: Focus group interviews, two per state, were conducted with selected Dalit women elected representatives. Similarly, two groups of Dalit women and Dalit elders and men from villages whose panchayats has Dalit women elected representatives were interviewed in each state.

These interviews were supplemented in each state by four individual interviews with other key stakeholders in Panchayati Raj, such as state-level panchayat officials, block/taluka development officers, election officers and police officials handling cases of panchayat-related atrocities against Dalit women. Individual interviews were also held with two dominant caste female and male panchayat representatives in each state.

Case Studies: Out of the 200 Dalit women who participated in the research, the narratives of 10 women in each state were compiled as case studies. The women were either panchayat presidents, panchayat members, or those who had attempted but failed to access a panchayat post due to external obstructions. Their narratives illustrated the numerous ways in which impunity factors into the access, participation and impact of Dalit women in Panchayati Raj, as well as enabling factors for political participation by independent Dalit women elected representatives.

SELECTION AND TRAINING OF FIELD INVESTIGATORS

The state coordinators identified two junior researchers and around 10 field investigators in each state. The junior researchers and field investigators had to be Dalit woman possessing, at a minimum, a graduate degree and 10th standard education respectively. They had to have field experience of at least a year and be able to relate to women in rural settings. Their orientation had to be towards Dalit and women's rights, and Dalit movements. They also had to have a working knowledge of the panchayat system.

All the junior researchers and field investigators underwent training on the Panchayati Raj system as well as how to administer the survey questionnaires, and interviewing skills. The final choice of field investigators was made after the training, based on their understanding of the objectives of the research and a human rights approach to assessing political participation.

PHASES OF DATA COLLECTION

Data collection occurred in two phases. In Phase I, junior researchers and field investigators interviewed the Dalit women and completed the questionnaires, returning to the field to cross-check or re-check data where necessary. Care was taken regarding the risk of contacting women and conducting interviews, as well as the possibility that questions might be perceived to be threatening. The field investigators did their best to ensure that the research participants were not put at any risk and were given full information about the research objectives and process prior to their consenting to the interviews. Reliability depended on participants not finding the questionnaire too threatening or invasive.

The state coordinators and research associate in Gujarat monitored all the fieldwork in their respective states with the help of their junior researchers to ensure that adequate and accurate data was collected. After each field investigator had completed several questionnaires, the coordinating researchers held one monitoring session in each state. Further clarifications were provided on how to fill in the questionnaire, review the interview process, overcome difficulties arising from the fieldwork and ensure a common understanding of the survey questions. Each questionnaire was manually checked to ensure it had been filled in correctly.

In Phase II, state coordinators, the research associate in Gujarat and junior researchers sat with the coordinating researchers to select the Dalit women to be interviewed for the case studies in each state. They also identified the focus group and individual interviews to be conducted to attain a deeper understanding and broader perspective of the research topic. Following the individual interviews and focus group sessions, which were conducted by the junior researchers and field investigators, all the case studies and interviews were reviewed and any gaps were filled, before they were translated into English.

Challenges and Limitations of this Research

Challenges were experienced in collecting adequate and accurate data for this research topic, leading to unavoidable delays in the fieldwork in both states. Dalit women in general were hesitant to share experiences of political participation, given the politicised nature of the research topic and issues of social status attached to panchayat positions. Particularly at the taluka/union and district panchayat level, it was hard to get women to share the obstacles they faced due to the party politics present in these panchayat tiers.

Certain issues were often invisible in the panchayats, 'untouchability' practices being one. Field investigators therefore had to ask a lot of questions and cross-check data with several sources before they understood the real situation. Another difficult issue to gauge was that of benami candidates who functioned on behalf of others, but sometimes talked as if they had actively participated in the panchayats. This gave rise to occasional contradictions in the women's answers to the questionnaire. Consequently, interviews with the women often had to be cross-checked with others in that village to ensure accuracy and objectivity, to the extent possible.

The detailed nature of the questionnaire resulted in several difficulties. Field investigators had to cover a large number of questions on complex issues in situations where many interviews progressed more smoothly if the questionnaires were not visibly filled out on a question and answer basis. Some elected panchayat representatives also found the lengthy interview sessions tiring and the field investigators had to be sensitive to other demands on the women's time.

Another set of practical problems was encountered in trying to interview the women. It was often difficult to interview the women alone, especially in their homes where other family members, and husbands in particular, sought to be present and occasionally interfered with the interviews. On the other hand, when some current elected panchayat representatives were interviewed in panchayat offices, the difficulty was then their lack of freedom to openly share their experiences with other panchayat representatives nearby. Field investigators also had to visit villages several times before being able to interview some women, with no phone numbers available to fix times for interviews.

Likewise, the field investigators, being Dalit women themselves, had problems juggling this fieldwork with commitments to their respective organisations and families. Some field investigators encountered familial displeasure at their staying overnight in unknown places with unknown people. Fear for the safety of young female investigators led to some families preventing the women from conducting interviews or trying to persuade them to stop the fieldwork. The field investigators faced physical difficulties as many of the panchayats were located at a distance from each other and lacked frequent public transport facilities. Others cited a lack of food and proper accommodation at night, ill-health and the weather – both the summer heat and then the monsoon rains (in Gujarat) – as impacting their fieldwork.

Finally, in several cases chosen for the detailed case studies, women who had related their experiences of political participation in Phase I of data collection later retracted their statements, denied that problems had occurred, or gave contradictory versions of events. Intimidated by the local dominant castes, restricted to conducting interviews with family members present, or worried about the possible implications of their recorded statements (in the case of current panchayat representatives), several women refused to speak openly to the field investigators. This meant that some women had to be met more than once, and more women had to be approached to find those willing to further share their political experiences.

There are also limitations in the scope of this research, given the time and resources available. More detailed research could have delved deeper into each component of access, participation, impact and responses by Dalit women elected representatives to ensure, for example, greater quantification of development benefits or further details on the responses of various actors. A more comparative piece of research could have been undertaken through interviews with a sample of Dalit men and dominant caste women to ascertain the extent to which these two social categories recorded experiences in the panchayats that differed from those of Dalit women. Furthermore, a wider cross-section of relevant stakeholders in the panchayats could have been interviewed. All these limitations, however, do not restrict the ability to draw general conclusions considering the primary and secondary data collected. This research does not claim to provide a complete picture of Dalit women's participation in Panchayati Raj. Instead, it highlights trends and patterns that impact Dalit women in their efforts to access and participate in local governance institutions.

Data Analysis and Research Report Writing

The questionnaire data was analysed and tabulated before the research team met for a three-day workshop to debrief on the research process and collectively analyse the preliminary trends emerging from the questionnaire data. Additional and detailed discussions were held on three key emerging issues: the enabling factors and obstacles to Dalit women independently participating in the panchayats; the factors surrounding benami representatives; and the impact of Dalit women's participation in the panchayats. Being a piece of action research, discussions also focused on the recommendations to state and non-state actors flowing from the research findings, and the development of a concrete action plan for each state organisation to take forward the research findings. The research thus draws on the questionnaire data, interviews, case studies and analytical points emerging from the three-day workshop to build an overall picture of the experiences of Dalit women when asserting their right to political participation.

Readers should note several points in relation to the presentation of the research in this book. First is that the names of all the women and other key actors have been changed to preserve their anonymity. Reference is made only to the panchayat tier and the actual names of the districts and states. Secondly, a comparative understanding of different Dalit communities across the two states, or different sub-communities within one state, or between North and South India, is not the purpose of this research. Instead, all the Dalit women are treated as one group. Thirdly, this research employs the term 'dominant caste' to refer to those castes which are socially, politically and economically dominant from the perspective of Dalits. In this usage, not only 'upper' or 'Forward Castes' but a whole range of 'Backward Castes' are termed 'dominant caste' because they wield real political, social and economic power over Dalits. While this usage collapses distinctions among the 'touchable' castes that would be important to more general sociological research, this reflects an important Dalit reality that must be recognised. Finally, to avoid confusion arising from the different terminology used in Gujarat and Tamil Nadu for panchayat positions, the research uniformly adopts the terms president, vice president and member to denote the head, deputy head and members of a panchayat.

3

PROFILE OF DALIT WOMEN IN PANCHAYATI RAJ

First of all, women need education. Training should be given to them. Then women should get organised... In order for Dalit women to participate in the panchayat, they need education, freedom in the family, leadership and administrative training, and economic access.
— Dalit women villagers in Madurai district, Tamil Nadu

[There is a] need to make [women] more aware and to educate them... Dalit women should get government trainings, and changes should be brought in social norms and practices. Awareness trainings should be organised for Dalit women so that they become independent in handling the panchayat administration.
— TDO from Surendranagar district, Gujarat

Before looking at Dalit women's experiences of Panchayati Raj, it is important to first understand who these women are. This chapter profiles the 200 Dalit women who participated in this research from Gujarat and Tamil Nadu. It describes their personal background and socio-economic status, their involvement in the social concerns of their communities and prior political activism. It also details their understanding of the Panchayati Raj system and legal awareness of caste-based offences.

Socio-Economic Profile of Dalit Women

CASTE REPRESENTATION

Table 3.1 illustrates the caste composition of the 200 Dalit women. In Gujarat, 30.0 per cent were from the Vankar sub-caste, reflecting their position as the largest Dalit sub-caste in the state. Rohits were the next most represented sub-caste at 9.5 per cent, followed by Valmikis (5.0 per cent), Senva (3.0 per cent), Garoda (1.5 per cent) and finally one member each (0.5 per cent each) from the Mochi[1] and Sadhu sub-castes. In Tamil Nadu, the majority Dalit sub-caste – the Paraiyar/Adi Dravidar – was once again the most highly represented (24.5 per cent). The Pallar (15.0 per cent) and Arunthathiyar (9.5 per cent) sub-castes also figure significantly. One member each of the Koliyan and Kuravan sub-castes (0.5 per cent each) were also included.

These sub-caste groupings reflect the major Dalit sub-castes in the two focus states. They were also largely included in the same proportion as their presence in the population of each state, with the following exceptions: a higher proportion of Vankars and a lower proportion of Rohits were included (as compared with their population in Gujarat).

Table 3.1: Sub-Caste Representation of Dalit Women

Dalit Sub-Caste	Gujarat	Tamil Nadu	Total	%
Vankar	60		60	30.0
Rohit	19		19	9.5
Valmiki	10		10	5.0
Senva	6		6	3.0
Garoda	3		3	1.5
Mochi	1		1	0.5
Sadhu	1		1	0.5
Paraiyar/Adi Dravidar		49	49	24.5
Pallar		30	30	15.0
Arunthathiyar		19	19	9.5
Koliyan		1	1	0.5
Kuravan		1	1	0.5
Total	100	100	200	100.0

AGE

Table 3.2 shows that the majority of contesting Dalit women were relatively young. The majority were in the age group of 26-45 years (33.5 per cent between 26-35 years, and 38.5 per cent between 36-45 years). Another 22.0 per cent were between 46-60 years. This trend is confirmed by a series of other studies,[2] and indicates a progressive change from the time before the *73rd Constitutional Amendment Act*.[3]

Table 3.2 Age of Dalit Women

Age Group	Gujarat	Tamil Nadu	Total	%
20 – 25 years	2	6	8	4.0
26 – 35 years	35	32	67	33.5
36 – 45 years	41	36	77	38.5
46 – 60 years	20	24	44	22.0
Above 60 years	2	2	4	2.0
Total	100	100	200	100.0

MARRIAGE STATUS

Table 3.3 sets out the marital status of Dalit women. As to be expected given the age group of the women, the vast majority (90.5 per cent) were married. A further 6.0 per cent were widowed and another 2.5 per cent were separated from their husbands, leaving only 1.0 per cent single. Across both Gujarat and Tamil Nadu, this data is largely identical. Thus, the Dalit women seeking election to panchayat posts were largely women of some maturity with family

Table 3.3 Marital Status of Dalit Women

Marital Status	Gujarat	Tamil Nadu	Total	%
Married	91	90	181	90.5
Widowed	7	5	12	6.0
Separated	1	4	5	2.5
Single	1	1	2	1.0
Total	100	100	200	100.0

responsibilities of their own. The implications, however, are that many elected representatives had to juggle their household and panchayat responsibilities.

EDUCATION

Education plays a critical role in breaking the vicious cycle of poverty and exclusion, and is a fundamental human right of every woman, man, girl and boy, enshrined both in international law and the Indian Constitution. Yet Dalit women continue to face gross violations of this right, embedded in multiple layers of discrimination based on their gender, caste and class. This has major implications for their enjoyment of the right to political participation.

Table 3.4 details a striking educational profile of Dalit women contesting for panchayat representation. An average of 26.0 per cent had no education at all, while 20.0 per cent were educated only up to the lower primary level (1st-5th standards). A further 19.0 per cent were educated up to the upper primary level (6th-8th standards). A comparable percentage (18.5 per cent) had reached 9th-10th standards and 9.5 per cent had gone on to complete 11th-12th standards. Finally, a small number (6.5 per cent) had completed higher education.

Table 3.4: Educational Level of Dalit Women

Education Level	Gujarat	Tamil Nadu	Total	%
None	30	22	52	26.0
1-5th std	18	22	40	20.0
6-8th std	19	19	38	19.0
9-10th std	18	19	37	18.5
11-12th std	10	9	19	9.5
Vocational training		1	1	0.5
Graduate degree	5	8	13	6.5
Total	100	100	200	100.0

While one-quarter of the women (26.0 per cent) were illiterate, three-quarters were fortunate enough to have enjoyed some schooling. However, of this latter group, the fact that almost one-third of them stopped with primary schooling seems to indicate a comparatively low level of education that is not commensurate to the level required to manage panchayat governance (including the ability to read, understand and critically analyse the various schemes, powers, functions, reporting, funding, and so on in the panchayats). This is amply evidenced in a subsequent question, where 59.0 per cent of the women said that they could read and write, while 41.0 per cent said they could not.

Even on the basis of these figures, however, a high percentage of Dalit women contesting were literate. This is higher than in a number of other studies on women and Panchayati Raj and highlights a positive trend emerging.[4] There is a particularly high number of women with high education levels (16.5 per cent). This shows a strong potential for these women to assume the powers of panchayat posts. By contrast, those not educated or with little education were more prone to becoming benamis and being used at the behest of others' interests and control. They were also severely limited in their ability to understand their roles, responsibilities and powers. Ghajraben, a village panchayat president in Anand district in Gujarat, for instance, did not understand the government training she attended because she could not read and write. Likewise, Kalaben, a village panchayat president from Vadodara district in the same state explained that she did not participate in any of the training sessions because she is illiterate.

OCCUPATION

Table 3.5 reveals the primary occupation of Dalit women seeking election to the panchayats. The majority of women were labourers, including household labour (48.5 per cent) and agricultural labour (29.0 per cent). This high proportion of women engaged in the domestic or 'private' sphere as housewives has implications on the women's confidence and ability to move freely in public spaces, as well as their capacity to speak and engage with others – including panchayat members, district administration officials, contractors and so on – in public fora. The high dependency on wage labour employment also leaves Dalit women with a poor economic base and a higher rate of under-employment. This results in a higher level of poverty. The data on primary occupation reflects the ongoing struggle against poverty most Dalit women experience. This was also reflected in the responses concerning average per capita annual income, as per the data presented in Table 3.6.

Table 3.5: Primary Occupation of Dalit Women

Primary Occupation	Gujarat	Tamil Nadu	Total	%
Housewife, household work	55	42	97	48.5
Daily wage labourer*	24	34	58	29.0
Cultivator	10	16	26	13.0
Small business operator**	3	5	8	4.0
Salaried worker***	5	2	7	3.5
Cattle rearer	2		2	1.0
Semi-bonded labourer		1	1	0.5
Sweeper, scavenger	1		1	0.5
Total	100	100	200	100.0

* Daily wage labourer includes agricultural labourer, beedi roller and other daily wage work.
** Small business operator includes petty shopkeeper, phone booth operator and tailor.
*** Salaried worker includes LIC agent, teacher, NGO and anganwadi worker.

A consequence of this level of poverty is that most Dalit women did not have the option of leaving waged labour to take up panchayat duties, for which there is little or no remuneration. This also raises the risk of dominant caste employers exploiting the employer-employee relationship and the poverty of these women to reinforce caste discriminatory norms, forcing Dalit women to become their benamis.

INCOME

The Dalit women contesting panchayat elections remained in an extremely low per capita annual income bracket. Note that this data is only a rough estimate, given the difficulties in accurately calculating annual income due to factors such as seasonal work, lack of knowledge of the income of other family members, and illiteracy. As per Table 3.6, 11.0 per cent of women mentioned per capita incomes of up to ₹5,000. This does not even amount to ₹14 per person per day (or ₹420 per month), and is below the official poverty line at the time of this research.[5] A further 23.5 per cent of women noted a per capita income of between ₹14 and 27 per day (₹5,001–10,000 per year) and another one-fifth (21.5 per cent) an income in excess of that up to ₹55 per day (₹10,001–20,000 per year). This means that 56 per cent of the Dalit women were in households which earned below US$ 1.30 per capita per day. The majority of the women were thus in households which enjoyed very little economic stability. At such precarious subsistence levels, the question arises as to how a Dalit woman panchayat representative could possibly assert herself as an active, independent leader. The basic struggle for survival renders one vulnerable to manipulation by those in stronger economic positions, and mandates extended hours per day directed towards securing basic sustenance.

Table 3.6: Average per Capita Annual Income

Average per Capita Annual Income	Gujarat	Tamil Nadu	Total	%
Up to ₹5,000	9	13	22	11.0
₹5,001 – 10,000	25	22	47	23.5
₹10,001 – 20,000	24	19	43	21.5
₹20,001 – 30,000	11	14	25	12.5
₹30,001 – 50,000	10	12	22	11.0
₹50,001 – 1,00,000	13	10	23	11.5
Above ₹1,00,000	3	10	13	6.5
Not known	5		5	2.5
Total	100	100	200	100.0

In a higher income tier, 12.5 per cent of Dalit women and their families earn ₹20,001–30,000 per capita annually; that is, a maximum of ₹82 per person per day (or US$ 2.08). Another 11.0 per cent were in the bracket of ₹30,001–50,000 (up to ₹137 per day). A comparable percentage (11.5 per cent) had larger per capita annual earnings of ₹50,001–1,00,000 and a further 6.5 per cent mentioned a per capita annual income in excess of ₹1,00,000. Women in the higher family income brackets enjoyed greater economic stability and a resulting independence from dominant castes. This may also enable more mental space and time to commit to participation in processes such as panchayat governance. At the same time, this must be viewed in the broader economic, social and political context of the woman vis-à-vis her family and society.

LAND OWNERSHIP

Given the strong correlation between land and economic status in rural India, the status of household landholdings is set out in Table 3.7. Almost half the Dalit women (48.0 per cent) contesting panchayat seats were landless. A further 42.5 per cent were landowners, 6.5 per cent tenants and 2.0 per cent both landowners and tenants. These low land ownership figures reaffirm the data on income and employment. The land holdings of Dalit women in families with land were also very marginal.

Table 3.7: Land Ownership Status

Land Ownership Status	Gujarat	Tamil Nadu	Total	%
Landless	49	47	96	48.0
Landowner	43	42	85	42.5
Tenant	5	8	13	6.5
Both landowner and tenant	1	3	4	2.0
Both landowner and user of government revenue land	1		1	0.5
User of government revenue land	1		1	0.5
Total	100	100	200	100.0

Ultimately, the majority of Dalit women panchayat contestants and representatives were of poor economic status. They were landless labourers earning a low income. Only 29.0 per cent earned more than US\$ 2.00 per person per day and about one-quarter were non-marginal landholders. This data offers insights into the economic dependence of Dalit women and their families, and suggests a paradox in that the exercise of independent authority in panchayat governance demands economic stability and independence. Political power cannot come without sufficient economic strength to negotiate freely at the relevant panchayat tier. This requirement is even more pronounced in a hierarchically structured society built on caste.

Panchayat Profile of Dalit Women

PANCHAYAT LEVEL

Rural Panchayati Raj institutions operate at three tiers: village, taluka/union and district. Table 3.8 reveals that most of the 200 Dalit women sought election to panchayat posts at the village level. A total of 82.0 per cent sought representation here, with 74.0 per cent of women in Gujarat being elected at this level,

Table 3.8: Panchayat Tier to Which Dalit Women Contested Elections or Were Elected

Panchayat Tier	Gujarat		Tamil Nadu		Total	%
	Tried to Contest or Contested and Lost Elections	Elected to Panchayat	Tried to Contest or Contested and Lost Elections	Elected to Panchayat		
Village panchayat	13	74	17	60	164	82.0
Taluka/ union panchayat	1	8	2	14	25	12.5
District panchayat		4	1	6	11	5.5
Total	14	86	20	80	200	100.0

and 13.0 per cent trying to contest, or contesting and losing, the elections. Similarly, in Tamil Nadu, 60.0 per cent of Dalit women were elected to village panchayats and 17.0 per cent tried, but were unsuccessful in winning seats at this level.

APPOINTMENT TO PANCHAYAT POST

Table 3.8 also indicates that 86.0 per cent of the women who stood for elections in Gujarat were elected. The remaining 14.0 per cent were nominated for election, but either withdrew their nominations before the elections or were not successful in the elections. In Tamil Nadu, 80.0 per cent were elected to a panchayat post while 20.0 per cent failed or withdrew their nominations.

PANCHAYAT SEATS FOR WHICH DALIT WOMEN SOUGHT ELECTION

Within the Panchayati Raj system, the four types of seats to which Dalit women can nominate themselves are: (a) seats of the general constituency, open to everyone; (b) seats that are reserved for women only; (c) seats that are reserved for scheduled castes (SC) only; and (d) seats that are reserved specifically for SC women only.

Table 3.9 details figures on the reserved constituency to which Dalit women sought election. The vast majority, in both Tamil Nadu and Gujarat, contested seats reserved specifically for SC women (81.5 per cent). By comparison, 8.0 per cent of women contested seats reserved for SCs and 10.5 per cent were nominated for seats reserved for women.

Caste and gender discrimination reinforce a strong assumption that general women reserved seats are for dominant caste women and SC reserved seats are for Dalit men. Dalit women are then relegated to the seats specifically reserved for them. This has the potential to circumscribe rather than encourage active participation, particularly with the rotation of reserved seats. Dalit women eager to actively participate in the panchayats faced enormous challenges in pushing beyond these assumptions to contest other seats. Shantaben, for example, was forced to

withdraw her nomination for a general women's reserved member
seat in a village panchayat in Surendranagar district in Gujarat
due to pressure from dominant caste village leaders who were
advocating for their benami candidate.

**Table 3.9: Reserved Constituency to Which Dalit Women
Contested Elections or Were Elected**

Panchayat Position	Gujarat		Tamil Nadu		Total	%
	Tried to Contest or Contested and Lost Elections	*Elected to Panchayat*	*Tried to Contest or Contested and Lost Elections*	*Elected to Panchayat*		
SC women reserved	7	71	16	69	163	81.5
SC general reserved		7	3	6	16	8.0
General women reserved	7	8	1	5	21	10.5
Total	14	86	20	80	200	100.0

Seats are reserved for members and also for panchayat
presidents at all panchayati tiers. Accordingly, women can seek
direct election as members or presidents at the village panchayat
level, while presidents of the taluka/union and district panchayats
are indirectly elected by the elected members of their respective
panchayats. Vice presidents at each of the three levels in both
states are elected indirectly by members of the newly elected
panchayat. Table 3.10 depicts the panchayat positions to which
the Dalit women successfully or unsuccessfully sought election.
The majority contested the post of president.

The very small proportion of Dalit women elected indirectly
as vice president reflects the powerful status of that position.
Examining all the panchayats into which the Dalit women were
elected, a Dalit woman was a vice president in only 1.5 per cent.

The only woman from Tamil Nadu in this post, Jayalakshmi, in a union panchayat in Thirunelveli district in Tamil Nadu, was elected as vice president with the support of her political party. Nevertheless, after the election, she faced obstructions and a complete lack of respect from the dominant caste president and members, who ignored her and verbally abused her in meetings.

Table 3.10: Panchayat Position to Which Dalit Women Contested Elections or Were Elected

Panchayat Position	Gujarat		Tamil Nadu		Total	%
	Tried to Contest or Contested and Lost Elections	Elected to Panchayat	Tried to Contest or Contested and Lost Elections	Elected to Panchayat		
President	8	57	17	62	144	72.0
Member	6	27	3	17	53	26.5
Vice president		2		1	3	1.5
Total	14	86	20	80	200	100.0

ELECTION PERIOD

The election process is different in Tamil Nadu and Gujarat. In Tamil Nadu, panchayat elections for all three tiers were held across the state in fixed years, 2001 and 2006 in this case; whereas in Gujarat, panchayat elections for each of the three tiers as well as within a panchayat tier were staggered across several years after 2000. This was due to various delays by the Gujarat government. In practice, the trends of earlier elections affect later elections, increasing the level of politics in the election process: that is, whoever dominates earlier elections influences the remaining elections.

Table 3.11 indicates the periods over which the Dalit women contested panchayat seats. It shows that 68.5 per cent of women were elected between 2000 and 2003. In total, 31.5 per cent sought election in 2005 or 2006. This was generally the third period of panchayat elections since the enactment of the *73ʳᵈ Constitutional Amendment Act.*

Table 3.11: Year in Which Dalit Women Contested Elections or Were Elected

*Year**	*Gujarat*		*Tamil Nadu*		*Total*	*%*
	Tried to Contest or Contested and Lost Elections	*Elected to Panchayat*	*Tried to Contest or Contested and Lost Elections*	*Elected to Panchayat*		
2000–2003	4	57	9	67	137	68.5
2005–2006	10	29	11	13	63	31.5
Total	14	86	20	80	200	100.0

Prior Experience and Knowledge

PRE-PANCHAYAT EXPERIENCES

Of the Dalit women contesting the elections, 30.0 per cent had a family member who had previously held a panchayat post. This number was higher in Gujarat (43.0 per cent) as opposed to 17.0 per cent in Tamil Nadu. The disparity may be explained by a stronger hold of traditional power in Gujarat, with less space for new faces and a higher number of consensus-based elections. By contrast, more women in Tamil Nadu had previously held a panchayat post. Another explanation may be that in Tamil Nadu reserved seats rotate after two panchayat terms, whereas in Gujarat reserved seats rotate with every election. A mere 16.0 per cent of women had previously held a panchayat post, with 11.0 per cent elected in Gujarat and 21.0 per cent in Tamil Nadu. Over two-thirds of these women (68.8 per cent) had previously assumed the post of president. Thus, the majority of Dalit women had no previous direct political experience, nor were they from established political families.

PRIOR SOCIAL ACTIVISM

Seventy per cent of Dalit women who sought election to the panchayats had never previously approached a government official concerning village problems. A further 4.0 per cent had approached an official only once, while just over one-quarter of the women (26.0 per cent) had approached government officials either a few or many times. Although overall quite low, this is nevertheless a reasonably high percentage given that only 16.0 per cent of the women had previously been elected panchayat representatives.

Table 3.12 indicates Dalit women's affiliations with and leadership within different types of political and socio-economic organisations. Of the Dalit women contesting a panchayat post, 33.5 per cent formally belonged to a political party, of which almost half were active members. The significant discrepancy between formal and active membership ostensibly reveals the family, in particular the husband, driving the woman's political participation. There is quite a contrast here between formal and active membership for all issues. Active membership implies some personal knowledge of local political structures, roles and functions, as well as economic and political benefits of governance, and would suggest greater potential for substantive leadership in the panchayats. These results are similar to other research. One piece of research undertaken across three states, for example, found that only a small percentage of elected women at all three panchayat tiers had any previous experience in politics, despite a majority being elected as candidates of political parties. Participation in social organisations and, to an even greater extent, engagement in political activities at school/college levels was also very low.[6] This data reflects women's seclusion and isolation from public life.

A similarly low level of active membership was noted in relation to involvement in women's self-help groups (SHGs): only about half of the 32.0 per cent of women who held membership saw themselves as active members. This was significantly higher than the number of women involved with a women's association or the women's movement in general. Only 16.0 per cent of the women were members of such organisations, with just

Table 3.12: Women's Organisational Membership

Organisational Membership*	No. of Members			No. of Active Members		
	Gujarat	Tamil Nadu	Total (% of 200 women)	Gujarat	Tamil Nadu	Total (% of 200 women)
Formal member of political party	22	45	67 (33.5)	14	16	30 (15.0)
Women's self-help group	27	37	64 (32.0)	19	14	33 (16.5)
Dalit association/ movement	41		41 (20.5)	25		25 (12.5)
Women's association/ movement	23	9	32 (16.0)	15	4	19 (9.5)
Women Panchayat President's Federation		2	2 (1.0)		2	2 (1.0)
Women's wing of political party		2	2 (1.0)		2	2 (1.0)
Other non-governmental organisation	2	1	3 (1.5)	2	1	2 (1.0)

* Some women were members and/or active members of several organisations

under two-thirds actively taking leadership, organising events or otherwise contributing to association activities. Engagement with women's movements in some form denotes an awareness of gender issues and some inclination towards challenging gender norms. Affiliation to a SHG, however, was the most common form of involvement and is the least confronting. Numerous studies have highlighted ways in which SHGs provide women with specific skills important in building a women's constituency and promoting leadership.[7] Further, membership in collectives for women that address similar problems or are collectivised around a common mandate cannot be underestimated given their capacity to expand a woman's mental space, the space that facilitates the 'power within', a critical condition for empowerment to take place.[8] Nevertheless, some still argue that the experience gained by participating in SHGs is not adequate to function in formal political structures that are largely male dominated.[9] Overall data from current research indicates a low involvement of Dalit women in women's issues.

Finally, 20.5 per cent of Dalit women were formal members of a Dalit association or movement, of which just under two-thirds were active members. This entire representation was drawn from Gujarat alone, and it must be qualified that this research focused on districts in Gujarat where a Dalit NGO is prominent. Overall, in terms of Dalit women's knowledge and social awareness, Gujarat has strong representation in Dalit movements and Tamil Nadu in political parties.

KNOWLEDGE OF PANCHAYAT ADMINISTRATION AND CASTE-BASED OFFENCES

The knowledge of Dalit women who contested panchayat elections regarding specific areas relevant to effective political participation as panchayat leaders was also a focus of this study. As is evident from Table 3.13, this reinforces the data on their political and social activism. Eighteen per cent of women had a good knowledge of the electoral rules and process for nomination for a panchayat position, leaving 82.0 per cent without a good working knowledge, and 53.0 per cent of women with no knowledge at all. This suggests that someone else was the driving force behind the latter's nomination for political representation.

A nominal 6.5 per cent of the Dalit women had a good knowledge of the provisions of the governing state panchayat act that prescribes the structures, roles, responsibilities, functions and funds of panchayat governance. The lack of knowledge of a majority of the women in this area is striking and of such a level as to preclude effective understanding of panchayat administration, local politics and development opportunities. One cannot direct local governance where one has no knowledge of the operating system.

Table 3.13: Women's Level of Knowledge of Panchayati Raj

Woman's knowledge of:	No. of Women with No Knowledge			No. of Women with a Little Knowledge			No. of Women with a Good Knowledge		
	GUJ	TN	Total (% of 200)	GUJ	TN	Total (% of 200)	GUJ	TN	Total (% of 200)
Electoral rules and process for nomination for a panchayat position	52	54	106 (53.0)	33	25	58 (29.0)	15	21	36 (18.0)
Provisions of the Gujarat Panchayats Act 1993/Tamil Nadu Panchayats Act 1994	65	81	146 (73.0)	31	10	41 (20.5)	4	9	13 (6.5)
Roles and functions of the three tiers of Panchayati Raj, and relationship between them	48	62	110 (55.0)	43	21	64 (32.0)	9	17	26 (13.0)
Roles and responsibilities of elected representatives at their panchayat level	34	62	96 (48.0)	52	19	71 (35.5)	14	19	33 (16.5)
Development programmes and schemes in the panchayat	35	60	95 (47.5)	47	22	69 (34.5)	18	18	36 (18.0)
Government officials who deal with these development programmes	38*	48**	86 (43.0)	36*	14**	50 (25.0)	12*	18**	30 (15.0)
Sources of funds available to implement these development programmes	55*	52**	107 (53.5)	21*	13**	34 (17.0)	10*	15**	25 (12.5)

Woman's knowledge of:	No. of Women with No Knowledge			No. of Women with a Little Knowledge			No. of Women with a Good Knowledge		
	GUJ	TN	Total (% of 200)	GUJ	TN	Total (% of 200)	GUJ	TN	Total (% of 200)
Legal provisions penalising misconduct during the elections period and misconduct of elected representatives	58	69	127 (63.5)	26	15	41 (20.5)	16	16	32 (16.0)
Whom to approach during panchayat elections as well as during period as elected representative regarding any misconduct or discrimination	59	61	120 (60.0)	29	19	48 (24.0)	12	20	32 (16.0)
SC/ST (Prevention of Atrocities) Act 1989	41	78	119 (59.5)	51	12	63 (31.5)	8	10	18 (9.0)
Protection of Civil Rights Act 1955	81	76	157 (78.5)	16	14	30 (15.0)	3	10	13 (6.5)

* Out of 86 elected panchayat representatives (Gujarat)
** Out of 80 elected panchayat representatives (Tamil Nadu)

More women, however, did convey some knowledge of specific panchayat issues when these issues were broken down. Thirteen per cent of women reported a good knowledge of the roles and functions of the three panchayat tiers and the relationship between them, and 16.5 per cent conveyed a good knowledge of the roles and responsibilities of elected representatives at the level for which they contested. Still, considering the fact that 59.0 per cent of these women have basic literacy skills, this knowledge is extremely poor. Given the literacy skills and livelihood needs of women, it is likely that their information stems from informal interaction or more practical training that prioritised content rather than the legal sources from which the rules are drawn. While this speaks loudly of another driving force behind the women's participation, it may also indicate Dalit women's lack of exposure to these issues, the lack of training opportunities for them and a lack of self-confidence to seek out further knowledge for themselves. Later chapters will further explore these issues.

The Dalit women's knowledge of local development processes was also assessed in terms of available development programmes and schemes, the government officials responsible for them, and sources of funds for the implementation of these schemes and for core panchayat needs. Approximately half of the women had no knowledge of these issues (47.5 per cent, 43.0 per cent and 53.5 per cent respectively concerning development programmes, responsible officials and funding sources).[10] Only 18.0 per cent of Dalit women had a good knowledge of the schemes and programmes for the development of their area, whether it be at the village, taluka/union or district level. A mere 15.0 per cent of women knew which government officials to approach for the implementation of these development schemes and 12.5 per cent had a good knowledge of the sources of funding available to implement them. This suggests that the vast majority of Dalit women elected panchayat representatives did not have a working knowledge of the core functions and use of panchayat governance.

This research was concerned not only with the development aspects of Panchayati Raj, but also its potential to counteract discrimination on the basis of caste and gender. It was concerned with the perceived impunity with which the state system, and the dominant caste persons that run the system, act outside the law to perpetuate their own power at the expense of others. In this regard, Dalit women's awareness of legal mechanisms that regulate behaviour in panchayat elections and panchayat governance, as well as laws specific to caste atrocities and discrimination were probed. Only 16.0 per cent of Dalit women had a good knowledge of the provisions penalising misconduct during the election period, and the misconduct of elected representatives throughout the panchayat term. An identical percentage knew whom to approach in instances of misconduct or discrimination, both during the elections themselves and their tenure as an elected representative. Around 60.0 per cent had no knowledge at all of these issues.

Only 9.0 per cent of contesting Dalit women had a good working knowledge of the *SC/ST (Prevention of Atrocities) Act 1989 (SC/ST (PA) Act)* and 6.5 per cent of the *Protection of Civil Rights Act 1955 (PCR Act)*. The number of women with no knowledge of the *SC/ST (PA) Act* was significantly higher in Tamil Nadu, with 78.0 per cent of women having no knowledge as opposed to only 41.0 per cent of women in Gujarat. Still, those with a good knowledge were of a comparable number (8.0 per cent in Gujarat and 10.0 per cent in Tamil Nadu). It is apparent from this that Dalit women elected representatives had little capacity to take a substantive, active role in redressing caste-based offences or imposing pressure to overcome impunity through the use of the legal system.

GOVERNMENT AND NGO TRAININGS

The women's knowledge on the above-mentioned issues has to be viewed in relation to the number of trainings they were provided with. As can be drawn from Table 3.14, 44.6 per cent of Dalit women elected representatives had not participated in any government-run trainings on panchayat administration. On the other hand, it is quite positive that 41.5 per cent have received two or more trainings from government bodies. Officials interviewed affirmed the poor state compliance with its training responsibilities to Dalit women. According to a TDO

from Surendranagar district in Gujarat, "the state government
organises a training programme in Ahmedabad once in five years,
especially on the panchayat administration. It is for four to five
days only. And there has been no special concentration on Dalit
women in those training programmes." He further noted that, "in
the conference of elected representatives[11] very little, inadequate
information is given. All the government officials emphasise
women's participation and their empowerment, but no specific
training is given at any time. [The conference] happens once
just after the election. Different political parties organise their
separate meetings with their party candidates. Other than this,
some information to improve women's participation is given to the
talati in his meetings with officials."

**Table 3.14: Number of Trainings on Panchayati Raj Elected
Women Received**

Number of Trainings	Number of Women Trained by the Government			Number of Women Trained by NGOs		
	Gujarat	Tamil Nadu	Total (%)	Gujarat	Tamil Nadu	Total (%)
None	49	25	74 (44.6)	62	63	125 (75.3)
1	13	10	23 (13.9)	9	5	14 (8.4)
2 – 5	20	34	54 (32.5)	13	9	22 (13.3)
More than 5 times	4	11	15 (9.0)	2	3	5 (3.0)
Total	86	80	166 (100.0)	86	80	166 (100.0)

Even when training was provided, gender and caste-based
discrimination often prevented Dalit women from enjoying
the benefits. While this may be directly due to their husbands'
demands or the women's lack of confidence, it was reinforced
by state officials, leaving them in breach of their human rights

obligations. For example, in the cases of Ratha, a village panchayat president from Madurai district in Tamil Nadu, and Soniben, a village panchayat president from Ahmedabad district in Gujarat, their husbands would attend the government training programmes in their place. Group interviews with Dalit women elected representatives made it clear that this was a common practice. Even more disturbing, government officials occasionally reinforced assumptions that Dalit women cannot learn and are incapable of understanding panchayat matters when they do seek to participate. Chanchalben, a village panchayat president in Kheda district in Gujarat, once went to a government training programme. However, when she informed the officials that she could not understand anything, they told her to just sign the register, and then send her husband to attend the training in her place.

Other bodies such as NGOs, political parties, and women's and Dalit associations are also failing to reach Dalit women and provide the required basic support. Table 3.14 shows that 75.3 per cent of Dalit women had not participated in any training run by NGOs, and only 16.3 per cent had received training twice or more times from NGOs. Some NGOs, though, also move beyond technical participation in Panchayati Raj institutions to issues such as fighting against social injustice within the panchayats, making independent decisions and resolving problems, atrocities against women, and legal provisions relating to the rights of Dalit women and other social groups.

Conclusion

Preetikaben, a village panchayat president in Anand district in Gujarat, captures the importance of awareness and knowledge for Dalit women's empowered participation in Panchayati Raj:

> Women need some support when they face development and social justice problems in the panchayat. Dalit women, in particular, need different kinds of support from the system because they face untouchability practices from the dominant castes. Dalit women need awareness and detailed information

about the panchayat because they have always been isolated from panchayat administration and they lack awareness. As president, for effective participation, women should get training on the administrative and development projects of the panchayat, the financial system and grants.

She also felt that there should be special training on the state's panchayat act and development schemes from the government, and not just NGOs. She further discussed the importance of education – that this helps a woman assert her authority in the panchayat, gain respect in the village and increases her personal confidence. Finally, she said family support, particularly from one's husband, is also crucial. Reality is a far cry from this state of affairs for most Dalit women elected representatives. Information is a source of power and takes on even more importance when considering the context of the caste-gender-class bias that has served to exclude and isolate Dalit women.

Overall, however, there are many positive factors suggesting the potential for Dalit women to start confronting existing systems of power and achieve development objectives through political participation. The data reveals that the Dalit women contesting panchayat elections are young, but married and thus somewhat mature. Just over half also have basic literacy and at least some education. These are positive factors for potential leadership, despite nearly half of them currently being illiterate. Their economic dependency, however, remains strong. These women remain highly economically vulnerable, with a majority in low income families from the labour class, 56.0 per cent earning under US$ 1.30 per capita per day and 48.0 per cent being landless. This has major implications for their participation in Panchayati Raj. Economic vulnerability is compounded by a lack of political experience and low levels of social activism and leadership, captured by the approximate 20 per cent of women active in one or more groups or associations, whether focusing on women, Dalits or something else altogether.

The knowledge of panchayat election processes is very poor, allowing dominant forces to influence and exploit these women's political representation. However, once in power, Dalit women may be more motivated to educate themselves. This is evident from the fact that approximately half the women possess at least some knowledge of their own responsibilities, development programmes, officials responsible and funding issues; and between 10 and 20 per cent have more solid knowledge.

A majority of the Dalit women who participated in this research were elected in the period between 2000 and 2003. This gave them significant time to participate in and influence the panchayats, and grow into their roles before being approached. The remaining low levels of knowledge are then striking and paint a very poor initial picture of Dalit women's participation in panchayat administration. Despite the depth and magnitude of entrenched oppression and discrimination that Dalit women continue to face, there are still enormous possibilities for political and social leadership from the profile of the women. The following chapters explore how these women have been able to access and participate in local governance in Gujarat and Tamil Nadu, and will identify enabling and disabling factors to build on, and redressal mechanisms to support these women in assuming their rightful role of free and empowered political participation.

Notes

1. Note that while the Mochi sub-caste is now removed from the Scheduled Caste list in Gujarat, at the time when the one Mochi woman contested elections, her sub-caste was still within the list. Hence, her case is considered as part of this sample.

2. Kaushik, S., *Participation of Women in Panchayati Raj in India: A Stock Taking* (New Delhi: National Commission for Women, 1998); Santha E.K., "Political Participation of Women in Panchayati Raj, Haryana, Kerala and Tamil Nadu", *Occasional Paper Series 24* (New Delhi: Institute of Social Sciences, 1999) – for which Kerala and Tamil Nadu had drawn a majority of women under 40 years and Haryana a majority over 40 years.

3. Datta, B. (ed), *And Who Will Make the Chapattis? A Study of All Women Panchayats in Maharashtra* (Calcutta: Stree, 1998); Singla, P., *Women's Participation in Panchayati Raj: Nature and Effectiveness* (Jaipur: Rawat Publications, 2007), pp. 139-140, focusing on Haryana.

4. Kaushik, supra note 2; Buch, N., "Women's Experience in New Panchayats: The Emerging Leadership of Rural Women", *Occasional Paper No.* 35 (New Delhi: Centre for Women's Development Studies, 2000), focusing on Madhya Pradesh, Rajasthan and Uttar Pradesh.

5. National Sample Survey Organisation, *Differences in Level of Consumption among Socio-Economic Groups 1999–2000*, NSS 55th Round, (New Delhi: NSSO, 2000).

6. Santha, supra note 2.

7. Mohan, S. et al, *Facilitating the Fulfilment of State Obligations towards Women's Equality: Baseline Report on Women and Political Participation in India* (Kuala Lumpur: NIAS et al and coordinated by IWRAW Asia Pacific, advanced unedited version, undated), p. 33.

8. See Deshmukh-Ranadive, J., *Women's Participation in Self-Help-Groups and in Panchayati Raj Institutions: Suggesting Synergistic Linkages*, paper presented at conference A Decade of Women's Empowerment through Local Government in India, 20-21 October 2003 (New Delhi: Institute of Social Sciences, South Asia Partnership Canada, International Development Research Centre, 2003).

9. Ibid.

10. Note that only elected panchayat representatives were questioned about sources of funding and officials responsible for the implementation of schemes.

11. The first meeting at the taluka panchayat level, called through a government order, where all elected representatives are meant to be given information about the panchayat and their roles and responsibilities.

4

GETTING A FOOT IN THE DOOR

In the patriarchal system, there are lots of struggles for women to win the election. And within the system, Dalit women struggle more than other women. It is very difficult for them to win the election because nobody believes that they can carry out panchayat work. Everyone plays politics with them and against them just because they – dominant castes and men – never want Dalit women to control the panchayat administration... Men never accept women's leadership, and there is a need for specific attention to this by making proper use of the reservation policy as Babasaheb [Ambedkar's] blessing to us. Dalit women have to reap the benefits of this opportunity by actively engaging themselves in creating models of leadership.

– Lakshmiben, village panchayat president,
Vadodara district, Gujarat

Lakshmiben expresses the struggles that Dalit women, disadvantaged by their caste and gender, undergo to access positions in panchayat governance. A 37-year-old agricultural labourer, she was educated up to the 8th standard and lived in Vadodara district in Gujarat. She spoke from her experience of contesting the post of village panchayat president in an SC women reserved constituency. Her struggle arose out of the contest for power between Dalits and dominant castes over control of the village panchayat and its developmental resources.

Previously, the local Dalit agricultural labourers went on strike under the leadership of Lakshmiben's husband, Sumanbhai, over the demand for a wage increase. Sumanbhai then decided to contest the post of village panchayat president. However, he lost the election to a FC Patel man after his co-worker was kidnapped, and the Patels openly threatened the co-worker's community, telling them not to vote for Sumanbhai. 'Untouchability' is still prevalent in this panchayat, where FC Patel landlords dominate in numbers, wealth and power, alongside the slightly less influential FC Darbars.

Then, for the next panchayat elections, the panchayat president's post was listed as reserved for SC women. Sumanbhai encouraged Lakshmiben to enter panchayat politics to test their community's strength against the dominant castes, and she filed her nomination for the post. Lakshmiben was already a familiar face in the villages. As an *anganwadi* worker, she met women regularly regarding health problems. She also knew the roles and responsibilities of elected representatives and the types of panchayat schemes available. Financially, her family was reasonably well off, with her brother-in-law being able to meet all her canvassing expenses. Hence, she felt confident facing dominant castes in the election. Lakshmiben also felt that it was important for her to win, the reasons for which are mentioned in her quote above. According to her, "Dalit women have to understand all this politics and accordingly convince people that they are capable of panchayat administration equal to men. Our participation in the panchayat is necessary because it can surely bring about change."

Despite stiff opposition from a rival candidate belonging to her own sub-caste, whom the dominant castes had set up against her as their benami, Lakshmiben won the election with a margin of 74 votes. She averred that, apart from the backing she received from her family and the dominant caste vice president, who was a family friend, critical to her victory was the support from Dalit and Adivasi communities, women in particular. "They believed that if I became president," she said, "development works would be implemented easily for them, and that they would feel comfortable to approach me or tell me anything related to such works."

Lakshmiben's experience provides a useful starting point to examine whether affirmative action – reserving one-third of SC reserved seats in the panchayats for SC women – does in fact facilitate Dalit women's access to positions of authority in the panchayats. A number of supportive and obstructive actors, their actions framed by caste, class and gender power dynamics, emerge from the narratives of Lakshmiben and other Dalit women. These actors serve ostensibly as gatekeepers in accessing positions of authority, which is the first step towards the enjoyment of the right to participate in local governance institutions.[1]

The extent of the political space required for Dalit women to access governance positions depends on their level of enjoyment of five basic inter-related rights: the right to information; the right to equality of status and opportunities; the right to freedom of expression, assembly and of association; the right to development, which entails an entitlement to adequate resources; and the right to security of life. Access to information regarding electoral processes, local governance structures and functions is necessary for Dalit women candidates. Given their generally low literacy levels, information is essential to equip them with adequate knowledge about their roles and functions in the panchayats. Based on international human rights law and Indian constitutional provisions regarding the right to non-discrimination on the grounds of race, caste, religion and sex,[2] the reservation policy ensures these women equal opportunities to access positions of public authority.

Similarly, freedom-related rights are essential conditions for Dalit women to access public positions of authority: the freedom to contest elections; freedom of movement to canvass for votes; freedom of expression to debate public affairs; freedom of assembly in order to elicit electoral support; and the freedom to publish political material and advertise political ideas. Political contest also presupposes the ability to access adequate resources for nomination fees or deposits, and the opportunity to campaign and undertake other electoral processes for garnering support from the public. The right to political participation without discrimination, therefore, is contingent on one's financial capacity as well as the state imposing a reasonable limit on expenses to enable economically weaker sections of society to enter the political fray.[3] Finally, access to political participation implies a free and peaceful environment wherein those seeking political office enjoy safety and security both in law and in fact.

All these conditions are essential if Dalit women are to enjoy their right to political participation. However, unequal caste-

class-gender power relations produced and reproduced in the
caste system strongly counteract women's efforts to benefit from
the political spaces reserved for them. This is seen throughout
their attempts to access power highlighted in this chapter – their
manner of taking decisions to contest panchayat elections; their
efforts to file nominations; their freedom of movement to canvass
for votes; the social environment they experienced on the voting
day and after the announcement of the election results; and the
expenses they incurred for their campaigns. The experiences of
Dalit women who both accessed and failed to access panchayat
posts are analysed to unearth the forces at play in determining the
women's entry into the panchayats.

Deciding to Contest Panchayat Posts

Of the 200 Dalit women interviewed in this research, only 30
(15.0 per cent) had decided freely and independently, without any
undue influence, to contest the panchayat elections. For instance,
Rajakumari from Madurai district in Tamil Nadu voiced her
independence, and determination to achieve something significant
through the panchayat:

> Soon after the demise of my husband, my union panchayat was
> declared an SC women reserved constituency. No one forced me
> to contest. I decided on my own. I was born, grew up and live here.
> After all, all of us have to die as human beings. But before I die,
> I wanted to achieve something significant. This was the passion
> with which I contested the elections. Who are Dalit women? Are
> they to remain bonded? I wanted to prove that no Dalit woman is
> a servile person. That is why I contested the panchayat elections.

For Vanitaben from Ahmedabad district in Gujarat, who had
previously been a panchayat member, was a little educated, an
active member of a Dalit organisation and known for taking
up social issues, the announcement of the reservation of the
president's post in her village panchayat for SC women was the
fulfilment of a long cherished desire. In her words, "I was elected
once as a panchayat member. But this time I decided to contest for

the post of president and so I filed my nomination on my own for the development of my Dalit people."

For a few women like Kamachi from Coimbatore district in Tamil Nadu, access to local governance proved to be a turning point in their lives. She twice contested and was elected village panchayat president. Her entry into the political fray provided an opportunity to shift from being overly dependent on others to taking an independent decision to access political power. Importantly, she learnt the art of 'doing politics' from her previous panchayat term. In her words:

> When my village panchayat was declared an SC women reserved constituency previously, I had no thought to contest the election. The former panchayat president, a dominant caste man, wanted to keep his hold on the panchayat and filed the nomination for another woman, Maheshwari. Meanwhile, the AIADMK-MDMK political party front approached me. I was reluctant in the beginning, but due to pressure from my parents and relatives, who are AIADMK supporters, I agreed to contest. The party members told me when I went to file my nomination that I would not have to do any panchayat administration, and that they would run the panchayat with me as president. They then decided to elect a dominant caste man from MDMK as vice president. Since I did not realise the power politics involved in the fixing up of panchayat positions, I did not find their proposal in any way a hindrance to my position as president. But the five years of obstructions and harassment I experienced from the dominant castes and political parties during my first term in office made me reconsider my stand in the next elections. Hence, for those elections I contested as an independent candidate. Being single and a Dalit woman, I thought I was best placed to work for the welfare of my community, especially women. I forged an alliance with the Congress party and made five Dalit members file their nominations for membership posts and helped them win.

In contrast, the 170 remaining women indicated the influence of individuals or multiple people over their decision to contest panchayat posts – for example, husbands and relatives, husbands and dominant caste villagers, Dalit and dominant caste villagers,

Dalits and political party members, dominant caste villagers and
political party functionaries. Nearly half the women (94 women
or 47 per cent) mentioned their husbands playing the main role
in their decision to content panchayat elections. Dalit women
villagers in Vadodara district, Gujarat noted that, "Unless we get
permission from our families, we cannot contest elections. We
need to get permission from our husbands. If it is a general seat, a
woman is expected not to contest. If she does, she cannot and will
not be allowed to go alone for canvassing. Hence, she has to keep
her husband beside her." Taking both the women who mentioned
their husbands (47 per cent of women) and those who indicated
their family members and relatives, mostly men (26 women or
13 per cent), it is clear that male kinship plays a major role in
women's decisions to contest panchayat posts.

Also significant was that dominant castes, especially dominant
caste men, played a relatively strong role in determining Dalit
women's entry into the political domain. The next largest
influential group after husbands was dominant caste villagers (65
women or 32.5 per cent), followed by political party functionaries,
of whom the majority were dominant caste (23 women or 11.5 per
cent). For example, the dominant caste and traditional panchayat
elders suggested that Selvi from Coimbatore district in Tamil
Nadu contest the SC women reserved post of union panchayat
member. They also told her that they would meet most of her
election expenses and ensure additional financial support from the
AIADMK political party. Where the dominant castes' influence
wasn't direct, as in the case of Selvi, it occurred indirectly through
the women's husbands. Either way, it evidenced a male influence
over the women's decisions.

A striking point is that the Dalit community played a minimal
role in the women's decision-making process (mentioned by only
18 women or 9 per cent), an influence not even on par with that
of political parties. The influence of Dalit men beyond the family
over these women's decisions is illustrated by the selection process
undergone by Priya from Thirunelveli district in Tamil Nadu.
Two candidates filed nominations for the SC women reserved
post of village panchayat president – Priya from the majority

Dalit sub-caste and her rival candidate from a minority Dalit sub-caste. However, men from Priya's sub-caste and the Dalit *nattanmai* (head of the community) drew lots to decide which of the two candidates would be allowed to stand for the elections. Priya was thus declared the candidate. This selection process exposes the social norms that legitimise male decision-making on behalf of Dalit women candidates.

When it came to supporting the women in filing their nominations, except for the 30 women who did so independently, a larger number of women received external support: from dominant caste villagers (124 women or 62.0 per cent), followed closely by husbands (123 women or 61.5 per cent), then family members and relatives (92 women or 46.0 per cent), Dalit villagers (89 women or 44.5 per cent) and political party functionaries (47 women or 23.5 per cent). Highlighting both the role of husbands and the gender gap in political education, a group of Dalit women elected representatives in Gujarat shared the following:

> Husbands always go with women to file nominations. Women hardly know anything about the panchayat and related activities, like filling up the nomination forms or arranging for the certificates. Husbands only know all such procedures. But the women learn these things by doing them with their husbands, thanks to the reservation policy. Then the husbands continue to guide the women on how to do things after being elected to the panchayat. They even tell them what to do – as the women still do not know anything more than the earlier experience of filing a nomination with the help of their husbands.

Comparing the women's decision-making regarding electoral participation and the support received at the nomination stage, husbands played a greater role than dominant castes in the women's decision to contest. However, the margin of difference in support at the nomination stage from these two groups was negligible. One explanation is that once the woman's candidature was decided upon, the dominant caste villagers rallied behind her nomination to ensure that, once elected, she would safeguard their interests. That husbands still held the predominant position both in influencing the women's decisions and in rendering support at the nomination stage points to the domestic sphere as the primary locus for decision-making and support for the women. The women either felt more confident and comfortable relying on their husbands, or were socialised to accept the decisions their husbands made on their behalf. Either explanation points to patriarchal power over the women.

In terms of the roles of Dalit villagers versus dominant caste villagers at the nomination stage, dominant castes clearly had a greater influence on the women in both decision-making and support. Whether the dominant castes did this independent of the husbands or in collaboration with them, what appears clear is the determined pursuit of their own interests, or interests in congruence with those of the husbands. In this situation, the question of whose interests – dominant castes', the husband's, or the Dalit community – the women would represent in the panchayat, if and when they were elected, becomes relevant.

DECISION UNDER EXTERNAL INFLUENCE AND BENAMI POLITICS

The majority of the 170 women whose decision to contest panchayat posts was influenced by external actors can be divided into two categories. The first category consists of women who took decisions based on the suggestion, request, instruction or persuasion of others. For example, 53-year-old Chanchalben from Kheda district in Gujarat did not want to file her nomination for the post of village panchayat president as she did not want the stress and strain of undertaking panchayat duties. However, she said, "I had to convince myself of the importance of contesting the election for my husband, who wanted to get into the panchayat. This time he could not as the seat was reserved for SC women, and hence he did not have any choice except to make me contest. Knowing that my husband is active in the village and because the whole village and the OBCs told me to contest, I filed my nomination." Being requested, instructed or persuaded to contest panchayat elections by others, these women may have had the freedom to refuse, but felt obliged to accept the proposal. Common reasons were feeling unable to reject the request of their husbands, feeling respect for their dominant caste employers, or being beholden to them for their livelihoods.

The second category belongs to those women who faced pressure or were forced to function as benamis for their sponsors. Benami politics in democratic electoral processes refers to the power dynamics operating between two parties – the dominant and the dominated, as determined by an unequal social context – leading to a dominated person being pushed to occupy a position of authority as the dominant's surrogate nominee. This surrogate nominee is then used to fulfil the interests of the dominant caste/class person/s who, in effect, is the one who exercises political authority. Benamis had no opportunity to freely decide whether or not to contest panchayat posts. Instead, they were forced to accept the decision made for them by their 'sponsors'.

A group of Dalit women elected representatives from Cuddalore district in Tamil Nadu identified three types of actors responsible for benami politics:

> Whether it is a panchayat election or state assembly election, the first helping hand is our family leader (husband). He is at the same time a stumbling block to us, for if we are uneducated or less educated, he makes use of us to earn money. The exception is only when we have the capacity to act independently. Our own relatives are the next stumbling block for us. The third group is the dominant castes. If we are able to dance to their tunes, they use us indirectly for their own benefit and needs. If we act freely and independently, they will directly confront and go against us. The reservation policy is an opportunity for us to achieve liberation from this kind of 'benami slavery'. Hence, Dalit women must make use of this policy to develop their skills and increase their power.

By contrast, Dalit individuals, Dalit elders or the Dalit community played a minimal role in applying pressure or force on the women to contest elections as their benami.

Compared to husbands, family members and other Dalit community members, those who had a more decisive say were a third set of sponsors comprised of dominant caste villagers, dominant caste vice presidents, dominant caste panchayat members and dominant caste political party functionaries. For example, Mookammal from Madurai district in Tamil Nadu contested the SC women reserved post of village panchayat president as the benami of the dominant castes, the panchayat vice president and clerk in particular, through her husband. In the village *katta panchayat* (traditional system of rural governance) attended by all the dominant castes, the dominant castes decided that they would only support Mookammal for the panchayat post; and, therefore, she would not need to do any canvassing. She had the support of only three households of her Dalit sub-caste whereas the majority Dalits of another sub-caste put up their own candidate.

Gangaben, by contrast, experienced a single dominant caste individual forcing her as well as the entire panchayat to accept her as the village panchayat president. Dominant caste Lakshmanbhai, a politically influential person and local *rowdy* (criminal element) who inspired fear in his and surrounding villages imposed his will on Gangaben from Anand district in Gujarat. She narrated,

> Lakshmanbhai quietly decided on my name as president by 'consensus' and signed the nomination form on my behalf. He also decided the names of all 12 women for panchayat membership and made his wife the vice president. Only two days before the closing date for filing nominations, the regional newspapers carried the news of the 'consensus' election of the all-women panchayat council. The night before the news became public, he came to my house to tell me that I had been elected president. His dominant caste community supported him in whatever he did. He selected me as a benami president because he wanted to exploit the Dalit community through me. I work as a manual scavenger and my husband is a sweeper in the panchayat. Lakshmanbhai knew that he would be able to control the panchayat administration effectively through me. My Dalit community is very much suppressed and he used threats to cut off my husband's livelihood. We could never even think of speaking against him or doing anything without his permission. He knew this, and that was why he selected me.

Important to note is that in several cases there were multiple benami sponsors cutting across family, caste and party lines and wielding power over the women candidates – for example, husbands and dominant caste villagers or political party functionaries, husbands and Dalit community members, Dalit and dominant caste villagers, dominant caste villagers and political functionaries, and so on.

A number of strategies and factors influence benami politics in specific social contexts. A straightforward strategy for husbands and male relatives is to exploit kinship ties to the women. Another strategy employed predominantly by dominant castes, is to exploit the women's vulnerability, be it old age, widowhood, physical disabilities like blindness, dependency as daily wage labourers and/or illiteracy. Kailashben of Surendranagar district in Gujarat, for instance, was propped up by the dominant castes to contest the post of village panchayat president in the general women constituency. According to her, they supported her candidature because she was illiterate and had no knowledge on the panchayat administration. The case of bonded labourer Vijaya from Madurai district in Tamil Nadu also merits attention for the manner in which the livelihood concerns of the working class are exploited in benami politics:

My family works as bonded labourers on the land of dominant caste Subramaniam and his relatives. He enjoys great authority in the area and was village panchayat president previously for two terms. When the panchayat was declared an SC women reserved constituency, Subramaniam told me that this time he would get me elected as president. He said, 'I will look after all election expenses, but you should not talk to anybody on any panchayat matter. You should not sign any paper without my knowledge. For the entire five-year term, you must be under my control.' Since I work as a bonded labourer for his family, people of his caste agreed by consensus to my candidature; so I did not have to do any campaigning. Because of Subramaniam's influence, I won the election. The day after the election results were announced, he told me, 'Trusting you, I spent two lakhs for the elections. Therefore, you should not affix your signature on any document without my permission. If your relatives come to meet you, you should inform me in advance about them, and only then will you be allowed to speak to them.' Subramaniam became the vice president of the panchayat and undertakes all panchayat responsibilities. To date, I have not seen the official green ink pen and the stamp meant for the president. They are with him, and I have nothing to do with the panchayat administration at all.

Factional rivalries, either among dominant castes, or between dominant castes and Dalits, also add another dimension to benami politics. This strategy often exploits and reinforces factions among Dalits in order to promote the interests of the dominant caste sponsors as well as to maintain control over them and the panchayat. In the case of Shardaben, she was placed in the crossfire of factional politics between Dalits and dominant castes. In her village in Vadodara district in Gujarat, the forward castes (FCs) were in conflict with one Dalit sub-caste over a caste atrocity and, therefore, did not want to support a woman candidate from that sub-caste for the SC women reserved post of village panchayat president. Hence, the dominant castes supported Shardaben from another Dalit sub-caste instead, and had her contest as a rival benami candidate in order to maintain control over the panchayat and isolate the other Dalit sub-caste. Shardaben said, "The FCs convinced my husband to make me contest for the post of president. Because my husband works as a *safai karamchari* in the panchayat, the FCs knew that he would never go against them due to fear of losing his job. As for me, I never wanted this post."

In many such conflict situations, the Dalit community faces a predicament because of their dependence on dominant castes for employment. This makes it difficult for them to remain united enough to counter dominant caste manipulations. Dalit women villagers in Surendranagar district in Gujarat articulated this dilemma as follows:

> All the three dominant sub-castes in our panchayat create internal conflict among us [Dalits] by propping up benami candidates from our communities in order to control the panchayat administration. We Dalits know this, but are unable to do anything because we are not united to challenge their domination. Whatever the dominant castes do, the entire village has to support them, including us, because most of us depend on these dominant castes for our daily livelihood and other monetary requirements.

Electoral democracy also provides scope for penalising Dalits for alleged past wrongs. An example of this is where the dominant castes use a benami Dalit woman from one sub-caste to punish another Dalit sub-caste by denying the latter entry into the panchayats. This is best illustrated by an incident in Kheda district in Gujarat narrated by a dominant caste vice president:

> Some time ago, one Dalit sub-caste in my village demanded that they sit and eat with us [dominant castes] at a public function of the village temple. This was an outrageous proposal, and hence we rejected it outright and cut off our relations with them. We then made it clear in the village that no one should elect or appoint anyone from this Dalit sub-caste to the post of village panchayat president. We are enemies, as the members of this Dalit sub-caste are educated job holders and hence feel independent. Moreover, this sub-caste has filed two atrocity cases against me, one of which concerns my efforts to stop a 20-year-old woman of this sub-caste from becoming panchayat president. So instead, my (FC) community supported a Dalit woman candidate from another Dalit sub-caste, got her husband's consent and ensured her victory as panchayat president. I played a major role in deciding who the president should be and in getting the village consensus on this.

Finally, a significant strategy for benami politics is for dominant castes to use consensus elections to maintain control over the panchayats through a proxy Dalit woman candidate. This research revealed two types of consensus politics. One type is the traditional village benami politics operative in both Gujarat and Tamil Nadu wherein dominant castes effectively decide on the one Dalit woman candidate allowed to contest the elections. A typical example in which the dominant castes imposed their collective authority on a Dalit woman to serve as their benami is recounted by Leela, an agricultural labourer from Madurai district in Tamil Nadu. She was elected by consensus as village panchayat president in 2006:

> When for the first time the post of president was announced as reserved for SC women in my panchayat, the dominant caste landlords, one of whom holds a district level political party

position, held a katta panchayat in the village. Therein they decided to make me contest the post of president. My husband and I did not know about this meeting being held or what they discussed. A messenger was sent to call us to the meeting. All the men and women belonging to different dominant castes in the entire panchayat were gathered there. I was afraid, for normally it is only when they want to punish somebody for any mistake committed that they gather like this. On reaching the venue, they told me, 'We have decided to make you contest the election. As soon as you win, you must resign, like what happened in Pappapatti and Keeripatti village panchayats. Till then you must be under our control.' At that time, I saw no one else go with this diktat; so I agreed. They also decided that no other Dalit should stand in the election except me.

Leela's experience illustrates a number of aspects comprising dominant caste imposed benami politics played out through 'consensus' elections. The imposition of 'consensus' candidates is executed in a pre-planned and non-transparent manner. It prevents any other Dalit woman from contesting as an independent candidate. It also forestalls any other dominant caste from propping up another Dalit woman candidate. In addition, the Dalit community is further subjugated by the dominant castes and exploited in a politically legitimised manner. This 'consensus' politics helps those with socio-political power in rural areas to maintain control over the panchayats. The dominant caste vice president effectively decides on all panchayat matters. And finally, to ensure that the Dalit woman acts as a benami, dominant castes maintain control over her and her husband's livelihood. In this regard, Dalit elders and male villagers in Surendranagar district in Gujarat commented:

In some villages, reservations are not productive at all. Even where it is an SC reserved seat, we are not allowed to contest the elections. The dominant castes just want to fill the reserved seat. They manipulate the entire village opinion by their domination through a 'consensus' decision of putting up a benami candidate for them. Even where an active Dalit man somehow enters into the panchayat, they keep creating problems for him or bring a no confidence motion against him very quickly. They think that reservation is a hurdle to their dominance over the village and the panchayat.

The second type of 'consensus' politics is found only in Gujarat where the state *samras* (consensus) scheme offers awards of up to ₹1,87,500 for establishing consensus panchayats. The experience of Rekhaben from Kheda district in Gujarat exemplifies how the dominant castes skilfully manipulate Dalit women candidates into accepting the samras scheme to suit dominant caste interests. A complete benami for her husband, who himself had been a benami for the FCs in the previous panchayat, Rekhaben was chosen by the FCs as their benami candidate for the position of village panchayat president. The FCs used village meetings to pressurise two other Dalit women candidates into withdrawing their nominations so that Rekha could be elected unopposed and the panchayat could get money under the samras scheme. Once these two women withdrew, Rekhaben's husband put her name on the nomination papers without even asking her.

The critical question is whether the state consensus scheme and traditional consensus practices are in line with democratic norms and practices. The Dalit women elected representatives and government officials interviewed favoured consensus politics emerging from below and not imposed from above, if at all. As a taluka development officer in Gujarat pointed out, "the consensus method is good in principle because it avoids unnecessary conflicts within and between different communities of the same village. But how good it is depends on the village community's composition and the way the process is conducted. Above all, what should be considered important is that the people should have the freedom to enter into consensus agreements." Freedom, however, is the critical missing element in consensus politics as currently practised. A group of elected Dalit women representatives in Ahmedabad district in Gujarat commented,

> There is no proper meeting of the whole village to decide on a real consensus candidate for the post of president. The consensus candidates who get selected are usually illiterate, poor

people who are influenced by the dominant castes on whom the candidates depend for employment... The dominant castes, who are experienced in manipulative politics, set the Dalit sub-castes against each other when an SC reserved post is announced and never allow them to come together and hold meetings like other castes. Hence, consensus method, as it is practised now, should not take place. There should always be elections so as to provide opportunities to any person to exercise her/his constitutional and electoral rights and only eligible persons should be allowed to vote.

Echoing this analysis, a group of Dalit women elected representatives from Cuddalore district in Tamil Nadu stated:

It is completely wrong to be elected unopposed or unanimously. This method of conducting elections is meant to strengthen the power of the dominant castes. Not only this, it is against democratic rights, freedom and equality. This is another kind of violence that dominant castes use against us [Dalits]. Hence, there should be a general election. Only then can the elected representatives take all the welfare measures to the people freely and independently without fear.

A deputy mamlatdar of the election branch in Gujarat was forthright in his view that the state supported consensus scheme should be abrogated because of its utilisation to make women subservient in panchayat politics.

The congruence in the observations of Dalit women elected representatives and government officials regarding consensus panchayats highlights how this strategy violates citizen rights and reinforces caste, class and gender inequalities. The only difference between traditional and state types of consensus politics is that in the latter case, the state legitimises the traditional dominant caste based village rule under the guise of maintaining social harmony. What this points to is the need to unpack local power dynamics as one examines the implementation of state schemes or reservation policies. Doing so highlights how Dalit women in benami politics, by virtue of their caste, class and gender status, serve as a mediating body through which dominant political actors exercise control over the panchayats.

Main Motivation for Accessing Panchayat Posts

Two main motivations drove the 200 Dalit women who sought to enter the electoral fray. They were either asked by others to contest (140 women or 70.0 per cent); or wanted to bring development benefits to Dalits (42 women or 21.0 per cent). The remaining 18 women (9.0 per cent) mentioned various other factors motivating them to access panchayat seats.

The first group of women were those who were requested, instructed or persuaded to contest a panchayat seat, and so were not fully independent candidates. In addition were those women who experienced pressure or force to file nominations as full-fledged benami candidates. Referring to her husband's role in her decision, for example, Vasantha of Cuddalore district in Tamil Nadu said, "I did not want to contest. I don't like all this politics… But my husband assured me that he would see to it that no problem would occur for me; and, therefore, that I should give my consent to contest the election. I was aware that this post would enable him to get his hands on the panchayat contracts."

What this shows is that while the reservation policy aims to ensure free access and fair representation in local governance for the development of Dalits and women, social inequalities lead to its subversion in practice.

While the second group also contained some women who were requested, instructed or persuaded to file nominations, the majority made independent decisions to access panchayat posts. Aside from viewing entry into the panchayat as important, these women viewed political participation as opportune to bring development benefits to Dalits. Vanitaben from Ahmedabad district in Gujarat, for example, wanted to tackle the larger issue of weeding out corruption in the panchayat so as to ensure that development resources intended for Dalits actually reached the community. Likewise, in deciding to contest elections, Jayashree from Thirunelveli district in Tamil Nadu was clear, "I contested the elections on my own effort in order to develop my Dalit people who were utterly poor in my area. I wanted to bring about an upsurge from among the Dalit community." The significance of Dalit women's decisions to access panchayat posts, given their oppressive social context, is well illustrated by the case of Reshmaben from Ahmedabad district in Gujarat:

> Some economically powerful dominant castes had been controlling our panchayat without elections for around 45 years. They threatened us with violence and stopped my (Dalit) community from using any public facilities in the village, like grazing lands for our cattle and government land for building houses. The dominant castes also encroached on all the grazing and empty lands of the village. All kinds of untouchability practices exist in the village and the panchayat area... This was the situation until 2001, when my community became so fed up that they wanted a change. They felt it was necessary for a Dalit to enter the panchayat so that work could be done for the community.
>
> In 2001, my husband Lakshmanbhai was elected panchayat president with support from all the other communities except for the powerful dominant castes. Much to the anger of these dominant castes, he took control of the panchayat administration and started doing work for village development – focusing on the poor among all caste communities including the Dalits. He struggled and managed to implement a few development works. Besides confronting them on some small issues, he took action against the dominant castes for their encroachment on government land. They therefore resorted to threats against panchayat members. Despite their opposition, my husband succeeded in doing his work effectively for four years and three months. Then the dominant caste members, being the majority in the panchayat, removed him from the president's post using a no confidence motion. Because his term was almost getting over, he did not appeal against his removal. His panchayat term was the first in which development work for the poor and the Dalits in the panchayat took place.
>
> Despite the opposition he experienced, in the next elections in 2006, my husband asked me to file my nomination for a panchayat member's post in a general women constituency. To divide the Dalit vote, the dominant castes supported another woman from my sub-caste as their benami candidate. My husband and others were convinced that only our family could really challenge the dominant castes due to our relatively sound economic status. I

filed my nomination because I felt it was very important for a Dalit woman to enter the panchayat at this time.

A number of other motivating factors drove the third group of women, who by and large made independent decisions to access panchayat authority. For women like Ramilaben from Vadodara district in Gujarat, the opportunity to participate in panchayat governance through reservations was a historic opportunity to be seized as a matter of right. She said, "It was important for a Dalit woman to win the election because for the first time in 54 years, there was an SC reserved seat in my taluka. If it was a general seat, the dominant castes would never have given Dalits the opportunity to participate. So if the panchayat seat is set aside for us, we must take it." The need to bring development benefits to the entire panchayat, including Dalits, was another such motive, as Kalaimani from Nagapattinam district in Tamil Nadu explained. A former union panchayat member, Kalaimani said the following regarding her interest in contesting the next election: "My target was especially the poor. I also wanted to implement all the development projects meant for my panchayat, in particular improving road facilities." Pushpa from Thirunelveli district in Tamil Nadu, however, contested the panchayat by-election in order to avenge her husband: he had been wrongfully arrested and dismissed from the post of panchayat president due to the forgery of panchayat cheques perpetrated by the dominant caste vice president and clerk. Finally, there were other Dalit women for whom the electoral contest was an opportunity to hold public office, initiate Dalit women's leadership in the panchayats and be a source of inspiration to other women.

Nominating for Panchayat Posts

The filing of a nomination is the first step towards entry into the panchayats. Given the number of Dalit women who were either supported or pressurised by others to contest the elections, it was not surprising that 175 women, or 87.5 per cent, filed their nominations unhindered.

OPPOSITION AT THE NOMINATION STAGE

However, access to the panchayats was obstructed at this stage for 25 women (12.5 per cent), most of whom being those who decided to contest as independent candidates. Those seeking to prevent the women from filing their nomination ranged from dominant caste villagers (reported by 12 women), to rival Dalit women candidates and their supporters (10 women), to Dalit villagers (7 women), to political parties and their supporters (3 women), and for some Dalit women, the obstruction occurred from multiple sources simultaneously. Two trends emerge from a further consideration of this list.

For about half of these women, dominant castes were the main stumbling block. Aiming to get their benami candidates elected, these castes sought to divide, or exploit the conflicts within, the Dalit community. Commenting on this situation, Dalit women elected representatives in Ahmedabad district in Gujarat highlighted how non-Dalits use internal conflicts among Dalits to benefit from the process: "Lack of unity among Dalits makes them vulnerable to easy manipulation by the dominant castes by setting up candidates against each other rather than the Dalit community itself building consensus on a Dalit woman candidate."

The other half faced obstructions primarily from rival Dalit women candidates. These candidates either wanted to utilise the democratic opportunity that reservations offered them, or were benamis for their husbands. Both situations point to identity politics based on the women's caste and gender, around which the negotiations for power take place. The identity politics of the former group of women was characterised by independence and the assertion of their agency. In the case of the latter group of benamis, the assertion was marked by a dependence on and willingness to be proxy candidates for others. Pushpa's experience from Thirunelveli district in Tamil Nadu illustrates how a rival Dalit woman candidate and benami for her husband sought to prevent Pushpa from filing her independent nomination in the panchayat elections:

I was put through many obstacles by Chinnasamy, my rival candidate's husband. He obstructed me from filing my nomination using threats of murder. His threats continued during the election campaign with the help of *goondas*. He did not allow my election posters to be pasted around the villages and made many threatening anonymous telephone calls. Even though I went to the local police station many times, the police showed no interest in my complaints. To date no action has been taken and I heard that this was due to Chinnasamy having bribed the police. But I did not lose hope. I campaigned with more vigour with the help of my son and relatives as I was unable to move about alone due to Chinnasamy's threats.

As Pushpa's case demonstrates, threats were a form of obstruction at the nomination stage. For the 25 women, a combination of one or more of the following obstructions occurred. One level was outright damage to their public image, by labelling the women as 'of immoral character' (seven women), subjecting them to verbal abuse of a caste-based or sexual nature (five women), and publicly pointing out the women's weaknesses, such as her ignorance of panchayat administration (one woman). A second level of pressure, enticement and threats included women being pressurised into accepting a consensus decision of the village in favour of their rival contenders (seven women). It also included threats of physical assault, destruction of property, or denial of employment (six women), women being offered bribes to not file their nomination (three women), or pressure to obtain political party tickets and not independently contest the election (one woman). A third level involved more direct actions against the women and their families. This included physically assaulting a woman's husband in an attempt to murder him, damaging a woman's house and property in order to frighten her, and physically preventing a woman from entering the government office to file her nomination papers.

Independent candidate Rajakumari from Madurai district in Tamil Nadu spoke of the multiple forms of pressure and obstructions she faced from dominant castes in her locality.

When I went along with my supporters to file my nomination [for the post of union panchayat member] at around 3:00 p.m.

on the last day for filing nominations, three dominant caste men from the neighbouring villages prevented me from entering the gate. Then they, together with all the dominant caste villagers in the panchayat, abused me with sexually vulgar words and my caste name, said things like, 'Hey, daughter of a Pallar, how dare you come to file your nomination!' They chased me away from the place and frightened all my supporters. By then some news reporters had reached the spot, and I gave an interview to a Tamil newspaper and a news channel, which broadcasted the incident in the 8:30 p.m. news hour. On hearing the news, the three dominant caste men, together with their caste community men and youth, rushed to my house and pelted stones on the roof, breaking the tiles and damaged the walls with their sticks and iron rods. They once again abused me using my caste name.

The primary reason behind these obstructive actions was the issue of whose interests the women would serve in the panchayats. Over two-thirds of the women facing opposition (17 women) highlighted the dominant castes' apprehension that the women, being Dalits, would not represent or serve their interests, or the Dalits' perception that the women would fail to represent their interests due to dominant castes nominating them as candidates. Fifteen women spoke of the dominant castes preferring their own choice of benami candidate instead of women who were viewed as too independent, or the Dalits favouring other Dalit women candidates belonging to their own sub-castes, or rival Dalit women contestants wanting to ensure they won the elections instead of the women. Identity-based discrimination was also evident for seven women, where dominant castes considered their Dalit female identity as equating to an incapacity to contest panchayat posts or a capacity to upset the status quo by advocating for Dalit development.

Similarly, opposition to three women's nominations stemmed from perceptions that they would be too active and vocal on social issues that might adversely affect the interests of the dominant castes, or the political parties dominated by these castes. This was especially the case in villages with established units of Dalit political parties, as in Tamil Nadu, where these units could support candidates who would act independent of the dominant castes. Contesting in a general women reserved constituency in Anand district, Gujarat, Sunitaben highlights the need for counter-strategies to thwart dominant caste obstructions.

> Before filing my nomination there was an attempt by one dominant caste community to convince me at the outset not to contest the post of panchayat president. This was done with the aim of fielding another woman candidate of their own caste as a benami. To strengthen their electoral chances, they promised a male candidate belonging to another Dalit sub-caste with the vice president's post and made him convince the entire Dalit community to support the dominant caste woman candidate for president. Although I was afraid of the dominant castes doing some mischief, the election process passed off peacefully without any obstacles for me while canvassing as well as on the voting day. This was mainly due to my supporters always keeping a watchful eye on the polling booth so as to stop any kind of illegal or bogus voting.

In sum, the above analysis highlights how, on the one hand, in order to protect their interests and preserve social inequalities, dominant castes resort to engineering panchayat elections from the nomination stage itself. On the other hand, Dalit women who are socially aware, critical and articulate in their views, and keen to see the development of their community and others, attempt to use reservations to assume positions of authority. In doing so, they face various kinds of verbal and physical obstructions intended to prevent them from filing nominations. An underlying assumption is that these women, because of their low social, educational, class and gender status, do not have the capacity to govern, and thus can be made subservient to dominant forces. As regards those Dalit women who have a stable economic base, are educated and articulate, their nominations also threaten dominant caste interests and hence must be prevented at all costs. Either way, a denial of the women's right to freely access political positions in local governance results.

Unfortunately, not all government officials overseeing Panchayati Raj understand this reality on the ground. An assistant director of panchayats in Tamil Nadu, when questioned about the relevance of monitoring to ensure a free and independent nomination process for Dalit women, replied, "In our country and in the Panchayati Raj system, there is no caste or gender discrimination. Only when there is discrimination or trouble, we will have to look for a solution. When there is equality in our country, where is the need for monitoring?" He also dismissed the use of threats against Dalit women who put forward their panchayat nominations as false news. A block development official (BDO) in Tamil Nadu further affirmed, "It is not our responsibility to monitor whether the candidates are free to submit their candidature or not for elections." An explanation of this bureaucratic mind-set came from a deputy mamlatdar from the election branch in Gujarat: "We do not have any special arrangements for Dalits and women to file their nominations freely. All arrangements are equal for every candidate. We accept the nomination forms which are brought to the office. There are no separate procedures followed for reserved panchayats at all. We do not go to the village panchayats. All the election related activities are done in the office only." Given the reality of the multiple obstructions faced by Dalit women, the lack of government monitoring mechanisms during the nomination process points to a failure by the Indian state to guarantee its Dalit women citizens an equal right to stand for local governance posts.

In the absence of state oversight over the nomination process, Dalit women are left to deal with any obstructions based on the assumption that they know the law and administrative procedures, and are able to face the consequences. As a BDO in Tamil Nadu said, "If anyone is unable to function freely and if this is given in writing, only then the Election Officer will intervene." The role of the police, then, as a police sub-inspector in Gujarat explained, is to "maintain law and order... to avoid conflict between parties" and "protect the ballot box on the voting day". Ensuring that socially marginalised groups such as Dalit women enjoy their right to freely access the panchayats, however, is not viewed as falling within the ambit of electoral responsibilities. Herein lies a fundamental difference of views on state obligations in relation to the right to political participation. Officials perceive their duty as simply 'to ensure a peaceful environment by maintaining law and order'. However, for Dalit women to enjoy this right in a complex society structured along highly unequal caste-class-gender lines, they require officials to create 'an enabling environment for the enjoyment of this right'; that is, to put in place preventive measures to remove obstructions to the women freely contesting panchayat positions.

PRESSURISED TO WITHDRAW NOMINATION

Having successfully filed nominations for panchayat positions, Dalit women then faced hurdles while canvassing for votes, thus pressurising them into withdrawing their nominations. Bearing in mind the predominance of benami candidates, and the one woman who was prevented from filing her nomination, 29 women, or 14.5 per cent, faced pressure to withdraw their nominations. Sareekaben from Surendranagar district in Gujarat was one such woman. She was previously removed from the village panchayat president's post through a no confidence motion because she refused to submit to the control of a dominant caste. After she put in her nomination for the next elections, this dominant caste community then applied pressure on her and other Dalit women candidates to withdraw their nominations in favour of their benami candidate.

For two-thirds of the women (19 women), the pressure to withdraw nominations came primarily from rival candidates and/or their family members or supporters. A significant trend here was the role of caste politics in the pressure applied by dominant castes. An illustration is the experience of Tejuben from Kheda district in Gujarat. She knew how difficult it would be for her to win the post of president in the village panchayat elections because of a weakened electoral base caused by three competing candidates from three different factions in the Dalit community. The husband of one of her rival candidates also pressurised Tejuben to withdraw her nomination. The dominant castes further divided her sub-caste's vote, one faction supporting her while the other faction supported a rival candidate. She did not succumb to the pressure, however, and eventually won the election.

Rival candidates aside, other villagers and even political parties, despite ostensibly not playing any role at the village panchayat level, applied pressure on the women. Dominant caste villagers were implicated in pressurising 13 women to withdraw their nominations, as were political parties for three women. Less common, reported by only five women, was pressure from Dalit villagers where the women were benami candidates for dominant castes. For example, when Suguna of Madurai district in Tamil Nadu contested the post of village panchayat member in a general women constituency as the benami candidate for the dominant castes, her Dalit community tried in vain to persuade her to withdraw her nomination and instead accept their consensus Dalit candidate.

The four common methods used to pressurise the women into withdrawing their nominations mirrored those used to prevent women from filing their nominations in the first place. Nine women experienced verbal abuse of a caste-based or sexual nature in public, eight women encountered threats of physical assault or property destruction, denial of employment or social boycott against the women and/or their families, five women faced the denigration of their public image by associating their public involvement with immorality, and three women were offered or told to offer bribes in exchange for the withdrawal or retention of their nominations respectively. Arulmani of Cuddalore district in Tamil Nadu contested for the SC women reserved post of village panchayat president. The day after she filed her nomination, the BC village elders persuaded the Dalit elders to support their demand of ₹1,25,000 from Arulmani if she wanted to contest the election. Their motive was to select a candidate who would allow them to control the panchayat. Due to financial constraints, Arulmani had to withdraw her nomination. On discovering that Reshmaben from Ahmedabad district in Gujarat had filed her nomination for the post of panchayat member in the general women constituency, some dominant caste villagers unsuccessfully tried to persuade her to withdraw her nomination. They were afraid that if she came into the panchayat, she would raise the issue of their encroachments on panchayat lands. Another smaller

Dalit sub-caste was then pressurised to swear before their local deity that they would not vote for Reshmaben, while another Dalit woman was set up as a benami candidate. Finally, two dominant castes boycotted everyone in Reshmaben's sub-caste community except her rival candidate's family; they were refused employment, essential livelihood supplies and all social interactions were cut. Despite this opposition, Reshmaben won the election by a margin of 53 votes.

More direct pressure on four independent candidates found expression in physical assaults, destruction or damage to homes and property, social boycotts of women and their families, and the foisting of false cases against their family members. For Shantaben from Surendranagar district in Gujarat, active in the village and in gram sabhas, she filed her nomination for the post of village panchayat member in the general women constituency. The dominant castes, however, set up her nephew's wife as the consensus candidate and then pressurised her into withdrawing her nomination. In return for her withdrawal of her nomination, they promised Shantaben they would drop the case they had filed against her sister, a nurse, for allegedly killing a child while administering polio drops. They also stated they would support her candidature in the next elections.

Behind the pressures on two-thirds of the women to withdraw their nominations was often a clash of interests between Dalits and dominant castes. Eighteen women mentioned how dominant castes wanted to have a say in the selection of the woman candidate – for example, through deciding on a consensus benami candidate or the removal of a woman candidate – so as to maintain their caste authority over the panchayat and village in general. Sometimes this was expressed through the short term advantage of obtaining the Gujarat State Government's cash award for consensus panchayats. In the case of Jasodaben from Surendranagar district in Gujarat, previously only the dominant FCs were village panchayat presidents. When the panchayat was announced as an SC women reserved constituency for the first time, many Dalit women wanted to contest the elections. However, the previous FC president and his brother called a village meeting to decide on the entire panchayat going in for consensus in order to avail of the state's cash award. Accordingly, all the panchayat posts, including that of vice president, were allotted to different people. Jasodaben acknowledged, "I was selected for the president's post because I am 50 years old, illiterate, do not go outside of my home, do not know anything about panchayat administration and am not at all outspoken. Hence, they found it easy to have control over the funds and the administration through me."

For eight women, dominant castes felt threatened by Dalit women candidates who were vocal or active on social issues. For another six women, it was dominant caste displeasure at seeing Dalit women rising up to positions of status and authority on par with them. As stated by a group of Dalit elders and male villagers in Surendranagar district in Gujarat, "The dominant castes don't give any value to outspoken or educated Dalit women, nor do they allow them to come into the panchayat... They in fact manipulate the entire decision-making process to maintain their domination so that no one will question their supremacy in the panchayat."

The assertion of Dalit sub-caste identities through multiple Dalit women candidates, as mentioned by 15 women, also propelled negotiations on panchayat posts. In other cases, Dalits targeted the dominant caste sponsored Dalit women candidates to try and ensure their own Dalit women candidate/s would win and represent the community's needs. Take the case of Vimala from Madurai district in Tamil Nadu. Following the murder of the Dalit male panchayat president by dominant caste villagers because of his independent functioning in the panchayat, the dominant castes pressurised Vimala to contest the post as their benami. The Dalits, however, were unhappy with this strategy and tried without success to persuade Vimala to withdraw her nomination. While Vimala's case highlights an unsuccessful assertion, what is significant in many cases is that Dalit assertions of a liberating identity against dominant caste power reveal positive trends towards inclusive democracy.

COPING WITH OBSTRUCTIONS AT THE INITIAL STAGES

In dealing with obstructions at the early stages of nomination and campaigning, most Dalit women drew upon the support of their families and their Dalit community. Others handled the challenges alone. Ratha from Madurai district in Tamil Nadu, for example, came from a family who had incurred the hostility of the dominant castes after they filed a police case against the dominant castes for the murder of Ratha's in-laws. Despite their hostility, Ratha contested as an independent candidate for the post of village panchayat president in the SC women reserved constituency with her family's support. While the dominant castes divided the Dalit votes by putting up a rival Dalit woman candidate, Ratha successfully countered this move by canvassing for wider support and won the election. In contrast to this growing political empowerment, the strong weight of pressure imposed on one woman pushed her not to file any nomination in the end. A further three women were forced to withdraw nominations.

Canvassing for Voter Support

Constituencies with a majority Dalit population provide a larger electoral base to Dalit women candidates for the independent and free exercise of their electoral rights. As Dalit elders and male villagers in Thirunelveli district in Tamil Nadu noted,

> Because in this area we are the majority and the dominant caste people are only a minority, the dominant castes agree to cooperate with us [in the panchayat elections] without any strong opposition. Even during the time of canvassing, they do not do anything against us when we go to their area for canvassing. We not only request their votes, but also later implement some welfare measures for them.

Conversely, panchayat constituencies with a minority Dalit population pose a greater challenge to Dalit women in garnering electoral support. Dalit elders and male villagers in Surendranagar district in Gujarat commented on the structure of panchayat wards:

> The small Dalit population means that we must rely on the dominant castes for votes. Even if they assure their support, they will manipulate the entire votes in favour of the candidate of their choice, thereby making the Dalits contest in opposition

to each other with consequent internal division. This results in the increase of dominant castes' influence and the number of votes for their candidate. As we are less in number, we do not get enough votes. It is only those Dalits with more family members and those who contest with the support of dominant castes that get more votes.

It is for this reason that a group of Dalit women elected representatives in Ahmedabad district in Gujarat suggested:

The wards should be constituted in such a way that Dalit votes are not divided. If there are more Dalit households in one ward, then a higher number of panchayat posts should be created in that same ward so as to enable Dalits to nominate persons for member and president posts at the same time. It is only such an arrangement that can ensure an all-Dalit panchayat and make sense of SC women reserved constituencies.

What these elected representatives suggested gains weight in light of the afore-mentioned positive experience of the Dalit elders and male villagers from Thirunelveli district.

Therefore, the size of the Dalit electoral base has an impact on Dalit women's access to the panchayats. Considering the Dalit population base in the 164 village panchayat constituencies wherein Dalit women contested positions, in the majority of constituencies (127 constituencies or 77.4 per cent) it was below 50 per cent; for only 37 constituencies (22.6 per cent) was it above 50 per cent. These women therefore faced challenges in building a voter base outside their Dalit community, particularly among the various dominant caste groups. This is in addition to the occasional challenge of sub-caste politics among the Dalits. Moreover, against the background of caste and gender-based discrimination they experienced, livelihood concerns and household responsibilities, their electoral burden in seeking voter support and managing electoral politics was significant. Given these constraints, it is important to examine the freedoms they enjoyed and the ways they built a voter base during their election campaign.

Few Dalit women could safely canvass for votes with freedom and independence. The right of 27 women to canvass for votes was appropriated by others in two ways: either they were pressurised to withdraw their nominations, or a village gathering presided over by dominant castes imposed the decision to have a consensus candidate. This aside, gender norms circumscribed women's freedom of movement to a large extent. Moreover, Dalit men were generally better known among the voting public, were more educated and had more contacts with government officials, politicians and political party members than the women. Conversely, the women, generally being less educated, not so well known in the village and devoid of social contacts, felt unable to move around in public for political activities without accompaniment. Consequently, only 11 women, or 5.5 per cent, canvassed for votes alone. In contrast, over half the women (105 women or 52.5 per cent) were accompanied by their husbands and/or male relatives, and two women (1.0 per cent) by female relatives. In many cases, the men joined the women as a protective shield against caste and gender-based harassment and intimidation, especially in dominant caste habitations and in villages far away from their own.

Aside from enabling the women to freely canvass for votes, in some cases husbands and/or male relatives had high stakes in women family members holding panchayat positions; for example, gaining panchayat development work contracts or preparing to contest elections in future. The men, therefore, thought it necessary to be publicly visible while canvassing with the women. For example, Vasantha from Cuddalore district in Tamil Nadu was forced to contest the elections as a benami for her husband who wanted to take up panchayat development contracts:

> My husband, family members and party workers accompanied me during the election campaign consecutively for fifteen days. To solicit votes, many times I had to bend down and fall at the feet of SC and BC village elders and important functionaries of various political parties. I was pregnant and found it very difficult to do this. I even feared a miscarriage. My pregnancy made me feel unwell while campaigning. But I canvassed for votes because I had to. On the day I was announced the winner, I had a miscarriage. On the one hand I felt happy to have won the

election, but on the other hand it was a painful experience for me. I simply hated life at that time.

At the other end of the spectrum were women who either did not try to canvass for votes (five women), or were denied this right (50 women or 25.0 per cent). As a Dalit woman elected representative in Kheda district in Gujarat remarked, "However much women are organised, the men stop us from going out for canvassing. Even the dominant caste women never go out for canvassing." It was therefore not surprising that most of these women had other people, mostly husbands, male relatives or Dalit men, canvassing for them instead. Commenting on the gender discrimination in this situation, Dalit women elected representatives from Ahmedabad district in Gujarat stated, "Women do not get votes because both Dalit and non-Dalit men do not believe that women are able to do panchayat work unless they have a husband or male relative behind them, especially during campaigning." Dalit male villagers in Thirunelveli district in Tamil Nadu confirmed how gender biases affect the women's ability to canvass for votes: "Not to speak of the dominant castes, even a Dalit man questions how, being a man, he can listen to a woman's voice. Hence, as his wife's representative, he takes upon himself her responsibility of fulfilling electoral tasks... Apart from this, it is the commonly accepted understanding in the village that a wife is not equal to but dependent on her husband; and, therefore, she has to heed whatever he says."

In a few cases, political party cadres or dominant castes did all the campaign work on the women's behalf. Mangalam from Nagapattinam district in Tamil Nadu, for example, contested the election at the request of a local political party unit. Her husband, a party member and previously panchayat vice president, spoke on her behalf in all election meetings, and because of his political status, the party cadre did all the canvassing for her.

A further reason for women's limited capacity to canvass votes was the gender constraints on their freedom and independence. Almost half of the women denied canvassing freedom (23 women) spoke of a lack of time given household chores and child care, alongside doing remunerative work; or felt ashamed or uncomfortable to go out in public places to perform public activities. Chanchalben from Kheda district in Gujarat, whose husband campaigned for her, explained, "I did not do any canvassing because I am illiterate. Hence, I felt shy and uncomfortable to go out in public spaces and speak in public. Moreover, since in reality it was my husband who contested the election, I was not bothered about doing any vote campaigning for he told me that he would take care of everything." Similarly, although she had been village panchayat president in the previous term, Saroja from Nagapattinam district in Tamil Nadu lacked the self-confidence to canvass for votes in the next elections. Hence, her husband, the AIADMK party supporters and some Dalits did it for her. Explaining this lack of self-confidence, a group of Dalit male villagers from Thirunelveli district, Tamil Nadu, traced the reason to "the husbands keeping them under their thumbs and failing to help their women grow in self-confidence by always being behind them." There were other women who were not allowed to go out in public, or were pressurised by their husbands or male relatives not to move around campaigning.

In the case of 13 Dalit women, fear of or actual obstructions from the dominant castes curtailed their freedom to canvass for votes. Some were barred from entering dominant caste habitations in the villages, as Thilagam from Coimbatore district in Tamil Nadu experienced: "During the election campaign, I could not enter, nor get any vote, in the villages of my opponent (dominant caste) Ramanujam and his benami (Dalit) candidate Subbuthai... In the dominant caste areas where people earlier had asked me to contest the election, I could not enter and canvas for their votes. I could do so only in the Dalit area." In certain cases, dominant caste supporters of the women's rival candidates simply tore away their campaign posters, thereby violating their freedom of political expression. Meenakshi from Thirunelveli district in Tamil Nadu, contesting the post of district panchayat president in the SC women reserved constituency, refused to accept the ₹3,00,000 bribe offered by her rival candidate's husband in return for Meenakshi withdrawing her nomination. Hence, her campaign posters were torn down. Fearing that she would go against their interests, the dominant castes supported her rival candidate and bribed voters in order to defeat Meenakshi. Threats or assaults from dominant castes also made some women abstain from any canvassing activity. Women like Annammal from Madurai district in Tamil Nadu, though a benami candidate for the dominant castes, faced threats and verbal abuse because of the stringent conditions placed on her while canvassing. These conditions included prohibitions on her wearing sandals and on entering some of the dominant caste localities.

Given the above constraints on women's ability to canvass for votes, it is unsurprising that for 139 women (69.5 per cent) their families played a major role in their campaigning. Two other significant groups campaigning for the women were dominant caste villagers (reported by 107 women, or 53.5 per cent) and Dalit villagers (reported by 100 women, or 50.0 per cent). For example, Kalaimani of Nagapattinam district in Tamil Nadu had both Dalits and some dominant castes campaigning for her. She attributed this, and her eventual electoral victory to the post of village panchayat president, to her previous performance as a union panchayat member. She said, "When I was a union panchayat member, I brought electricity to one dominant caste neighbourhood and had roads laid in the Dalit area. So, supporting me for the second time, these groups canvassed for me." Lakshmiben of Vadodara district in Gujarat, referred to at the beginning of this chapter, listed multiple reasons why she received campaign support from Dalits and Adivasis, especially women: her service to the village as an anganwadi worker; her husband's earlier agitation against landlords for a wage increase of labourers; her brother-in-law distributing notebooks and stationery to children in her village; the dominant caste vice president being a family friend and supporting her; and her rival candidate being a benami for the dominant castes and so losing the support of the Dalits.

Apart from the above groups, Dalit women also received campaign support from civil society and political organisations. While six women mentioned Dalit or women's groups such as Dalit village welfare associations and women's self-help groups, nearly a quarter of the women (47 women or 23.5 per cent) pointed to a political party cadre or supporters canvassing for votes for them. The latter points to the larger political dynamics that operate, especially at the taluk/union and district panchayat levels. At these levels, political parties took the initiative to select the women who would contest elections. Women also sought alliances with political parties, either directly as informal supporters or active members of political parties, or through their family members. Alternatively, women took initiatives to strike alliances with certain political parties to counter opposition from other parties. Village panchayat president Kamachi of Coimbatore district in Tamil Nadu provided an example of this. In her first panchayat term, she endured the control of the dominant caste-led AIADMK and MDMK parties over her authority. Consequently, she said, "In the next elections, with the Dalits' undivided backing and with the Congress party willing to bring in dominant caste votes, I made an alliance with this party and encouraged five Dalits to file their nominations for membership posts."

Financial Cost of Contesting Panchayat Elections

Given the mostly poor economic backgrounds of the Dalit women, their electoral spending patterns are a significant factor in assessing the operation of the reservation policy in guaranteeing the right to free and independent political participation. At the time of this research, the government of Tamil Nadu had stipulated for SC candidates a nomination fee of ₹100 for the post of village panchayat member, ₹300 for the post of village panchayat president and union panchayat member, and ₹500 for a district panchayat post. As per the State Election Commission's rules, there was a cap on election canvassing expenses: ₹3,750 for village panchayat members, ₹15,000 for village panchayat presidents, ₹37,500 for union panchayat posts, and ₹75,000 for district panchayat posts.

Of the 100 Tamil Dalit women, 77 were panchayat members and presidents, 16 were union panchayat members, and 7 were district panchayat members. In terms of total canvassing expenses incurred for their respective posts, 15 women (11 village panchayat members/presidents and four union panchayat members) had their expenses fully met by dominant castes. For some of the other women, dominant castes and Dalits outlaid some money for them. From the information the women furnished on their total expenses, all those who canvassed for village panchayat member posts had spent within the cap of ₹3,750, except for one woman spending ₹8,900. A total of 38 village panchayat presidents had crossed the expenditure cap, some spending over ₹75,000. At the union panchayat level, eight women had spent within the expenditure cap, while four women had spent on average over double the cap. Finally, at the district panchayat level, four women had spent within the limit while three women had spent beyond ₹75,000 for their electoral campaign.

Contrast this with the situation in Gujarat. According to the amounts notified by the State Election Commission at the time, the government of Gujarat fixed the following nomination fees for SCs: ₹250 for village panchayat member's post, ₹500 for village panchayat president's post, and ₹1,000 for a post in the taluka and district panchayats. According to the State Election Commission's rules, no cap was set for election canvassing expenses at the village panchayat level. Limits were set only for taluka panchayat seats at ₹60,000, and for district panchayat seats at ₹1,25,000.

Of the 100 Dalit women in Gujarat, 87 were panchayat members and presidents, nine were taluka panchayat members and four were district panchayat members. The electoral expenses of 18 of the village panchayat members/presidents were met fully by dominant castes. The 20 women who were elected through consensus did not incur any canvassing expenses. As for the remaining women, dominant castes and Dalits did, in a few cases, outlay money for some of them. From the information women furnished on their electoral expenses, 58 of the 87 women campaigning for village panchayat member/president's posts had spent up to ₹60,000 each, and seven had spent between ₹60,001 and 1,25,000; while the expenses of four women were unspecified. Of the nine women at the taluka panchayat level, six had spent within the prescribed limit whereas two had spent between ₹60,001 and 1,25,000, and the expenditure of one woman was unknown. At the district panchayat level, three women had spent within the limit while one woman had crossed the limit of ₹1,25,000.

Taking the available data as a whole for the two states, dominant castes met all the election-related expenses for 18 per cent of women in Tamil Nadu and 15 per cent of women in Gujarat. In terms of spending within the stipulated limit, 40 per cent of women in Tamil Nadu and 13 per cent in Gujarat did so, whereas 45 per cent of women had crossed the cap in Tamil Nadu and only 3 per cent in Gujarat. The reason for this wide gap is that where election expense caps are in effect at all three panchayat tiers in Tamil Nadu, in Gujarat they are in force only at the taluka and district tiers (and, therefore, applicable to only 13 per cent of the women panchayat members). This, thereby, gave Gujarati women and their sponsors unlimited scope for expenditure in village panchayat elections.

Where did the Dalit women source election funding in both the states? For just over three-quarters of the women (152 women, or 76.0 per cent), they themselves or their households paid for election expenses. Reshmaben of Ahmedabad district in Gujarat, for instance, mentioned how her husband spent around ₹85,000 from the family savings for her to contest the post of village panchayat member. Two-thirds of the women had to take out loans. For the remaining one-third (66 women, or 33.0 per cent), financial support came from their relatives or friends. Although such close kinship ties presented a semblance of financial independence, enough for women to contest the election, the reality for many women was patriarchal pressure from male family members and relatives who controlled financial resources and, thereafter, the women's actions in the panchayats.

The election expenses for 38 women (19.0 per cent) were either partly or wholly borne by dominant caste villagers, while the financial sponsors of 12 women (6.0 per cent) were their husbands' dominant caste employers. Benami candidate Mangalam of Madurai district in Tamil Nadu, for instance, is blind and a widow. Dominant castes forced her to contest the election, paid for her nomination and canvassing expenses, and canvassed for her as well. On the day of filing her nomination and again on the voting day, they warned her that she should not attempt to interfere in panchayat matters, nor entertain any ambitions about her status in the panchayat. Sunitaben of Anand district in Gujarat mentioned how the FCs initially met all her campaigning expenses because they wanted to prevent the OBCs' benami candidate from entering the panchayat. After she won the election, they came to Sunitaben with their bills, and she repaid them by selling her buffalo. By contrast, only six women (3.0 per cent) mentioned the solidarity financial contribution of their Dalit community. Given the fact that Dalits in rural areas are largely daily wage labourers, it is not surprising that they were not in a position to match the financial and political clout of the dominant castes.

Finally, eight women reported financial support from political parties, or a former minister in the case of Ramuthai from Nagapattinam district in Tamil Nadu. While two Dalit women wanted to contest the post of village panchayat president, the dominant caste former minister did not want any election in his panchayat and so told them to decide between themselves who would fill the post. As neither woman was willing to withdraw, the former minister then offered money to Ramuthai's husband and employee to file the nomination for his wife. After being elected unopposed, Ramuthai acted as a benami president for the former minister, ensuring his political power over his constituency. Similarly, Gitaben of Surendranagar district in Gujarat was elected as a taluka panchayat member in an SC women reserved constituency. She and her husband were Congress party members; and a dominant caste village panchayat president, a Congress party member himself, wanted to make her a taluka panchayat member in order to cement the Congress party stronghold. He both supported her politically and gave her money for vote canvassing on the understanding that her holding a post at the taluka level would enable him, at the village level, to access development funds and schemes through her.

On the one hand, therefore, women and/or their supporters justified their efforts to ensure the women's election by spending large sums of money, even if it meant financial trouble or falling into debt. Significant in this regard are the 33 women who reported spending more than their annual household income, thereby driving them to loans or donations; and a further 30 women whose election expenses were significant enough, given their household income level, to pose a risk to their livelihoods. On the other hand, a lack of sufficient campaign finance rendered women vulnerable to benami politics, thereby serving the interests of dominant actors in the political system. This highlights the dangers of ensuring political representation through reservations without effective political and administrative monitoring mechanisms in place to prevent benami politics and stringently enforce regulations curtailing electoral spending. Without these measures, economically vulnerable Dalit women will continue to experience limited access to free and independent political participation.

Right to a Safe and Secure Vote

The next stage in accessing political participation is the election (voting) day. By this stage, 31 of the 200 women (15.5 per cent) had withdrawn their nominations, had been elected unopposed, or there had been no voting due to consensus decisions on candidates. Of the remaining women, 21 (10.5 per cent) faced obstructions on the election day, mainly from dominant castes (reported by 14 women) and/or from the rival candidates and their supporters (nine women). Problems from opposing political parties, by contrast, were minimal (indicated by only one woman). This trend is important as it highlights once again the political clout of the dominant castes and their critical role as gatekeepers to accessing panchayat posts.

These 21 women experienced three broad types of obstructions, with some experiencing multiple obstructions. First, women candidates were directly targeted. Their freedom to vote or to enter the election booth was impeded through threats of physical assault or destruction of property (nine women), or verbal abuse of a caste-based or sexual nature (eight women). Three other women also faced serious obstructions such as harassment or assault, verbal arguments at the polling booths meant to chase them away, and harassment by polling booth agents. Take, for example, Natya from Nagapattinam district in Tamil Nadu, who was both an active political party member and a former union panchayat member, and hence knowledgeable about panchayat administration. She faced harassment from the polling booth agent on the election day due to the booth being in the opposing candidate's village. She was also verbally abused by the defeated rival candidate once the results were announced.

The second type of obstruction was directed at the women's supporters, and included threats as well as physical prevention from voting, as indicated by nine women. The impact of such obstructions can be seen in the case of Sooriya from Madurai district in Tamil Nadu. Knowing that she was independent, outspoken and would not serve their interests, the dominant castes tried to pressurise her into not contesting the elections and instead supporting their consensus benami candidate. Sooriya's refusal provoked strong opposition in the form of physical obstructions to her vote canvassing, verbal abuse and threats of physical assault and social boycott. On the polling day, threats to her supporters (and her) made them abstain from voting and ensured her defeat.

In the third type, those opposing the women resorted to illegal voting practices, as reported by nine women. These practices included actual as well as attempted bogus voting, bribes given to voters to vote for rival candidates, and attempts to remove ballot boxes from the voting booths. For instance, Kuyil from Cuddalore district in Tamil Nadu, a Dalit party (DPI) supporter, contested the post of village panchayat president in the SC women reserved constituency. A local landlord's family placed pressure on her, first not to file her nomination and then to withdraw it, with threats of physical assault, destruction of her home and murder. Her entry into the dominant caste locality for canvassing also was barred. On the election eve, taking advantage of the Dalits' poverty, the dominant castes bribed them to vote for their benami candidate as well as threatened loss of employment, house burning and social boycott so as to ensure Kuyil's defeat.

Another method mentioned by Vanitaben from Ahmedabad district in Gujarat was the fraudulent withdrawal of her nomination without her knowledge and consent. Her experience illustrates the collusion of dominant castes and political parties in preventing independent Dalit women from accessing panchayat posts. On panchayat elections being announced with the president's post reserved for women, the FC BJP party members informed the villagers about the government's monetary award for village panchayats that adopted consensus candidates. Their motive was to push a candidate of their choice for the president's post. Two Dalit women candidates, including Vanitaben, filed nominations, however. Each of the other four dominant caste groups put up their own candidates as well. According to Vanitaben,

> No one knew for sure who would win the election, but it was certain that the FC woman would not win because she was not known in the village and was seen as a benami. Hence, the FCs started playing politics. After I filed my nomination, they sought to entice me with money to withdraw my nomination. When I refused, they abused me. They then used one of their relatives who is a higher official in the state government to pressurise one of the four dominant caste groups to support their benami candidate. Then they promised to share the consensus award money with the remaining three dominant caste groups and some Dalits. At this new move, one of the dominant caste groups agreed to withdraw their candidate's nomination. At a meeting with another dominant caste group, the FCs requested them to forget all past conflicts and come together to stop a Dalit from holding the president's post. An agreement was reached, according to which this dominant caste group was promised the vice president's post. The FCs then roped in a few Dalits to convince some Dalit families about supporting the FC consensus candidate on the reasoning that the consensus decision was an order of the BJP high command. The consensus decision, therefore, was not the agreement of the whole village, as it was taken by the dominant castes without the consent of half the Dalit community.
>
> I did not relent in my decision to contest. I withstood pressure from the FCs to withdraw my nomination in favour of their consensus candidate. However, ten days before the

election day, an FC withdrew my nomination by affixing a forged signature without my knowledge. The FCs then called a village meeting and declared their FC candidate, Lakshmiben, elected as president by consensus. Only when the news of the consensus vote appeared in the newspaper did I discover that my nomination had been withdrawn without my consent. Lakshmiben currently functions as a benami for the FCs... As long as 'samras' (consensus) is upheld and legitimised by the government or the caste system, the rule of the FCs will continue to prevail in my panchayat.

These transgressions of the democratic electoral process turn attention to the enforcement of law and order. A police sub-inspector in Gujarat gave a positive assessment of the role of the police: "According to my experience, the police have always helped and fulfilled their responsibilities. They start working before the panchayat election itself and visit all the villages. Generally, we have to go patrolling, but it becomes compulsory during election days to visit the villages and maintain law and order during the polling time as well." However, a head constable at the SC/ST cell in the office of a deputy superintendent of police in Gujarat suggested a more complex situation in enforcing law and order: "Politically, there is a lot of pressure – pressure from political parties and MLAs of the ruling party – and yet the police have to maintain law and order. Also, there is less neutrality in investigations. In Gujarat, even the deputy superintendent of the police is afraid of the taluka panchayat president."

The above analysis suggests, on the one hand, the need for the implementation of stringent electoral laws, the separation of law enforcement officials from politicians and political parties, and quality training and performance monitoring for the police. On the other hand, an assessment is required of whether the police are free of caste and patriarchal biases when dealing with obstructions, including discrimination and violence, against Dalit women electoral candidates. This assessment is provided in Chapter 8.

Right to Post-Election Safety and Security

A final point for analysis in the process of accessing panchayat posts is the extent to which Dalit women who win panchayat elections are accepted as elected representatives. For 25 of the 166 women (15.1 per cent) who made it through to the election day, the announcement of the election results was accompanied by further obstructions. Aside from the opposition arising from defeated rival Dalit women candidates and/or their supporters (mentioned by 14 women), the women faced two opposing social groups. One was Dalits, including other panchayat representatives; and the other was dominant castes, including panchayat representatives, talatis/ clerks and traditional village panchayat elders. The women's ascent to positions of authority triggered this antipathy from the dominant castes ostensibly based on their caste and gender; that is, the women were deemed unworthy to occupy positions of authority. The women's election also threatened the economic and political interests of these castes. Opposition from Dalits, in contrast, was rooted in gender dynamics wherein Dalit men contested the women's claim to equal political status, especially when it was an SC reserved seat. An example of the former is the case of Reshmaben of Ahmedabad district in Gujarat:

> On the same evening I was declared elected [as village panchayat member], around 100 people belonging to four dominant sub-castes attacked my supporters in the Dalit locality with sticks, stones and other small weapons. One dominant caste man held my neck and hit me on the head with a stick. All the 11 injured people, including myself, were hospitalised. Being land encroachers, the attackers were scared of the issue being raised in the panchayat when I won the election. I registered a case against them under the *SC/ST (PA) Act*. The original attackers also filed a counter FIR, which was a false case against me.

Apart from the three women who faced demands from defeated candidates for vote re-counts in constituencies where election results were very close, and the opposition mounted against one Gujarati woman panchayat president becoming chairperson of the Social Justice Committee, there were four main forms of obstruction.

Each was aimed at debilitating the women's capacity to govern on the threshold of their entry into panchayat institutions. First and predominant was personal identity-based attacks against 13 women in the form of verbal abuse of a caste-based or sexual nature, questioning their fitness for office as Dalit women.

Second, targeting their bodily integrity: eight women and/or their families experienced harassment and assault. Alamelu of Nagapattinam district in Tamil Nadu, for instance, contested for a union panchayat member's post in the SC women reserved constituency with support from the DMP party. On the election day, there was a clash between DMK and AIADMK party supporters after the latter attempted to take away the voting box. She also faced verbal abuse and threats when she went to cast her vote. On the announcement of Alamelu's election to the post, the losing AIADMK candidate and her party supporters chased Alamelu and tried to assault her. She was rescued by members of the DPI party, which was in alliance with the DMK party.

The third form of obstruction was social boycotts, which negated the women's social identity by cutting off their links with the village community. Four women from Gujarat mentioned the imposition of social boycotts in reaction to their being elected to panchayat posts. For one president, this included putting a stop to any communication with her during her entire five-year term in office.

The fourth form was false cases foisted on three women that questioned the women's personal probity and public standing in society. These were cases of alleged bogus voting, for disqualification as a Christian contesting an SC reserved seat, or in the afore-mentioned case of Reshmaben, for allegedly instigating her Dalit supporters to attack the dominant castes after her electoral win.

An overall analysis shows that apart from the Dalit political rivalries and sub-caste identity politics manifested throughout the electoral process, specific to the period following the announcement of election results was opposition directly related to the women's social status. As far as Dalit men were concerned, while the women may hold official positions and exercise authority in the panchayat as elected representatives, they are not expected (or allowed) to claim a position equal to that of men. For dominant castes, they expect the elected Dalit women to maintain their low caste and gender status by only exercising nominal panchayat authority. The dominant castes continue to hold executive authority to ensure their economic and political interests. Thus, evidence once again demonstrates how traditionally accepted caste and gender norms and practices influence political processes.

Entry into the Panchayats

SUCCESSFUL ENTRY INTO PANCHAYATS

In the end, 166 of the 200 Dalit women (83.0 per cent) entered the panchayats. Of these women, 83.7 per cent (139 women) did so through elections, 13.9 per cent (23 women) were nominated as consensus candidates, and 2.4 per cent (4 women) were elected unopposed as the sole candidates to file a nomination.

The women attributed their success to several factors. Not surprisingly, over one-third of the women (39.1 per cent) entering the panchayats cited voter support from dominant castes as the main factor, and in a few cases Adivasi and Dalit support. Critical to the women's reliance on dominant caste support, aside from the larger population of these castes, was their livelihood dependence on dominant caste employers and lack of financial resources to meet election expenses. Moreover, caste and gender hierarchies in a rural feudal context, while being critical determinants of social relationships, also allowed dominant castes to exercise control and authority over the electoral prospects of Dalit women. In situations where the Dalits were at loggerheads with the dominant castes, the latter swung into action to reinforce their power. The structure of dependent relationships becomes more complex when one considers the qualities women are expected to possess if they are to enter public life: education, knowledge on panchayat matters, experience with public or political life, an ability to communicate in public, and contacts and dealings with government institutions. A lack of these factors is a serious handicap for the women both in terms of their ability to perform their role in political governance and their ability to act independently. Though this issue of dependence on dominant castes is generally applicable to all Dalit women in varying degrees, its relevance to benami politics is high.

Aside from dominant caste backing, 13.8 per cent of the elected women reported that panchayat consensus politics, engineered mostly by the dominant castes, led to their election. Markedly different from this political engineering is the voluntary support received from villagers cutting across caste lines, which helped only 4.2 per cent of women to access panchayat posts. Interestingly, Dalit backing was considered a deciding factor by only 6.6 per cent of the women. This low percentage might be attributed to sub-caste identity politics or smaller Dalit populations. Compared to this, 9.6 per cent of the women spoke of their husbands, family members or relatives as a key reason for winning the election. A further 7.8 per cent cited membership of and/or support of political parties by the women or their family members, combined with party interests.

Only 9.6 per cent of the Dalit women listed personal factors such as their education, economic stability, experience on social issues, public visibility or good relations with villagers as enabling them to win panchayat seats. A further 8.4 per cent noted a combination of other factors responsible for their electoral victory, including voter belief that the woman would work to ensure development in the panchayat, and the women's previous good performance in the panchayats.

UNABLE TO ENTER PANCHAYATS

The remaining 34 Dalit women, or 17.0 per cent of the 200 women, were unable to access panchayats posts. Most had contested independently. Thirty of these women (88.2 per cent) lost the elections, three (8.9 per cent) were forced to withdraw their nominations, and one (2.9 per cent) was prevented from filing her nomination.

From the main reasons women proffered for their failure to access panchayat posts, three motives ostensibly drove different actors to contribute to the defeat of the women. The main motive of dominant castes was to safeguard and promote their economic and political interests. For instance, fearing that Parvathi would question their panchayat activities and corruption if elected village panchayat president, the dominant castes saw to her defeat in an SC women reserved constituency in Madurai district in Tamil Nadu. An ultimate say in the choice of candidates was often the best way for the dominant castes to protect their interests. Therefore, soon after she filed her nomination for the post of village panchayat member, dominant castes verbally abused and harassed Urvasi of Madurai district and then imposed a social boycott on her and her family for going against their choice of a benami candidate. She later had to withdraw her nomination after some dominant castes attempted to murder her husband.

Significantly, Dalit women who were independent candidates, educated, articulate on social issues and keen on Dalit development had reduced chances of successfully contesting the elections. For example, Rajakumari of Madurai district in Tamil Nadu was articulate about social problems and could speak well in public. The dominant castes prevented her from filing her nomination for the union panchayat member's post because they were aware that they would not be able to control her, and that their economic development would not be her focus. Moreover, some women were made targets for dominant caste politics due to their husbands' independence and public activism. This was the case for Samjuben of Kheda district in Gujarat, competing for the post of village panchayat president in an SC women reserved constituency. The dominant castes, assuming that she would not be easy for them to control due to her husband being an active union leader, bribed voters in order to ensure that their benami candidate won the election.

Dominant castes also blocked access to panchayat posts for several women who had previously confronted the dominant castes and defended Dalits when, for example, violence was perpetrated against them. For instance, dominant castes retaliated against Anitaben of Ahmedabad district in Gujarat for contesting the post of village panchayat president in the SC women reserved constituency by putting up a rival candidate to divide the Dalit vote and thus defeat her. They did so because she had previously supported Dalit women villagers in filing an atrocity case against dominant caste women regarding access to water. Likewise, Vasanthi of Nagapattinam district in Tamil Nadu lost the election for the post of village panchayat president after the dominant castes ensured that almost all votes went to their benami candidate. Behind this was Vasanthi's previous support of a Dalit survivor of violence, whom she helped to file a police case against dominant caste assailants.

These cases illustrate that while reservations in panchayat governance may be considered a strategy to restructure power relations in strongly hierarchical societies, its application in democratic electoral politics presupposes equality in status and fair bargaining between the negotiating actors. This is particularly important in the case of SC women reserved constituencies where Dalit women have a chance to decide the composition of the panchayat. A socio-political reality of unequal bargaining powers, however, is clear from cases where dominant castes used bribes, bogus voting or threatened voters to ensure the defeat of Dalit women candidates. Beyond this, dominant caste manipulation manifested through the use of their majority population to get the women candidates of their choice elected, or the engineering of factional politics within the Dalit community to ensure victory to their benami Dalit women candidates.

In the few cases where the Dalit community played a key role in preventing women from accessing panchayat posts, an important motive was the factional dynamics within the community, with rival candidates articulating their respective sub-caste identities and/or interests. In contesting the SC women reserved post of village panchayat president, Veena of Thirunelveli district in Tamil Nadu, a member of a minority Dalit sub-caste, was opposed by another majority Dalit sub-caste. Since Veena's candidature was supported by dominant castes, the majority Dalit sub-caste put up their own candidate against her; and, without their support, Veena lost the elections.

Political party politics was the third major motive behind the women's failed efforts to access panchayat posts. Women were placed in the crossfire between opposing political parties, resulting in their defeat. One such example was the case of Vandanaben of Kheda district in Gujarat, who contested the post of taluka panchayat member in the general women reserved constituency. Previously a member of the village panchayat and a Congress party supporter, she canvassed mainly with the help of Congress party supporters. However, she could not garner the Muslim vote as the Dalits there did not have amicable relations with Muslims following the 2002 Gujarat riots. Moreover, in a taluka dominated by the BJP party, she lost the election to the BJP candidate.

Conclusion

The right to free and fair access to local governance institutions is a necessary pre-condition for Dalit women to enjoy their right to political participation. The experiences of these 200 Dalit women highlight how the reservation policy has opened the doors to grassroots democracy for Dalit women who want to cross the boundaries of the domestic sphere to involve themselves in public affairs and test their personal capabilities, leadership skills and political acumen. In doing so, they challenge dominant caste, class and patriarchal forces which have traditionally foreclosed democratic freedom and independence for Dalit women. To gain entry to governance institutions, however, requires an inclusive democracy that provides political space for all citizens and guarantees equal access. In reality, as demonstrated throughout this chapter, Dalit women face a number of internal constraints or external obstructions arising from their social, economic and political context when accessing political authority. These obstructions occur at all stages of the electoral process and highlight a backlash against reservations by dominant social forces.

Lakshmiben's statement at the start of this chapter, "...nobody believes that Dalit women have the ability to carry out panchayat works... Men never accept women's leadership..." illustrates how the assumption of inclusive democracy is contradicted in practice. For Dalit women like Lakshmiben, caste and patriarchy constantly challenge their efforts to access panchayat institutions; and the women are forced to prove their capacity to participate in the panchayats. The reservation policy has resulted in Dalit women being caught between two conflicting world views as they attempt to enter the panchayats: the first governed by a legal rights regime that opens avenues for individual and group mobility with the promise of progress in social, economic and political fields; and the other directed by the rule of hierarchical social groups, with entrenched vested interests benefiting those of higher status within the social system. While the former worldview is anchored principally in an individual's right to equality and freedom as pre-requisites for inclusive democracy, the latter presumes hierarchically dependent relationships among social groups as necessary for maintaining social harmony. This applies particularly to Dalits, especially Dalit women, structuring their relationship to dominant caste groups as one of dependence and subservience.

Set against this background, the reservation policy in Panchayati Raj is a socially engineered mechanism to resolve this conflict between two worldviews in favour of the legal rights regime. In principle, this policy should ensure Dalit women their right to equality, freedom and independence when accessing panchayats. In reality, the extent of the political space the women enjoy having realised these rights is in proportion to the extent of conflict between the aforementioned worldviews and interests the women encountered in their respective contexts.

The women had several responses to this conflict. The weight of the patriarchal caste system overpowered the efforts of a small group of women to access the panchayats with freedom and independence. A second slightly larger group of women were able to act with independence and freedom, navigating electoral politics in order to realise their right to access panchayat posts. This was due to various personal factors and external support. By contrast, the freedom and independence of a third group comprising the majority of women was circumscribed by the vested interests of those playing benami politics and exploiting the women's social and economic vulnerabilities. Cutting across these three groups was a fourth group of women for whom the democratic space panchayat elections provided opened up opportunities – for some as independent contestants, while for others as benami candidates opposing independent Dalit women competing candidates.

These patterns at the election stage highlight the remaining work to be done to ensure that the reservation policy does open a political vista of empowerment and emancipation for Dalit women. Change is possible. However, it requires efforts to increase the women's education levels, provide adequate information and knowledge on panchayat affairs, create adequate support systems and put in place effective election monitoring mechanisms. Such measures would improve the social environment and enable Dalit women's equal access to panchayats. Without such measures, the struggles Dalit women experienced at each phase of the panchayat electoral process were enormous.

The following chapters explore what happened to the women once they succeeded in entering the panchayats. The focus will be on whether the women were able to exercise their rights to non-discrimination, freedom and independence in political participation; and whether they were able to promote the developmental agenda of their Dalit community and women in particular, and the wider panchayat constituency in general.

Notes

1.   Article 25 of the *ICCPR*, detailing the right to political participation, requires the right to access public service positions as an essential component of citizenship rights in a democratic polity.
2.   Articles 2(1) and 25 *ICCPR* deal with the right to equality. Articles 14, 15 and 16 of the Indian Constitution deal with rights related to equality, and Article 17 refers to the abolition of 'untouchability'.
3.   Article 25 of the *ICCPR*.

5

FROM REPRESENTATION TO PARTICIPATION

Being the majority, the dominant castes could not accept the idea of being under a low caste Dalit leader. So, for namesake, they made me the president. The dominant caste vice president and other dominant caste members took away all my powers and responsibilities. I did not even convene a meeting. I went to the panchayat office only when I was asked to go… I functioned like this because I have no education and belong to a low caste. Though I was given training, I was in such a situation that I could not do anything at all.

— Thilagam, village panchayat president,
Coimbatore district, Tamil Nadu

Like Thilagam, who made this statement, 99 of the 166 Dalit women elected representatives interviewed, or 59 per cent, functioned as benami or proxy representatives in the panchayats. Just over a half of these women were benamis for dominant castes, as in the case of Thilagam, around a third were benamis for husbands and/or male relatives, and the remainder for others such as dominant caste ex-MLAs and political parties dominated by dominant caste members.

Thilagam was 40 years old, illiterate, and married with four children. She was engaged in household chores and grazing cattle when she won the post of village panchayat president in the SC women reserved constituency in Coimbatore district, Tamil Nadu. 'Untouchability' practices against Dalits are prevalent in her panchayat, where the dominant castes are a majority. The dominant caste leaders asked her to contest the election, and then ensured their man Kandramanickam became the vice president and indirectly wielded power. She functioned as a benami president. What follows is Thilagam's account of her term as president:

> I came to know about the panchayat meetings only through others. And only for namesake would I be invited to any meeting. The vice president fixed the agenda for discussion, conducted the meetings and decided on the resolutions. I signed the necessary documents. Since I do not know how to read and write, I would not get any information. In fact, in the beginning they said that they would look after everything. I had no chance to perform any administrative work at all. In gram sabha meetings, I did not perform any responsibility except to give a welcome speech. When the people in the gathering questioned me on panchayat matters, I would just keep quiet.
>
> I never attended any important meeting organised by government officials. Instead, the vice president and the clerk would tell me, 'It is an important meeting, so you need not come. We two will attend.' When important officials came to the panchayat office, they would invite me. But after introducing me, the vice president and government officials would leave to some other place without me. Even if I happened to meet these officials, the vice president and the clerk would always be with me, and only they would speak to the officials.
>
> It is not in the nature of my husband to control me regarding panchayat matters. However, sometimes when I went to attend meetings, I would return home rather late. If my husband was drunk, he would come to the meeting venue and accuse me of not paying attention to my household duties. While he provided support to me in my day-to-day activities, he also was a hindrance to me. My son used to help me in fulfilling my panchayat responsibilities; for example, helping me examine the panchayat accounts, read the cheques before I signed them, and so on.
>
> I faced a lot of discrimination in the panchayat. I could not sit equally and drink water or take tea with the [other caste] panchayat members. For a long time, I never sat on the chair meant for the president. I would simply stand or sit on the floor in the panchayat office. It was only when government officials came to the office that I would sit on the chair. I could do this only when the dominant castes told me to do so. Both the vice president and clerk, who was his relative, treated me disrespectfully. They

routinely addressed me by my name or caste name instead of using my official designation 'president'. If they happened to address me as 'president', then they did so ironically. Nadesan, a dominant caste panchayat member having some enmity with the vice president, and some of his supporters constantly degraded me based on my caste.

The contractors belonged to the vice president's dominant caste and all the welfare scheme contracts would go to whoever he decided. The benefits from schemes would go to the groups he decided on, or to those of his caste only. I simply abided by whatever he decided. He knew that for the past 50 years, the Dalit colonies in the panchayat needed basic amenities, but they got nothing. The exception was my Dalit colony which got some welfare measures like the free distribution of land *patta*, a road, public lighting and drinking water, because I accepted all his decisions.

I did not supervise any panchayat development works... Dominant caste men accused me often about the clerk's corruption and spoke derogatively of my caste both inside and outside the panchayat office. Some of them even gathered in front of my house drunk and shouted out accusations at me that the development schemes implemented by the panchayat were not up to the mark. All these were everyday occurrences.

I functioned like this because I have no education and belong to a low caste. The major challenges for me were the problems dominant caste members created in the panchayat and the clerk's corruption. But I managed the situation because of my cordial relationship with the vice president. Though I attended trainings organised by several NGOs as well as district level government officials, I was still in a situation wherein I could not do anything at all. We cannot speak against the dominant caste men. Even the officials do not care for us. When they come to the village or panchayat office, they do not force us to attend the meetings. They simply speak with the vice president, deal official business with him and then leave the place. How can Dalits function well in such a situation?

Thilagam's narrative makes clear her statement at the start of this chapter. She perceived the motives behind dominant castes selecting her for the president's post: to counter the prospect of a Dalit woman executing authority in the panchayat, and to maintain control over the panchayat's development resources. The only way to circumvent the reservation policy and achieve their objectives was to make Thilagam a proxy representative and nominal head while the dominant caste vice president exercised Thilagam's political authority. The dominant castes' selection of her as their candidate and payment of her election expenses was ostensibly a form of 'recognition' of her capacity for the post and a 'favour' bestowed on her. At the same time, once elected, she was discriminated against as a Dalit and a woman, and exploited because she was poor, and lacked knowledge and experience in panchayat institutions. The realisation of her predicament is evident in her question: "How can Dalits function well in such a situation?" This question opens a critique of the implementation of the panchayat reservation policy. Can this policy, set against the backdrop of an inequitable social order, ensure Dalit women their right to political participation in any meaningful manner?

Governance is defined as "the process whereby public institutions conduct public affairs, manage public resources and guarantee the realization of human rights."[1] There are five key constituents of good governance: transparency, responsibility, accountability, participation, and responsiveness to the needs of the people.[2] The right to political participation cuts across the other four attributes and is critical to the functioning of a healthy democratic governance system. As elected representatives, Dalit women have an obligation to exercise their right to political participation by undertaking their responsibilities as 'duty bearers' towards 'claim holders' – their constituents. As such, it is the quality of their participation in the panchayats that enables them to fulfil their obligations to the people who elected them.

Article 25 of the *International Covenant on Civil and Political Rights 1966* (ICCPR) stipulates the right to political participation as an entitlement for elected representatives to conduct public affairs. Precisely because of the representative nature of their position, Dalit women panchayat presidents and members both enjoy the right to exercise political power, and are accountable to their constituencies for the exercise of that power. In general, once elected they are entitled to the *direct* exercise of executive and administrative powers covering all aspects of public administration, and the formulation and implementation of policies and programmes at the local government level.[3]

The direct conduct of public affairs requires Dalit women's *active, free and meaningful participation*[4] in the panchayat administration. In keeping with the constitutional mandate to ensure equality and affirmative action, the *73rd (Rural Panchayats) Constitutional Amendment Act 1992* provides for reserved seats for SC women. Critical to active participation are elected representatives articulating views and taking decisions, as well as giving general direction to the panchayat administration. A pre-requisite to this is the enjoyment of the rights to information and capacitation. This enables the women to fulfil their responsibilities in accessing development processes, institutions, information and redressal or complaint mechanisms. Transparency, accountability and responsibility regarding decisions taken and executed, all being important attributes of good governance, also characterise active political participation.

Closely related to active participation is the women's freedom to discharge their duties. This implies multiple rights and freedoms: to 'freely communicate ideas about public and political issues';[5] independently make decisions; freely move to attend meetings and supervise development works; freely interact with their constituencies, other elected representatives and government officials; and operate free from discrimination, violence and other forms of obstruction.

Dalit women's active and free participation becomes meaningful in so far as it is directed towards the development objectives of the panchayat: meeting the needs of the most marginalised groups and the community concerns of the entire panchayat. Thus, the realisation of various rights related to development hinges on the effective exercise of the right to participation. Meaningful participation is also linked to other objectives, such as the political empowerment of Dalit women. Women's political participation is also expected to transform power equations in terms of caste-class-gender relations and resource distribution among social groups.

These three indicators for participation – active, free and meaningful – provide a framework to explore multiple issues. First is the ability of Dalit women elected representatives to actively and freely exercise their authority on all matters of panchayat administration. Second is their ability to execute panchayat works for the benefit of their panchayat constituencies, thereby effecting positive changes to the development and social status of Dalits and Dalit women. The first point is explored in this chapter, and the second will be dealt with in subsequent chapters.

Decision-Making Powers

Five factors help determine the extent to which the 166 Dalit women elected presidents and members freely exercised their decision-making powers in the panchayat: first, the caste and gender composition of the panchayats; second, the performance of panchayat responsibilities by Dalit women presidents; third, the relationship between Dalit women and other panchayat members that factored into the level of cooperation or confrontation they faced within the panchayat; fourth, the support Dalit women received for their participation in the panchayats; and fifth, who the women perceived to be the most important decision maker in the panchayat.

PANCHAYAT COMPOSITION AND DECISION MAKING

Just as the composition of the panchayat electorate – whether Dalits are a majority or minority – factors into elections, similarly the composition of the panchayat factors into Dalit women's ability to freely participate in panchayat affairs. Three-quarters of the Dalit women (124 women or 74.7 per cent) mentioned the representation of Dalits in their panchayat councils as being below 50 per cent. Most Dalit women therefore had to depend on the majority non-Dalit members for support in passing panchayat resolutions. Presidents also had to live with the possibility of no-confidence motions being passed with the vote of two-thirds of the panchayat members.

In this respect, the 166 Dalit women elected representatives frequently mentioned the critical role vice presidents played in decision making in the panchayats, or presidents where the Dalit women were members. In these panchayat councils, however, only 16 vice presidents were SCs (9.6 per cent) and only 20 were women (12 per cent). Analysing caste and gender data together, 145 dominant caste individuals, 90.3 per cent being men, constituted 87.4 per cent of vice presidents. Likewise, aside from the 119 panchayats with Dalit women presidents, in the remaining 47 panchayats, 32 (68.1 per cent) had dominant caste presidents, 62.5 per cent of whom were male. Five other panchayats with Dalit women members had Dalit male presidents. Therefore, when put together, the breakdown figures for presidents and vice presidents point to the predominance of dominant caste male power in the panchayats. This should be borne in mind while examining the spaces for Dalit women's free and active participation in the panchayats.

Dalit women confirmed that political authority is often vested in others in the panchayat. Only 35, or 29.4 per cent, of Dalit women presidents felt they played a critical role in decision making in their panchayat. For the remaining 84 Dalit women presidents, a significant proportion of whom were benamis, ultimate decision-making power was vested in the predominantly dominant caste vice presidents (53 women), husbands, brothers or sons (18 women), talatis/clerks (6 women), dominant caste villagers (5 women), and BDOs/TDOs/DDOs (2 women). A group of Dalit women elected representatives from Cuddalore district in Tamil Nadu explained, "In practice, it is only the vice presidents and some members that make decisions. It is only they who can do much because they are dominant castes… [Hence], for the vice president's post, the dominant castes buy over the panchayat members by bribing them. They may even kidnap the panchayat members to negotiate with them."

EXERCISING AUTHORITY AS PANCHAYAT PRESIDENTS

A president exercising authority in the panchayat administration has two core responsibilities: decision making and decision execution. Under these responsibilities fall a set of duties.

Panchayat presidents call and chair council meetings. They take decisions, including signing panchayat resolutions, authorising panchayat payments and approving panchayat contracts. They execute decisions by monitoring the panchayat administration and inspecting development works or services. They also evaluate the implementation of development schemes, including a review of all contracts undertaken. They organise, call and conduct gram sabha meetings. And finally, they generate financial resources by requesting funds for development from the higher tiers of the panchayat and the state government. Five of these duties have been chosen to assess the level of authority exercised by the 119 Dalit women panchayat presidents in the study: calling panchayat meetings; calling gram sabha meetings; signing panchayat resolutions of their own free will; authorising panchayat payments; and approving and reviewing contracts for panchayat development works.

Most Dalit women presidents did not call panchayat meetings. Only 42 women (35.3 per cent) could do so. This indicates that there were people holding greater power and authority than the presidents. These people either blatantly scuttled the efforts of some presidents to call meetings or prevented many presidents from initiating the process to hold meetings at the outset. Moreover, of the 70 women presidents unable to call meetings and the seven who tried but were prevented from doing so, 22 women were also not informed of these meetings. A similar situation applied to gram sabha meetings, which only 26 of the 110 village panchayat presidents (23.6 per cent) called. This data, taken together, signifies the lack of due recognition and respect for the Dalit women holding the panchayat president post.

When it came to voluntarily signing panchayat resolutions, only 33 of the 119 women presidents (27.7 per cent) could do so. A similar situation prevailed regarding the authorisation of payments in the village panchayats or monitoring the administration and supervising the work of BDOs/TDOs or DDOs in the higher panchayat tiers: only 31 Dalit women presidents (26.1 per cent) succeeded in doing so. Village panchayat president Shardaben from Vadodara district in Gujarat was not one of those women.

She said, "Those who secured my election and the panchayat members excluded me from key decision making and only expected, and at times forced, me to sign documents in my capacity as president. After deciding the resolutions, the dominant caste vice president and talati came to my house to get my signature on cheques and papers."

Even the 33 women who could sign resolutions often did so with great difficulty. Take the case of Sunitaben, a village panchayat president from Anand district in Gujarat. She reported opposition from all the panchayat members precisely because she was literate, economically independent, received training and support from social organisations and her husband, and actively participated in the panchayat administration:

> When I became president, everyone thought that I was not a very educated woman and that I knew only how to sign my name, but I knew very well how to read and write, and had my husband for guidance. That is why I not only independently signed on resolutions, but also fulfilled my responsibilities, whether writing resolutions or any other works. If I did not give control of the panchayat administration to my husband, why would I give it to other panchayat members? It is my right; and, as president, I take all the decisions and work independently. Although the vice president, talati and the dominant castes tried to create problems for me, I never let them prevent me from functioning.

The approval of contracts for development works at the village panchayat level and their review at the taluka/union or district level was undertaken by only 28 women presidents (23.5 per cent). Women had negative experiences in this regard because decisions on who received panchayat contracts for development works were either never decided in the gram sabhas, or were decided only rarely in the panchayat councils. Instead, many dominant caste members, members of the majority political party in the panchayat, or the panchayat members of the current ruling party in the state, secured the contracts in negotiations that took place outside the panchayats. Again, dominant caste male control over panchayat resources and ingrained discriminatory attitudes often translated into Dalit women being left out of negotiation over development contracts. The assumption was that they were incapable of undertaking such negotiations, as stated by a group of Dalit women elected representatives from Kheda district in Gujarat. Moreover, as these women noted and village panchayat president Thilagam in Coimbatore district in Tamil Nadu confirmed, where a Dalit woman was panchayat president it was inevitably the dominant caste vice president who negotiated to ensure that contracts went to dominant caste contractors. Only rarely, as seen in the case of village panchayat presidents Preetikaben from Anand district in Gujarat and Kamachi from Coimbatore district in Tamil Nadu, were contracts decided by consensus in panchayat meetings.

For the higher panchayat tiers, Ramilaben, taluka panchayat president from Vadodara district in Gujarat explained the process:

> Development contracts would be announced by the DDO for bidding and the DDO and TDO, with some influential dominant caste panchayat members, would decide which bidding contractors would succeed. Every taluka member got contracts for development of their area allocated in every meeting by the DDO and planning commissioner... [In my case] taluka panchayat members from my political party, the DDO and TDO kept all the contracts for themselves and gave me smaller sub-contracts to implement with the help of the *mandali* (registered body of contractors at the district level). It was mostly contracts for Dalits that I received... I never said much against this because I was afraid of a no confidence motion being brought against me.

As with the village panchayat level, efforts were made to sideline Dalit women in the allocation of large taluka development contracts. Their receipt of only smaller contracts for works in Dalit colonies served to further ghettoise them in the panchayat.

Overall, therefore, only around one-third of Dalit women presidents succeeded in exercising their authority. For a large majority, although vested with *de jure* political authority, they were denied the *de facto* authority to execute these duties. The authority they were expected to wield in practice was instead appropriated and used by others in the panchayat councils. For 44 of the presidents, overt obstructions, primarily from dominant caste panchayat members or vice presidents, were placed in their path as they sought to perform their duties. Behind this opposition was a discriminatory attitude leading to the non-acceptance of Dalit women occupying a position of authority. For a larger number of benami presidents, all their official duties were appropriated by men within or outside the panchayat. The result confirmed the majoritarian power of the dominant castes. Contrast this with the following statement by an assistant director of panchayats in Tamil Nadu: "As far as we are concerned, Dalit women representatives are working very well. The main reason for this is the government officials and their training programmes. Sometimes the [women] are administering superbly. They do better than the educated men in the administration."

THREE PATTERNS OF POLITICAL PARTICIPATION

Analysing the women's experiences further, three types of Dalit women presidents emerge. First were those who freely decided and executed decisions, making up approximately one-third of the women. Most were educated, and a few had previous panchayat governance experience. A few others were actively involved in social organisations and political parties and, as such, had established contacts with government officials. Many received support from family or community members. They were motivated, self-confident and astute enough to understand and negotiate panchayat power politics. For example, Keerthana from Tamil Nadu, a district panchayat president and active Congress party member, proved her capacity for work and achieved a lot at the district level. She astutely dealt with opposition from other panchayat members. Barring the district collector, even government officials above her in rank came to meet her. Though advised by her party, she made independent decisions. Another example at the village panchayat level is that of educated and financially well-off Jayashree of Thirunelveli district in Tamil Nadu:

> I exercise my duties without any restrictions and hindrances from any source. A great support for me, my husband helps me to make decisions through valuable suggestions... Members of

the panchayat accept all my proposals for they are assured of my abilities to perform well... Although there are not many SC Paraiyars in the panchayat, I am sensitive to the needs of this community, and try to fulfil them despite their initial opposition to me. Even though I belong to the DMK party, I represent all the people. If the party were to pressurise me to perform certain tasks, I am prepared to quit the party because for me what is important is the public welfare.

A striking feature of some women presidents' performance was their tactical moves, especially where they shifted from being benamis to being active and independent presidents. For instance, village panchayat president Kamachi from Coimbatore district in Tamil Nadu was educated, single, economically independent and had undergone NGO training. Looking back on her first term of office, she said, "Although the members of the AIADMK and MDMK parties told me not to bother with the panchayat administration, I allowed this situation to go on for only six months while buying time to understand the panchayat administration. By then I also understood the nuances of political pressures and decisions. I then moved to gain the trust of the former panchayat president and, through him, learned to deal with matters arising in the panchayat council." Referring to changes in her functioning during her second term of office, she said, "I handled my responsibilities independently... I was quite successful in the way I managed the administration and saw to it that people of all castes benefited."

Another feature of some women's functioning was the assertion of their role as elected representatives. When the government administration failed to respond to their demands on behalf of their constituencies, these women registered their protests through collective action. Village panchayat president Neelamben from Anand district in Gujarat managed to carry out development works for Dalits and other communities. However, when she failed in getting a road and public transport for her village, she held a hunger strike in front of the district collector's office until she got these facilities. Similarly, village panchayat president Aarthi from Cuddalore district in Tamil Nadu, knowledgeable on panchayat matters and a member of the state-wide Women Panchayat Presidents' Federation, lobbied the district administration for several development schemes for Dalits. At one stage of her panchayat career, however, she had to organise a protest in front of the district collector's office to get back common property land that had been encroached upon.

Some women presidents also were determined to function independently despite opposition from dominant castes, Dalit leaders and/or political parties. Some like village panchayat president Anjali from Madurai district in Tamil Nadu negotiated directly with political party leaders who sought to silence her in the panchayat council. Others secured support from government officials to counter opposition to their functioning. For example, village panchayat president Asmitaben from Kheda district in Gujarat functioned independently with the guidance of her husband, the previous panchayat president. Consequently, the FC vice president, the local BJP MLA and some panchayat members tried to remove her through a no confidence motion. Fortunately, on coming to know of this move, she and her husband rushed to make a complaint to the TDO, who immediately acted in her favour. Others like Subbuthai from Thirunelveli district in Tamil Nadu had to find alternative ways to access information on the panchayats. Subbuthai had her mail directly seized from the postman to prevent her from receiving information on schemes and other information from the BDO. She eventually had to get a separate phone connection to overcome this hurdle posed by the dominant caste vice president and a union panchayat member.

Tejuben of Kheda district in Gujarat succeeded as a village panchayat president despite constant opposition. She highlighted the significant challenges she faced as a Dalit woman:

> Sometimes I hated this post and wondered why I should face such a problematic situation. When there was financial pressure, or false allegations of corruption were levelled against me, or someone used abusive language or passed accusatory comments against me, I thought of resigning. But because I got full support from the villagers I gave up this idea and completed the panchayat works with determination. When their financial or power interests

were at stake in the decisions I took, dominant caste panchayat members accused Dalits of not asking for their opinion when making decisions. However, after the successful completion of development works, they stopped opposing me. My frustration was because I did not have any prior experience of panchayat administration. But as I became more experienced, I could solve the problems myself.

Ratha's experience in a village panchayat in Madurai district in Tamil Nadu likewise shows the strength of dominant caste opposition to Dalit women's leadership in the panchayats. After dominant castes murdered Ratha's in-laws in the 1960s, her family filed a case against the perpetrators. Hence, dominant castes in her village disliked her family for their lack of submissiveness. Ratha then contested the panchayat elections despite opposition from the dominant castes, who had put up their own benami Dalit woman candidate to counter her nomination. Still, Ratha won the election. Once elected, she attempted to function in the face of strong opposition from the dominant caste vice president and other dominant castes. At the beginning of her term, she was not allowed into the panchayat office, or to perform her duties. Instead, she was verbally abused and not allowed to conduct panchayat meetings, not informed of meetings convened by the dominant castes and prevented from attending meetings. The vice president and dominant caste panchayat members demanded that she resign her post. Her family was socially ostracised by the Dalits (out of fear) and dominant castes of her village. Only after the intervention of a local NGO did her case come to the notice of government officials. They intervened to work out a settlement, so that she could be allowed to function in the panchayat.

A second smaller group of Dalit women panchayat presidents, around 10 per cent of the women, attempted but failed to exercise their decision-making powers. Various factors curtailed their active and free participation in the panchayats. Women perceived their lack of education as a key handicap, justifying the domineering influence of husbands or dominant caste persons. Another perceived handicap was their insufficient experience in establishing contacts with government officials and civil

society organisations. For example, Jayshreeben demanded and
obtained the post of vice president in her village panchayat in
Surendranagar district in Gujarat on the grounds that no Dalit had
ever occupied this post. However, she participated only minimally
in the panchayat administration. Not being literate and not having
attended any capacitation trainings, she had to depend solely on
her husband for guidance to fulfil her panchayat duties. When
village panchayat president Arukkani from Coimbatore district
in Tamil Nadu attempted to act independently in fulfilling her
panchayat duties, the dominant caste clerk, panchayat members
and villagers silenced and ignored her. They also sought to bribe
her into being their benami and finally made her do what they
wanted. Some women also narrated how political parties used
their husbands to make them function as benamis even though
they attempted to act independently. In other cases, husbands who
were political party functionaries treated their wives as benamis
for their own political ends.

The silenced majority, over half of the women, constitute the
third type of Dalit women presidents. These women were unable
to execute their duties as president. As with access to panchayat
posts, the main issue again was benami or proxy representation
for dominant castes (especially vice presidents), the women's
husbands, or a combination of different actors. A group of
Dalit women villagers in Madurai district in Tamil Nadu stated,
"The stumbling blocks for [a Dalit woman's] involvement in the
panchayat are the vice president, clerk and other BC members.
The dominant castes consider the participation of Dalit women
to be an insult to them. They think that if they allow her to
function in the panchayat, she will work for the welfare of
the Dalits only. And if they allow this once, it will become a
tradition in the future, so she should continue to be subjugated
under them. Thus, they take all the responsibilities away from
her." Contrast this with the observation of an assistant director
of panchayats in the same state: "There is no need for us to
monitor [the panchayats] at all... There is no benami system
at all in Tamil Nadu. Here every panchayat president functions
freely and independently."

Commonly employed direct methods of control over the women included appropriating or divesting them of their authority, 'domestication', manipulative control, and caste and gender discrimination. The appropriation of authority is apparent in the case of village panchayat president Gangaben of Anand district in Gujarat. A dominant caste *rowdy* in her area manipulated the panchayat elections in such a way as to get only women who would be subservient to him elected. Lamenting this situation, she said, "I am a complete benami and am unable to do anything on my own... All the women in the panchayat, too, have been treated the same, and none dare to come to the office. To date, no panchayat meeting has taken place. He decides everything from outside. I only go to the office when called to sign the cheques. I am president only on paper."

For village panchayat president Leela of Madurai district in Tamil Nadu, her lack of education, poverty and her family working as bonded labourers for a local landlord made it easy for the dominant castes to appropriate her panchayat powers. Speaking of her situation, she said:

> Soon after the election, my husband and I were called for a meeting before the same members of that *katta panchayat* who had pressurised me to file my nomination. They demanded, 'We selected you for election with the intention to make you resign once you won. However, now we are thinking of something else. You must give [a guarantee] in writing submitting the title deeds to your house and to one acre of land.' We were forced to accept their demand. They also said to us, 'You must be under our control for the next five years. Only then will we return the bond paper to you. In case you go against our wishes, then your house and the land will belong to us.' They later told me, 'You have taken up leadership of the panchayat, but we are going to auction all the welfare programmes and your responsibilities. However, you should not reveal this plan to anybody. If you reveal it, you will lose your house and the land together.'

The auction took place at midnight one night with seven dominant caste landlords placing bids. Perumal won the auction for ₹2,16,000. After the auction, all Leela's political power went to Perumal. He constructed a road in the dominant caste locality and a bridge to facilitate grain transport from his fields to the village. Leela and other villagers know that Perumal must have swindled money through the welfare schemes, but no one knows how much. News leaked to the newspapers of the auction and the district government officials then acted. The police arrested those involved in the auction. Thereafter, bail was posted for the accused, and no further action had followed six months later, at the time of the interview with Leela. Meanwhile, she continued to function as a benami for the dominant castes. She felt caste discrimination and caste domination played a big role in depriving her of all her powers as a democratically elected representative.

Narrating how Dalit women village panchayat presidents can be divested of their authority, Vijaya from Madurai district in Tamil Nadu said:

> The day after the election results were declared, Bhoominathan, the dominant caste landlord and panchayat vice president who performs all my panchayat duties, met me and my husband who works in his fields. He said, 'Trusting you, I spent ₹2 lakhs for the elections. Therefore, you should not affix your signature on any document without my permission. If your relatives come to meet you, you should inform me in advance about them and then only will you be allowed to speak to them.' I have not seen the official pen and the stamp given to me as panchayat president. It is always with him. I have absolutely nothing to do with the panchayat administration. I know nothing about the panchayat system. As vice president, he handles all [the administration] by himself without any consultation. I do not even occupy the chair in the panchayat office. I do not affix my signature on the resolutions. And because I am Bhoominathan's bonded labourer, no one cares for me.

The method of domestication refers to the experience of women like village panchayat president Renuka from Thirunelveli district in Tamil Nadu. At the time of her nomination, and again when assuming her panchayat responsibilities, she was told to stay at home and only affix her signature on documents. The dominant castes looked after the running of the panchayat. Similarly, dominant castes told village panchayat president Anuradha from Cuddalore district in the same state that she need not do anything except receive ₹50-100 each time they asked her to sign a document. She also received ₹50, betel leaves or tobacco from the dominant caste panchayat members or clerk for attending panchayat council meetings. She did not dream of crossing the line demarcated for her as the dominant caste vice president controlled the panchayat.

Some women reported instances of dominant caste manipulative control: for example, threats of no confidence motions, threats against husbands or to deny the women employment; tutoring women on what to do; and offering bribes to the women. Both on the day of filing her nomination and on the election day, the dominant castes, panchayat clerk and vice president threatened village panchayat president Mangalam from Madurai district in Tamil Nadu with removal from office if she attempted to undertake her panchayat duties or interfered in any panchayat matters. Village panchayat president Vimala of the same district was elected with dominant caste support. The same dominant castes had murdered the previous Dalit male panchayat president because of his independent political stance in the panchayat. Mangalam was ignored, or bribed to do the bidding of the dominant caste vice president, who made most of the decisions in the panchayat.

Dalit women also had their political participation hindered through discriminatory treatment aiming to humiliate and degrade them. Discrimination is dealt with in detail later in this chapter. Here, reference is made to abusive language emphasising the women's low caste, class and gender status, or telling them to behave as befitting their supposedly low status. Thilagam from Coimbatore district in Tamil Nadu commented on how a dominant caste male village panchayat member constantly degraded her due to her low caste status and spoke negatively about her community. When panchayat decisions went against his interests, he would openly shout at Thilagam saying, "If we have a Chakkiliyar woman as our leader, we have to undergo such things." Another open expression of such caste abuse, despite being illegal under Section 3(1)(x) of the *SC/ST (PA) Act*, was seen in the case of panchayat president Kowsalya from Coimbatore district. The dominant caste clerk and dominant caste members, in addition to ignoring or silencing her in the panchayat, wrote caste abusive words against her on the walls of the panchayat office. Some women presidents were made so self-conscious of their social status that they did not dare to transgress prevailing traditional norms. In the village panchayat in Thirunelveli district in Tamil Nadu where Sathya was president, for example, there were only two male dominant caste members. These members rarely attended meetings and would bring their own drinking water from home precisely because a Dalit woman was heading the panchayat. Having faced some problems in the panchayat administration, she felt that, being 'only' a woman, she could not go against the dominant castes' wishes, nor function independently.

Significantly, aside from direct control over the women, dominant caste control occurred through the women's husbands. In the case of village panchayat president Revathi of Thirunelveli district in Tamil Nadu, she felt she should maintain peace and unity in the panchayat by not going against the wishes of the dominant castes. She therefore allowed her husband to undertake her panchayat duties under the direction of the dominant castes. She attended panchayat council meetings, but did not raise any issues due to being ignored and made to accept whatever the dominant castes decided. Similarly, village panchayat president Rekhaben of Kheda district in Gujarat would come once or twice a month to the panchayat office, or as required, to affix her signature on panchayat papers. Her husband, a benami for the dominant castes, would instead do everything on her behalf. Determined to keep his wife under his control, once he verbally abused her for signing things without his knowledge.

Aside from operating as a mediating benami of the dominant castes, a smaller number of husbands also wielded authority directly over Dalit women panchayat presidents. Chanchalben, a village panchayat president from Kheda district in Gujarat, was a benami for her husband. He was educated and a second-time panchayat member while his wife was now president. She was not aware of most of the work in the panchayat, and did not have anything to do with even the little she knew about. She never spoke in the panchayat meetings because her husband told her there was no need for her to do so. She did not have any understanding of the issues in the village either. In her words, "Why should I be bothered about issues in the village? My husband has told me that I don't have to bother about anything in the panchayat as he is there to take care of everything. It is enough that I sign the papers and cheques."

Another small group of Dalit women elected representatives were benamis for multiple actors including dominant castes, political parties and husbands. Significantly, every major political party, national (Congress, BJP and CPM) and regional (DMK, AIDMK, MDMK), was involved in making the women presidents benamis through their husbands. The dominant caste vice president, talati and the BJP party thus instructed village panchayat president Lakshmiben of Kheda district in Gujarat to sign on cheques and other documents through her husband, a BJP supporter. Her husband undertook all other panchayat duties for her. In Tamil Nadu, village panchayat president Uma of Coimbatore district highlighted the extent of the normalisation of benami politics. Her husband performed all her panchayat duties as directed by the CPM party, including meeting government officials in her stead.

RELATIONSHIP WITH OTHER PANCHAYAT MEMBERS

A pre-requisite for a panchayat president's or member's political participation is their ability to build relationships with their colleagues in the panchayat. The extent of the cooperation that exists among panchayat council members determines whether desired outputs result: that is, decisions for the benefit of the panchayat, the free and independent exercise of administrative responsibilities, and the execution of development projects. Given the women's caste, class, gender, education and their resulting position in society; the relationships they forged, both cooperative or conflictual, with other panchayat members are important to examine.

Both women presidents and members mentioned a wide range of relationships with other panchayat members extending from minimum contact, to cooperation, to conflict. Being a benami representative appeared to be an important factor in limiting their relationships with panchayat colleagues. For example, village panchayat president Anandhi from Cuddalore district in Tamil Nadu, a benami for the dominant castes through her husband, said, "I did not have much association with the clerk and other members in the panchayat office, because I did not play much of a role as president. I just knew them by face and acknowledged their presence whenever I met them outside." A similar situation seemed to prevail at the taluka/union panchayat level as well. Vasantha from the same district held a union panchayat member's post and was a benami for her husband. She said, "I related well with all my colleagues in the union panchayat. But I talked very little with the president, a Dalit man. I approached him only when necessary, when giving a petition regarding a village development programme." Both Anandhi and Vasantha evidence the extent of male control over the women's performance of public duties and consequent limits on the women's expansion of social space in the public arena.

In comparison, some women presidents and members reported successfully maintaining good relationships and cooperation with other panchayat members. This success, however, requires a qualified understanding. In certain cases, it was not the women but their husbands who received cooperation from mainly dominant caste panchayat members. For instance, village panchayat president Chanchalben from Kheda district in Gujarat was a benami for her husband. She did not face any obstructions from panchayat members because her husband maintained good relations with different caste communities and government officials. Being a two-time panchayat member, he was known to be active in panchayat matters.

At the same time, there were instances where women participated actively in the panchayats and received cooperation from other panchayat members. Village panchayat president Jayashree of Thirunelveli district in Tamil Nadu, presiding over an all-Dalit panchayat council, said, "I have established a very cordial and family-like relationship with all of the members. They offer their unconditional support to me." She had knowledge and experience from being panchayat president for three consecutive terms, her husband's support and a majority Dalit population in her panchayat constituency. These apart, she attributed her success mainly to "my honesty and integrity, and the good works I did in the panchayat. I exercised my duties without any restrictions and hindrances from any source… Members of the panchayat accept all my proposals for they felt assured of my abilities to perform well."

For a large group of Dalit women presidents and members, however, obstructive behaviour from other panchayat members hindered the performance of their panchayat duties. Examples of such obstructions appear throughout this chapter.

INFLUENCE OF OTHERS IN DISCHARGING
RESPONSIBILITIES

Another way to understand how Dalit women presidents and members performed their panchayat responsibilities is to assess the extent to which actors *outside* the panchayat council – self-help groups and women's associations, youth associations, NGOs, political parties, Dalit organisations and movements, dominant caste villagers, husbands and other male relatives – influenced them in discharging their responsibilities. Three levels of potential influence were noted. One was *capacitation support*, by providing information on the panchayat system and helping strengthen the women's organisational, negotiation and public speaking skills. Second was *logistical support*, including helping the women implement development programmes and rendering support when they faced obstacles. Third was *decision-making support* by way of advising the women or making decisions for them.

Of all the external actors, husbands and male relatives exercised the most influence over the women. Women, ranging from just under one-third (30.1 per cent) to just over half (51.8 per cent), acknowledged them exercising the above-mentioned forms of influence. In some instances, it was the women's close family members and relatives. Village panchayat president Thilagam from Coimbatore district in Tamil Nadu, for example, had her son help her by reading and explaining panchayat documents and accounts. Husbands, however, exerted the most prominent influence. At times, husbands crossed the line of the women's independent decision-making and undertook their duties in relation to the implementation of development schemes.

In certain instances, however, this influence was limited to minimum guidance. Independent village panchayat president Annammal of Madurai district in Tamil Nadu stated, "My husband is employed in a private company and never had the time to influence me. But he offered suggestions on how I should go about certain things. When I faced any problem, he never interfered nor opposed me. I myself would deal with panchayat issues." A similarly positive role husbands and family members played was noted by village panchayat president Preetikaben from Anand district in Gujarat:

> My husband and family supported me in performing my duties. They encouraged, discussed, offered suggestions and guided me to understand the politics in the panchayat as well as in the village. For example, when I was challenged by my opponents in the panchayat, my husband guided me in resolving these problems. He advised me to make sure that all matters were resolved through discussion. He also advised me to speak with people face to face. I took all my decisions independently and my family was happy with those decisions.

Women cited several reasons for their husbands' interventions in their panchayat work. Village panchayat president Kalaimani of Nagapattinam district in Tamil Nadu, a benami for her husband, noted that he was the one who kept in contact with the outside world and was quite knowledgeable about getting information. Another contributing factor was their ongoing social ostracism due to a land dispute with a dominant caste landlord: they were abused, prevented from paying village taxes (signifying that they were no longer members of the village) and her husband was attacked one day. By contrast, village panchayat president Sunitaben of Anand district in Gujarat faced stiff opposition from dominant caste village elders and panchayat members owing to her refusal to act as their benami. She therefore had to depend on her husband for support and guidance. Though she sought guidance from her husband for many of her decisions, she reserved her right to decide and act independently. The trainings she had attended equipped her with a knowledge of panchayat politics and the know-how to get herself out of trouble. Other reasons for spousal interventions included husbands having previous experience in holding panchayat posts; being members or supporters of political parties; working as labourers for, and hence acting on behalf of, prominent dominant caste villagers or panchayat heads; having cultivated contacts with government officials; and being actively involved in taking up social issues for the Dalit community.

The husbands' influential role in supporting the women in critical areas of capacitation and decision-making, however, must be interpreted considering the large number of cases where dominant castes influenced the women's husbands to direct the women's decision making. In other words, the husbands' direct influence over the women's decision making did not always mean their direct control over the panchayat administration. Power often lay with dominant castes who used the women's husbands as their intermediaries.

Husbands and male relatives aside, other external actors who also influenced Dalit women elected representatives included SHGs/*mahila sanghas*/NGOs/youth associations, political parties, Dalit organisations/movements, and dominant castes. Notably, the influence of SHGs/mahila sanghas/NGOs/youth associations was minimal. At most 17 women (10.2 per cent) received information on the panchayats from these actors. Twelve women (7.2 per cent) received help regarding their organisational, negotiation and public speaking skills. Less than 5 per cent of women reported other forms of influence. This raises an important question about the role civil society groups play in panchayat politics and Dalit women's political empowerment.

Political parties primarily provided capacitation and logistics in four important areas: supplying information on the panchayat system (for 26 women or 15.7 per cent), supporting them in implementing development schemes (23 women or 13.9 per cent), providing advice on panchayat decisions (15 women or 9.0 per cent), and extending support when the women faced obstacles (15 women or 9.0 per cent). When strong opposition arose from dominant caste panchayat members on issues like the construction of a water pipeline or the illegal logging of forest wood, village panchayat president Sunitaben from Anand district in Gujarat asked the Congress party state leader to intervene on her behalf. Village panchayat president Tejuben from Kheda district in the same state said, "I enjoyed full freedom in my family and was active enough to deal with any type of issue [in the panchayat]. I did get help, though, from dominant caste village elders, one of whom was a Congress party state minister. He helped me defeat the no confidence motion against me and always gave me guidance and suggestions regarding the functioning of the panchayat. These elders also assured me of their support and encouraged me to continue my work without fear." In general, political parties, normally dominated by dominant castes, seemed interested in equipping the women with information on panchayat administration and supporting them in overcoming obstacles. They wanted to ensure development projects were implemented in favour of their party supporters.

Significantly, a few women, while protecting their independent political participation, deftly made use of both their own and their husband's political connections for the betterment of their panchayat constituency. Village panchayat president Jayashree from Thirunelveli district in Tamil Nadu said, "I do not allow political influence in my leadership. I choose to remain dissociated from the DMK party. My husband, who works as a clerk in the DMK party union panchayat office, takes care of all political activities." While clearly demarcating her role as well as that of her husband, Jayashree added, "Although I have held membership with the DMK party for the past 15 years, only in the recent election did I contest on behalf of the party. Now I use this position for people's welfare. As I am also the union level panchayat secretary of the DMK, I have been able to acquire funds for development projects in my panchayat. However, I remain independent as one who makes every effort to get better facilities for my people."

The influential role of political parties in Dalit women's political participation was the most apparent in the taluka/union and district panchayats. The power dynamics of caste-class-gender within which local governance operates are such that the higher the level of political authority exercised and the greater the role different political parties play, the more intense the power struggles among party stakeholders for political visibility, social status and access to resources.

Irrespective of the women's electoral post at the taluka/union or district level and whether they were associated with political parties as members or supporters, two points determined their style of functioning. First, because the women chose, or were asked, to contest the elections on a political party ticket, they operated within the parameters of the party's hierarchical authority and a commitment to implement the party's agenda. Taluka panchayat president Ramilaben of Vadodara district in Gujarat, though not a party member, was required to consult the district president of the Congress party before taking decisions, especially in relation to finance and expenditure. She had been elected with the support of this party. Moreover, it was the practice for the dominant caste president of the Gujarat Congress Committee to take all major decisions in the taluka and district panchayats. In the case of district panchayat president Gauri from Tamil Nadu, as most members of her panchayat were from her political party, she cultivated a good relationship with all of them and did not encounter many obstructions to her independent functioning. She made sure, however, that all panchayat matters were taken up for discussion and decided with the input of the DMK party, and was careful not to delve too deeply into the local dealings of panchayat members.

Second, the women's success in functioning independently and effectively as elected members of their panchayat within the political party framework depended on several factors: the extent of their knowledge on public affairs; the range of their social and political contacts; the quality of their administrative and political skills; the strength of their voter base; the level of importance accorded to their official position in the higher tier panchayats; and their belonging to the ruling or opposition political party. At the same time, their social status still impacted how they were viewed by political parties. Educated, economically independent and socially active in a Dalit movement and social organisation, the aforementioned taluka panchayat president Ramilaben effectively dealt with the panchayat administration. However, she noted a contradictory party approach:

> Because I am an active woman and understand politics, and know whom to approach, the Congress party leaders gave me the ticket to contest the election. But the local party members in the panchayat did not support me and instead gave me trouble. The Congress leadership came to my help by sending a high-level leader to guide me and give advice. However, even after an order from the party higher officials directing the panchayat members to cooperate with me, the members did not respect me in the panchayat meetings. Knowing this, the Congress higher officials later wanted me to just remain as the face of the party and not be an active party worker because I am a Dalit woman. They did not make things change for me within the panchayat council.

When it came to Dalit organisations or movements, political parties tended to capacitate the women with information on the panchayat system (23 women or 13.9 per cent), or strengthen their organisational, negotiation and public speaking skills (18 women or 10.8 per cent of women). They also gave the women advice regarding panchayat decisions (16 women or 9.6 per cent of women), all to fulfil the developmental requirements of the Dalit community. The small percentage of Dalit women representatives receiving this support suggests a need for Dalit organisations and movements to play a much larger role in capacitating the women.

In contrast, for a small percentage of women (11 women or 6.6 per cent) dominant caste patrons or villagers exerted the most influence in terms of making decisions *for* them. However, benami dynamics are such that this small percentage must be read in relation to the higher percentage of women reporting their husbands or male relatives giving them advice on what decisions to make, or making decisions for them (some at the behest of the dominant castes). A slightly lower number of women noted dominant caste support for implementing development programmes and providing information on the panchayat system (10 women each, or 6.0 per cent).

Participation in Panchayat Meetings and Committees

ATTENDANCE AND PARTICIPATION IN MEETINGS

Another indication of the performance of panchayat duties is active participation in panchayat meetings. On the one hand, it is a positive sign that over half of the 166 Dalit women elected representatives (87 women or 52.4 per cent), especially taluka/union and district panchayat presidents, attended at least half of the panchayat meetings held during their term in office. The percentage of regular attendance may be greater when one accounts for the 35 recently elected Dalit women representatives who recorded attending either one or several of the meetings held so far.

On the other hand, over half of the remaining 47.6 per cent of women who claimed to have attended only a few panchayat meetings had completed their panchayat tenure or were a substantial way through their term. Not surprisingly, presidents recorded more regular meeting attendance than members. However, eight women, seven of them presidents, had not been to even a single meeting. One of these women was village panchayat president Gangaben from Anand district in Gujarat. The dominant caste man who forced a consensus on all the women panchayati candidates controlled the panchayat administration through his wife, the vice president, and stopped all meetings. Gangaben only visited the panchayat office to sign cheques for development works, while the other women representatives dared not enter the office out of fear. Lower attendance rates indicated the presence of benami elected representatives, or dysfunctional panchayats, or the overriding influence of caste and gender norms and discriminatory practices on the women's presence in meetings. As one dominant caste vice president controlling a village panchayat in Anand district in Gujarat openly admitted, "[The benami Dalit woman president] doesn't contribute in any way in meetings and programmes. I do everything related to organising meetings in the panchayat... and I take most of the decisions in the meetings. Only if any government officials come or we happen to call her does she come to the panchayat."

An equally disturbing trend was if women elected representatives were not present in many panchayat meetings, their husbands (66 women or 39.8 per cent), other male relatives (8 women or 4.8 per cent), or even dominant castes (2 women or 1.2 per cent) attended in their place. At the higher panchayat tiers, this trend was less evident due to government officials attending the meetings. Restrictive gender norms saw 12 Dalit women being told by other panchayat members or their husbands and families to stay at home and do their household duties instead, or simply not being allowed to attend meetings by husbands or families. Where Dalit women were benamis for dominant castes, some husbands attended meetings merely to be able to pass on information to their wives. For instance, the husband of Kasthuri, a village panchayat president from Madurai district in Tamil Nadu and benami for the dominant castes, attended meetings instead of her. He mainly did so just to collect the official documents for his wife to sign. Similarly, another benami village panchayat president, Shardaben from Vadodara district in Gujarat, never attended panchayat meetings except on some special occasions, like when government officials visited. Instead, her husband, who worked as a safai karamachari in the panchayat office, would sit outside the meetings so that dominant caste panchayat members could tell him anything that needed to be communicated to his wife. Respect for state laws concerning the panchayat responsibilities of these elected representatives, therefore, was observed only in instances where those controlling the panchayats could not evade the monitoring gaze of the government officials.

Moreover, gender norms continued to restrict the women's free movement in public spaces. Hence, if women attended meetings, they rarely went alone. They were usually accompanied by their husbands (80 women or 48.2 per cent) or male relatives (9 women or 5.4 per cent), and in one case by a woman's dominant caste patron.

Attending meetings does not evidence effective participation in and of itself. Participation by speaking is an important factor. Compared to attendance, fewer Dalit women elected representatives spoke in these meetings: only one-third of the women (56 women or 33.7 per cent) said that they spoke often in meetings, while just over one-third (59 women or 36.7 per cent) spoke only once or a few times. A further 49 women (29.5 per cent), most being presidents, did not speak at all in meetings and, therefore, had little or no say over the decisions made. The following example of Leela's experience from Madurai district in Tamil Nadu, captured by the Indian Express newspaper on the 19th of November, 2006, highlights this trend:

> [Leela] continues to struggle with her responsibilities as the panchayat president. During the two 'ordinary meetings' held so far, she sat quietly in her chair and moved only when she was asked to put her thumb print on cheques. 'I don't say anything. Others decide,' she said softly. Her Deputy [Kalimuthu], also a Dalit, said no one bothered to attend the meetings so far. 'The President, the other two ward members, the panchayat Clerk and myself are the only ones present at the meetings,' he said.

The indifference and lack of respect accorded to Dalit women elected representatives, especially benami presidents, is evident from the following examples. Kashiben from Kheda district in Gujarat would attend village panchayat meetings, but just come for a short while, sit down on the floor and then leave a while later without speaking. Thamilselvi from Coimbatore district in Tamil Nadu attended a few meetings in which she never spoke and no one was bothered if she attended or not. This lack of respect extended to outright discrimination, as in the case of village panchayat president, Usha from Cuddalore district in Tamil Nadu. She was a benami for the dominant caste vice president and only one of two women in the panchayat. She attended only one panchayat meeting when the BDO visited their panchayat office. Even then, she was seated on the ground during the meeting, whereas all the others had chairs, and she did not speak.

Taking the women's participation in panchayat meetings one step further, approximately a quarter of the women (45 women or 27.1 per cent) brought up many issues in meetings, while the same number mentioned raising only one or a few issues. That left just under half of Dalit women elected representatives (76 women or 45.8 per cent), mostly presidents, who had not raised any new issues during meetings. Again, putting aside recently elected women, over two-thirds of the women who never raised issues during their terms in office had either completed or were a substantial way through their term.

When those inside the panchayats with concentrated decision-making powers in their hands are viewed alongside those outside the panchayats who accompanied the Dalit women representatives to meetings or attended in their stead, a pattern of limited political participation becomes clear. Taking the 98 elected representatives who had someone either accompany them or attend meetings in their stead, 74 women (77.1 per cent) stated that this person spoke in meetings a few to many times. Further, 65 women (66.3 per cent) indicated that this person raised several or many new issues. In other words, the majority of accompaniers usurped or diminished Dalit women's participation in meetings by talking 'on their behalf'.

Other methods of controlling women's voice in meetings were also used. Several benamis were effectively coached before the meetings by dominant castes and/or their husbands as to what to say in the meetings and what issues to raise therein. For example, Amarben, a village panchayat president from Anand district in Gujarat, would sit with the dominant caste vice president and talati before each meeting to discuss what issues to raise in panchayat meetings, and what she should say or do. In a similar manner, village panchayat president Chandra from Coimbatore district in Tamil Nadu was tutored by the dominant castes to raise a few points in the meetings she attended, as if she was suggesting the points independently. Another 13 women were offered bribes in meetings. The bribes were to accept and support the suggestions of other members, especially dominant castes. Bribes were also a part of attempts to obstruct these women or make them abdicate their duties in approving contracts for panchayat development works. In several cases, dominant castes bribed women benami presidents to stay at home and just sign on resolutions as they directed.

Benami or proxy representation aside, several reasons lay behind the limited participation in meetings experienced by almost three-quarters of the Dalit women elected representatives (120 women or 72.3 per cent). Two frequently interconnected reasons were fear and lack of knowledge and self-confidence. Either the women felt anxious they would do or say something wrong in meetings and thereby incur the wrath of others, or they believed their lack of education and knowledge of panchayat administration limited their capacity to contribute to the discussions. A group of Dalit women elected representatives from Kheda district in Gujarat also alluded to the significance of social networks and information: "Dominant castes hold more control over social networks due to their multiple contacts and relationships with government officials at the taluka and district levels as well as the talatis, most of whom are dominant castes. This allows them to gather more information on development schemes, contracts and so on, all of which are required to consolidate their hold on panchayat administration."

Behind much of this lack of self-confidence and fear of public speaking lay unspoken caste and gender rules. According to Dalit elders and male villagers from Surendranagar district in Gujarat:

> In comparison to other women, our women live in more fear, thinking that their every step in the panchayat would be against the wishes of the dominant castes. The dominant castes don't like a Dalit woman being elected. Our women also fear the consequences of breaking social rules by coming into the panchayat administration. Most of the time she is the only woman in the entire council and it takes a lot of effort for a Dalit woman to sit in front of this male gathering and speak. Because of fear of all the dominant caste men sitting there, the lurking fear of all opposing her and no one cooperating with her, the women have no other option but to sign any paper placed in front of them. If the woman is president, then other Dalit panchayat members, numerically and/or gender-wise dominant, also

oppose her as no man would like to be under a woman. Besides, the women can't function on their own because of a lack of information and support from other panchayat members as well as the discrimination practised against them as women.

In the same district, Dalit women villagers mentioned how generally "if the woman is from the Valmiki sub-caste, then she won't even be allowed to enter into the panchayat office. If she belongs to another Dalit sub-caste, she can at least sit in the meeting but cannot speak because social rules restrict her from speaking in front of elders and dominant castes."

Confirming the enduring power of these social norms, a dominant caste vice president from Anand district in Gujarat stated that a Dalit woman elected representative "has to follow the village norms and traditions because she is a woman and belongs to the lowest caste... She can't speak freely in front of anyone in the village and cannot drink water or tea in the panchayat [office]." At an extreme, village panchayat members like Chellammal from Madurai district in Tamil Nadu reported that the dominant castes in her panchayat refused to allow the panchayat meetings to take place after Dalits were elected to panchayat seats following years of caste-based opposition to their political participation. Instead, the panchayat clerk came to her home to get her to sign that the meetings had been held, until she refused to sign one day.

Crosscutting caste are gender norms impacting women's freedom of movement and speech in relation to panchayat meetings. These norms were experienced both as obstructions and as restrictive gender roles and attitudes. For example, village panchayat member Ushaben from Kheda district in Gujarat, the only woman in the panchayat, was told by the dominant caste male members that women should not speak in meetings. Her successful rebuttal was, "You should not tell me that women must not speak. I know the law and I can see you being removed from your office by law. If you are not ready to listen to the advice of a woman, then why did you reserve the seat for women?" Gender norms also caused Dalit women to self-regulate their speech so as not to invite disapprobation from other male panchayat members. Women grew up in *purdah*[6] (in Gujarat) and, therefore, were constantly told not to speak loudly and directly in front of men, and to defer to the opinions of men (in both Gujarat and Tamil Nadu). Moreover, some women stated they could not afford to take enough time away from work or household duties to adequately participate in panchayat meetings. Thus, the economic freedom offered by household financial stability alongside a relative freedom from household responsibilities seemed to strengthen attendance at meetings. The lack of these two freedoms implied the converse.

Furthermore, social disapprobation of outspoken Dalit women and other discriminatory attitudes were occasionally expressed as overt attempts to stop women elected representatives (38 women or 22.9 per cent) from attending or speaking in meetings, or even outright opposition and stifling their voices during meetings. Silencing or ignoring women in panchayat meetings (30 women) was one common tactic. This tactic took advantage of the women's Dalit and minority status, as well as gender norms that legitimised men stifling women's voices. For instance, Jayalakshmi, vice president of a union panchayat in Thirunelveli district in Tamil Nadu, faced a complete lack of respect from the dominant caste president and panchayat members. They would ignore her attempts to speak and verbally abuse her in meetings. Despite this, she succeeded in ensuring a few development projects for the Dalit community. For 13 women elected representatives, many of them presidents, meetings were fraught with unnecessary questions or arguments and non-cooperation, if not outright opposition, to the resolutions they supported. One of these women was village panchayat president, Kamachi from Coimbatore district in Tamil Nadu. She managed panchayat meetings despite the dominant caste panchayat members, vice president and clerk demanding commissions on panchayat contracts, arguing in meetings, demanding contracts for development schemes, turning up drunk, and even threatening her with knives.

Despite such obstructions, some Dalit women presidents like Preetikaben from Anand district in Gujarat sought to establish good democratic practices in village panchayat meetings:

> I decided on the dates and agenda of our meetings and asked my
> colleagues to comment on this. The panchayat peon delivered the

meeting schedule, agenda and purpose to a dominant caste male member who often refused to attend the meetings. That man's presence was not crucial. However, his presence was useful because it was good practice to pass resolutions in the presence of all the panchayat members. When he attended meetings, he arrived at the last moment and opposed my proposed resolutions. I constantly had to bring him to order during the meetings because whenever he spoke he seldom had a clear plan or constructive interest in the panchayat work. His only intent and action was to oppose me.

When I faced obstruction from the supporters of my electoral opponent who was in the panchayat, and other dominant caste panchayat members, I always confronted them. When I confronted them, I took away any space they might have had to act corruptly. I forced them to settle issues in the meetings. They created problems for me by constantly disagreeing with my views and decisions in the panchayat. This was because they were unhappy with me for defeating their benami candidate, and because their dominant caste interests were not being fulfilled through me. But I was always true in panchayat activities. I was aware of the politics and aware that they were trying to suppress me. Part of my success was because of my outspokenness, and knowledge of the law and duties of government officials.

Preetikaben, however, was in the minority. Disturbingly, less than 5 per cent of Dalit women elected representatives indicated democratic practices in panchayat meetings, especially at the taluka/union and district level. At these higher tiers, political party control over panchayat decisions in some cases meant that union panchayat members were left out of decision-making processes, and decisions were made outside the panchayat.

The above analysis highlights the constricting influences of caste, class and gender norms and practices. The women's lack of education and information, and the economic exigencies affecting their ability to participate, are intrinsically linked to the patriarchal caste system that denies Dalits, and especially Dalit women, equal access to economic resources and education. Caste, class and gender norms enable dominant castes – almost always men – and Dalit men to appropriate the women's role in the panchayats, whether overtly through benamis, or by circumscribing their voice and agency. This allows undemocratic practices to thrive in panchayat meetings, with dominant caste men and, to a lesser extent, Dalit men, controlling meetings almost as a matter of right. This, in turn, reinforces the very norms which prevent future representatives from attempting to or succeeding in raising women's or Dalit issues in panchayat meetings.

ISSUES RAISED BY WOMEN IN MEETINGS

90 of the 166 Dalit women elected representatives (54.2 per cent) raised issues in panchayat meetings, and these related to several areas. The most common issues, mentioned by 88 women, related to development or economic issues: for example, the inclusion of families in the BPL (below poverty line) list, increasing basic facilities in the villages, focusing on the needs of the poor or Dalits or women, allowing Dalit use of common lands, and so on. Linked to these issues was neglect in the implementation of panchayat programmes or services, mentioned by 36 women. Women pointing out the latter is an important indication of good democratic practice: that is, demanding accountability for the implementation of panchayat development decisions.

A further issue for 11 women was land encroachments, be it encroachment on panchayat lands, burial lands, common lands, government revenue lands, or Dalit lands. Land in rural areas is a vital source of economic livelihood in terms of agricultural production, grazing space or the collection of minor produce. Land is also a social need in terms of housing space or space to bury the dead. More fundamentally for Dalits, land represents a physical space to belong to and live with dignity. Thus, the socio-economic power of the encroachers has an impact on the way in which the problem is dealt with. Where landed dominant castes are the encroachers, tensions become heightened if panchayats try to address encroachments. If Dalits are occupying land for their habitations or minor cultivation, as is often the case when they are landless, these 'encroachments by necessity' become a constant source of vulnerability for them. It was most often the former scenario of dominant caste encroachers which prompted Dalit women elected representatives to discuss

land encroachments in panchayat meetings or to make direct
complaints to government officials.

Notably, no woman took the opportunity in panchayat
meetings to raise social justice issues that aligned with strategic
caste-class-gender needs, such as the abolition of untouchability
practices, tackling sexual harassment or domestic violence, or
curbing alcoholism. One reason for this could be the limited
nature of schemes and funds available to the panchayats. In
Gujarat, it may have been that such issues were relegated to the
Social Justice Committees. Another reason could be that direct
or indirect caste-class-gender obstructions prevented Dalit women
from voicing social justice issues out of fear, or because of the
complexity involved in tackling such issues.

Raising issues in meetings, however, did not guarantee the
women's participation in discussions on these issues, nor approval
of the solutions proposed, nor the implementation of approved
solutions. For over half of the 90 Dalit women who raised issues
in panchayat meetings (47 women or 52.2 per cent), these issues
were never discussed, or were discussed and approved only a few
times. While the remaining 43 women (47.8 per cent) indicated
that several issues they raised were discussed and approved in the
meetings, what should be borne in mind is the number of women
directed by dominant castes or their husbands to raise certain
issues. Moreover, many Dalit women panchayat presidents had
to struggle to get their proposals approved. Village panchayat
president Tejuben from Kheda district in Gujarat narrated the
following: "I convened all the panchayat meetings and got an
opportunity to speak in every meeting. Except for the issue of
grazing land, all decisions were taken solely by me. This was
because I faced opposition to all resolutions no matter what I did.
However, I passed decisions, writing 'passed – with opposition'. I
did this because no work could have been done otherwise."

When it came to the implementation of decisions, fewer
women answered positively. For 13 women (14.4 per cent),
approved decisions were never implemented, while for another 35
women (38.8 per cent) only a few approved decisions were carried
through. The remaining 44 women (46.7 per cent) saw many of

their proposed issues approved and implemented, though it must again be noted that some of these women proposed issues at the behest of others. Jayashree, three-time village panchayat president from Thirunelveli district in Tamil Nadu, highlights how effectively some Dalit women raised issues in panchayat meetings. Jayashree heads an all-Dalit panchayat. As a self-confident, educated and economically well-off Dalit woman with strong family support, she actively participates in panchayat meetings. According to her, "In the panchayat, only the needs and problems of the people and the schemes coming from the BDO's office are discussed. Issues discussed in the panchayat are, for example, roads, drinking water pipelines and electricity. Decisions are taken if they are found to be legitimate needs. Subsequently, I visit the concerned offices – BDO or union panchayat office – to put forward these needs and get things implemented."

One particularly problematic proposal arose throughout the three terms she was in the panchayat:

Proposals were placed in the panchayat council for sand quarrying in the Thamiraparani river, which flows along my panchayat area. Although there were pressures from contractors for this proposal, I refused permission and withstood all outside pressures to force me to allow sand quarrying in the river basin. I pacified the contractors because sand quarrying would curtail the water flow and affect the environment. My people have understood my concern for ecology and accepted the decision to stop sand quarrying without opposition.

As the Dalits of the panchayat do not have regular sources of income – they are only agricultural labourers working under landlords, I suggested that they begin a cement factory, which would serve as a permanent source of work and income for the people. However, this idea was vetoed in the council due to concerns about pollution and the requirement of too much finance to start it. I keep continuing to look for ways and means of finding a permanent source of income for the Dalits of my panchayat from the district and union councils.

Contrast this situation with the 98 women representatives who had men either accompanying them to panchayat meetings or attending on their behalf. Of the issues they raised, over half of these men had a few or more approved and implemented. In other words, despite not holding a formal position in the panchayats, these men were treated as *de facto* members or even presidents. This subverted democratic governance and reinforced the women's marginal role in panchayat decision-making processes.

Overall, when Dalit women raised issues for discussion in meetings, in a greater number of cases at least some of these issues were approved, and a few were implemented. While on the one hand, this evidences Dalit women's capabilities in exercising their right to political participation in panchayat meetings, the number of benami representatives suggests that this participation was, to some extent, controlled to serve others' interests. By contrast, dominant caste and Dalit men's overt appropriation of women's rights to raise issues in meetings highlights the continuing relegation of many women's roles, reducing them to obligatory quorum fillers.

PARTICIPATION IN COMMITTEES

Aside from the panchayat councils, 66 Dalit women elected representatives (39.8 per cent) were members of panchayat committees for education, housing, health, water, watersheds, sanitation, planning, public distribution, village development, farmers, temple welfare, social justice, women elected representatives, panchayat presidents, atrocities eradication, or (in Gujarat) executive committees. One likely reason for more women being committee members in Gujarat (50 women) than in Tamil Nadu (16 women) is that Gujarat has Social Justice Committees comprised solely of Dalits and Adivasis, with at least one mandated female member. Significantly, in both states most women were on panchayat committees which examined issues traditionally considered to be 'female oriented': that is, education, health and water.

Women's participation was greater in these smaller issue-based committees than in the formal panchayat meetings. A third of Dalit women committee members indicated that they had raised several issues in these committee meetings, while another third had raised a few issues. The remaining third had never raised any issues either because they did not feel comfortable enough to do so, or because the committees they were a part of were dysfunctional. Of the 44 women who raised issues in committee meetings, 15 saw their issues approved on many occasions, while the majority (26 women) had only a few of their issues approved. Only three women never had their issues approved. It might be easier for women to create spaces for themselves in these smaller committee meetings and feel confident enough to raise issues, especially on 'female oriented' issues such as education or water. What remains questionable is how many of these issues were then translated into approved resolutions in the formal panchayat council meetings.

The Social Justice Committees in Gujarat are interesting to examine as their purpose is to secure social justice for the weaker sections of society, including SCs. Given the small Dalit population in the state and small Adivasi population in most of the sample districts, alongside the requirement of at least one woman member, almost all of the 86 Gujarati Dalit women elected representatives should be part of these committees. Only 26 of these women (30.2 per cent), however, were Social Justice Committee members. The majority (53 women or 61.6 per cent) were either not part of the committees, or did not know if they were members. In addition, another seven women indicated that these committees did not exist in their panchayats. This data casts doubts on the Gujarat government's commitment to promoting social justice for Dalits, aside from constituting a breach of duties under the *Gujarat Panchayats Act, 1993*.

Moreover, only 13 women Social Justice Committee members raised issues in committee meetings and eight women brought complaints to the committees for redress. The remainder either did not involve themselves, or their committees were not active. A TDO from Surendranagar district with authority regarding the social justice committees in his taluka confirmed that women rarely become part of these committees. He further commented that important issues such as atrocities are discussed in these committee meetings, and the committees give a report to the talati or related authority to assist them in taking further action.

However, the committee decisions are rarely implemented in the panchayat. Moreover, TDOs and DDOs do not undertake monitoring visits to these committee meetings. Instead, the talati acts as secretary to the Social Justice Committee and reports to the TDO or DDO every three months on the meeting resolutions and on the functioning of the committees. In effect, the Gujarat State Government appears to take little interest in the operationalisation of these committees and fails to monitor their functioning so as to effectively eradicate discriminatory practices at the local level.

Interaction with Government Officials and Higher Panchayat Tiers

Panchayat administration also involves interactions with government officials, the police or office bearers at the higher panchayat tiers. Not surprisingly, a larger percentage of panchayat presidents than members approached officials, given their executive authority. High levels of interaction with officials would indicate that Dalit women elected representatives have established networks to increase their knowledge of panchayat schemes and administration, obtain advice and help on issues, and negotiate for schemes and funds to implement development works in their constituencies. Such interactions should strengthen political participation as well as their responsiveness to people's needs.

Dalit women elected representatives from Ahmedabad district in Gujarat, however, revealed that such interactions were ostensibly the prerogative of men. Restrictions placed on the women, rooted in their caste, class and gender identities, and a lack of self-confidence linked to a lack of education and access to information on Panchayati Raj, prevented their interactions:

> Most Dalit women never go to meet government officials. Their husbands have good relationships with government officials, so they go and meet them. Women feel they should not or cannot go just because they do not feel comfortable or confident enough to interact with government officials, and because almost all officials are men. They also don't know much about the government schemes and the procedures to get them implemented. Their

education level is one of the obstacles which stops them from going, negotiating and arguing with these officials. The women think that their husbands, as men, are vocal and strong enough to deal with the officials. Dalit men do also face some problems due to their low caste status when meeting with officials, but then it is easier for them than for Dalit women. Only the husbands attend meetings organised at the taluka level or any training camp. Government officials never oppose this.

The first level of official interaction is with the block/taluka or district development officers (BDOs/TDOs or DDOs), who exercise executive and supervisory powers over the panchayats. On the positive side, 101 women elected representatives had visited these officials several times or frequently. Most went to discuss development and administrative issues, with very few women forwarding complaints. The remaining 65 Dalit women elected representatives (39.2 per cent), however, had never visited these officials. Instead, their only interaction was when the officials visited their panchayat offices and attended meetings.

Slightly fewer women elected representatives visited and interacted with presidents in higher panchayat tiers, including in a few cases the Social Justice Committee presidents at higher tiers in Gujarat. Just under half the women (74 women or 45.8 per cent) had interacted with presidents in higher panchayats on several or more occasions as compared to just over half (90 women or 54.2 per cent, almost equally presidents and members) who had never done so. While the lack of interaction may be understandable for panchayat members, the lack of interaction between presidents of lower tiers with those at higher tiers reveals poor coordination. In the absence of formal structures for interaction between executive authorities in the three tiers, the lack of any organic working link between these tiers means that the panchayats largely operate as almost independent entities, except for the provision of funds and schemes. This lowers the potential for coordinated and coherent development plans in their respective panchayat areas.

Dalit women elected representatives visited the district collectors and revenue officials – tahsildar or revenue divisional officer (RDO) – in relation to development or administrative issues, particularly land, as well as complaints. Their interactions with these officials were roughly comparable with that of higher tier panchayat presidents: 43.4 per cent (72 women) had interacted with these officials on several or more occasions as compared to 56.6 per cent (94 women) who had not met them. In contrast, Dalit women elected representatives interacted much less with police officials and other development officials – panchayat department officials, project officers (Tamil Nadu), district development commissioners (Gujarat) or mamlatdars (Gujarat) – or members of Parliament or Legislative Assemblies: over three-quarters of the women indicated they had never met these officials.

Moreover, the fact that Dalit women elected representatives visited these officials did not mean that they spoke to them. Just taking the main officials with whom the women interacted, the following numbers of women remained silent: 28 of the 101 women visiting BDOs/TDOs or DDOs (27.7 per cent); 16 of the 76 women visiting taluka/union or district panchayat presidents (21.1 per cent); and 21 of the 72 women visiting district collectors, RDOs or tahsildars (29.2 per cent). The large number of benamis and the gender norms inhibiting women's freedom of speech with primarily male officials meant that others often spoke on the women's behalf. Otherwise, the women merely delivered petitions which others had drafted to the officials. For instance, Thilagam, a benami village panchayat president for the dominant castes from Coimbatore district in Tamil Nadu, noted how in all the meetings with officials the vice president and clerk would only speak with the officials. Husbands, male relatives or other panchayat members escorted most of the women to meet these officials. This was partly due to safety issues where offices were located at a distance. This was also partly so that those accompanying the women to meet officials could speak on behalf of the women. Whenever district panchayat member Archana from Cuddalore district in Tamil Nadu went to meet government officials, for example, she took her husband, a government official himself, with her. He alone would talk to the officials. She felt the BDO was indifferent to her, and her presence was a mere formality.

The aforementioned cases hint at the complicity of state officials in allowing a situation where a democratically elected panchayat representative could be bypassed and others allowed to speak in her place. For example, Chanchalben, a village panchayat president from Kheda district in Gujarat and benami for her husband, only met the TDO several times. Each time the TDO discussed panchayat issues directly with her husband. On one occasion, a government official explicitly told her not to speak and to let her husband speak on her behalf instead. Another TDO in Surendranagar district in the same state did the same to village panchayat president Hiraben when she visited his office, telling her that she need not speak to him, and to just send her husband thereafter. These two cases and the examples above highlight how state actors reinforce benami politics and gender norms, which silence women's voices and limit their official interactions with others. In doing so, these officials breach their supervisory duties in the panchayats. The open acceptance of such patriarchal practices was evidenced in the following comment by a BDO in Tamil Nadu: "During my tenure, many Dalit women members and presidents sought my help. When they come to speak about their panchayat problems, their husbands accompany them and only they speak."

Where the women elected representatives spoke with government officials, it is a positive indication that many received the requested support: 39.3 per cent of women (46 women) had their invitations to visit their panchayats accepted by officials; 36.8 per cent (43 women) saw officials implement schemes requested by them or were themselves supported when implementing schemes; and 34.2 per cent (40 women) had officials take prompt action on their requests or complaints. Annammal, a village panchayat president from Madurai district in Tamil Nadu, for example, related well with officials and got their support in facing obstructions from most panchayat members. Referring to her contacts with government officials, some Dalits appreciated her, saying, "It's something to be proud of for an Arunthathiyar woman to do this. Then only the dominant castes will not speak about us in a derogatory manner as being incapable and worthless." In the case of village panchayat president Sunitaben from Anand district in Gujarat, she often met the TDO and DDO to ask for their help in getting government grants for development works for her panchayat. She said, "When the TDO or DDO came to check the resolution book and accounts, they gave me a lot of information and guidance on grants and schemes available, and instructed me about the relevant procedures to get the grants. I shared my panchayat experiences with them, too. They always gave me advice on ways to deal with obstacles in my panchayat. The TDO advised me to keep quiet and pretend to work together with the others when facing opposition, and then inform him about what was happening."

As Sunitaben's case illustrates, aside from advice on how to confront problems, several women elected representatives indicated how officials also increased their capacity to actively engage in their panchayat duties. Village panchayat president Tejuben from Kheda district in Gujarat, for instance, generally met with her local MLA, MP, district collector and the district panchayat president bi-monthly and received advice from them on various panchayat issues. Whenever she required their help, they would guide her over the phone or write a letter to her to ensure the effective implementation of development works. The local MLA was instrumental in defeating an attempted no confidence motion against her. Even panchayat members who cultivated good relations with officials strengthened their participation and impact in their panchayat wards. This was the experience of Rukhmini, a village panchayat member from Nagapattinam district in Tamil Nadu. She met her local MLA regarding sanitation facilities for her ward and got toilets built in her panchayat.

In contrast, some government officials also bypassed the proper lines of political authority and instead granted requests put forward by the women's husbands, or those with less authority and rank such as the panchayat vice presidents. Just over one-quarter of the women (32 women or 27.4 per cent) experienced this. In doing so, as mentioned above, these officials perpetuated caste and gender discriminatory norms in local governance structures, and subverted the democratic process.

A common scenario (for 27 women or 23.1 per cent) was
for officials to harass the Dalit women elected representatives
by asking them to make frequent trips to government offices to
deal with the same matter, or to delay the implementation of
schemes despite repeated requests from the women. Persistence
was required from women like Preetikaben, a village panchayat
president from Anand district in Gujarat:

I had the skills to deal with all the administrative officers and
any other officials. I was relatively well educated, had previously
worked in the village on social and development issues, had
visited government offices, was an active Congress party member
and was part of a women's and Dalit organisation. I knew the law
because I attended training programmes on the *Gujarat Panchayats
Act*, and my husband and family apprised me about the panchayat
and its rules. I also had chances to meet the taluka panchayat
president. I visited government officials repeatedly because no
project can be secured in a single visit. During these visits, all the
officials sat with me for long periods of time and listened to me.
They also guided me on relevant procedures and time periods for
the implementation of specific schemes. I think they responded to
me because they believed that I would go to higher authorities if
they didn't. I also maintained good relations with these officials by
regularly visiting them. When they came to the gram sabhas, they
often promised me support like providing various development
schemes to my village. However, oftentimes they never followed
through on these promises. Again, I had to visit them many times
and remind them of their promise to help with a project. In the
end, they helped me implement schemes related to housing,
school renovation and upgrading, water and health.

[For example] last year the village was destroyed by heavy
rains. Most Dalit houses were destroyed. All the concerned
officials refused to visit the village because it was waterlogged.
I went to the TDO and mamlatdar's offices twice and asked
them to visit the village, but they did not respond positively to
my requests. After this, I went to the Dalit community elders and
they helped arrange a tractor to take Dalits to meet the TDO and
DDO. I led the group and we argued with the TDO to support
us. Finally, that day itself, the TDO gave us a cheque for ₹1 lakh.
The District Collector also promised to construct 52 new houses

for the Dalit community. These houses have now been built.
Now I come to realise that only when a woman is educated and
understands the law can she get such work done... In my view, it
is necessary for a Dalit woman president or her husband to have
a good reputation and standing with government officials and
the police. This is one of the reasons they took my applications
seriously.

Likewise, 21 women (17.9 per cent) experienced lengthy
waiting periods to meet the officials to discuss official panchayat
matters. Furthermore, Kowsalya, a village panchayat president
from Coimbatore district in Tamil Nadu, was one of three
women who reported that government officials she met regarding
panchayat works all demanded large bribes from her to do
anything. Bureaucratic lethargy and corruption aside, behind the
officials' behaviour was also caste, class and gender prejudices.
As noted by Jasodaben from Surendranagar district in Gujarat,
a benami village panchayat president, "Whenever I approached
government officials, they never responded immediately and
they didn't do work fast. Only if they (dominant castes) apply,
do government officials attend to them quickly." Hence, when
she appealed against a no confidence motion brought in by the
dominant caste members against her after she tried to act with
some independence in the panchayat, the TDO did not support
her and did not conduct a proper investigation. She therefore lost
her seat as president.

Seven women also narrated that government officials either
received their complaints and did not take any action, or openly
showed indifference to their requests, or told them that certain
development projects could not be implemented due to a lack of
funds. Reshmaben, a village panchayat member from Ahmedabad
district in Gujarat, recounted how the TDO and DDO visited the
panchayat in response to her request for their intervention on a
land encroachment issue. Despite promises to consider the matter,
they did not take any action, nor did the district collector. Other
women recounted how government officials would not sanction
development works for their panchayats. In the case of Kalaimani,
a village panchayat president from Nagapattinam district in Tamil

Nadu and benami for her husband, caste discrimination also factored into her transactions with government officials:

> The BDO never gave full support to us because he was bribed by the [dominant caste] landlord and village head Alagesan. The tahsildar also opposed our initiatives all the time, but after visiting his office 12 times with the support of the people, we made him remove the landlord's encroachments... The union and district panchayat members also wouldn't respect us and didn't care about our representations to them. They refused to release any funds for my panchayat. One dominant caste union panchayat member never cooperated with me. He made sure, with the help of the BDO, that all the funds and developmental works meant for my area were siphoned off to the dominant castes instead. Besides, he and the local MLA are of the same caste, and members of the AIADMK party, and so they didn't support us. Both were also close to Alagesan. Hence, on the basis of caste, these three men aligned together to obstruct all my efforts in fulfilling my panchayat responsibilities. Unfortunately, the government officials were also in collusion with them. The district and union panchayats are completely ruled by the AIADMK party and since [I was not aligned with any political party], I could not establish a good rapport with them.

While Kalaimani experienced indirect discrimination, four other women experienced direct discrimination from government officials. Government officials spoke to these women in disrespectful terms using casteist language, or did not offer the women seats in government offices, or did not allow the women to speak, or just went ahead and addressed the men accompanying the women without showing any respect to the women's official position. The detrimental effect such discrimination had on women's political participation is clear. However, women like Kamachi, twice elected president of her village panchayat in Coimbatore district in Tamil Nadu, also strategised to overcome this discrimination and discharge their panchayat duties. Realising she was being discriminated against because of her caste and gender by the government officers and others in charge of panchayat related works, Kamachi approached the district collector directly for all matters.

What the above analysis highlights is both the necessity of official support to strengthen Dalit women's political participation, and the need for reforms and education to ensure that officials act promptly on the requests of elected representatives. Moreover, government officials must be reminded that their official duties do encompass investigating issues of caste and gender discrimination. Those complicit in perpetuating such discrimination by allowing others to speak on behalf of women elected representatives or by ignoring discrimination in the panchayats should be disciplined for this breach of their duties.

Discrimination in the Panchayats

The fundamental right to non-discrimination enshrined in Article 15 of the Indian Constitution notwithstanding, nine out of every ten Dalit women elected representatives (146 women, or 89.8 per cent) felt they were treated differently from other elected representatives in their panchayats. This reflects the findings of other studies.[7] The women most often attributed the discrimination to their core identities as women (90.6 per cent) and as Dalits (84.6 per cent). A group of Dalit women elected representatives from Thirunelveli district in Tamil Nadu stated:

> As we are Dalits *and* women, we are forced to bear the brunt of double discrimination unlike our male counterparts... Other members of the panchayat do not give respect to us because we are born Dalit and women, and they will even go to the extent of working against us. The dominant caste men do not let a Dalit woman function as an elected representative because of their wrong view that women are good for nothing, that they are simply a benami, that they cannot be involved in public life; and if they are, then they are immoral women. They say and do such things precisely because they cannot bear the sight of a Dalit woman occupying a position of governance over them... In general, we can say that Dalit women are forced to encounter more problems and more opposition than Dalit men, dominant caste men and women. That is, for a dominant caste woman, it is only her husband or a male member of her caste who can be a source of

irritation, pressure and obstacles. But for a Dalit woman, such opposition comes from Dalit men, dominant caste men and women. She must encounter three sources of obstructions. What is the reason? It is simply their anti-Dalit woman mindset; that is, these three sets of people are of the view that a Dalit woman is someone who need not be given any importance on any matter and hence can be easily dispensed with, who is ever submissive and patient with whatever is done or happens to her, who is incapable of asserting herself.

Government officials confirmed the above statement. A TDO in Gujarat stated, "Dalit women elected representatives are confronting problems of traditional gender and caste practices. They face all these challenges at the time of the election and even after the election as well. The caste system is an obstacle which exists at all the panchayat levels in many different forms." Even the assistant development commissioner in Gujarat openly stated that Dalit women faced multiple problems because "no elected representative supports Dalit women directly". The following opinion of a dominant caste village panchayat vice president from Kheda district in Gujarat evidences this: "It is *impossible* for Dalit women to become capable elected representatives. As a president, a Dalit woman is not at all capable to work at the taluka and district panchayat levels. She doesn't understand any issues or questions. And if I make her capable, then she will go against me, so better not make her capable." In other words, behind discrimination is the protection of dominant caste economic and political interests.

Thus, women such as village panchayat president Priyaben from Vadodara district in Gujarat suffered discrimination from all the men as well as the dominant caste women in the panchayat. Pooncholai and Priya, both village panchayat presidents from Thirunelveli district in Tamil Nadu and benamis for their husbands, noted how gender discrimination was evident in the way other Dalit and other caste male members slighted or ignored the women, or how Priya had no role in the panchayat's public programmes. Even in the higher panchayat tiers, discrimination remained, though sometimes less overt. For example, Keerthana, a district panchayat president in Tamil Nadu stated that while she faced no direct discrimination, she was treated disparagingly because of her gender in that other members made snide comments behind her back about how she spoke, dressed, and so on. A further nine women faced discrimination for being outspoken in their views on social issues, thereby contradicting caste and gender norms that prescribe the women's submissiveness and lack of voice in any male-dominated forum. Dalit elders and male villagers from Surendranagar district in Gujarat noted in this regard, "If a woman opposes anything [in panchayat meetings], then it becomes an issue and men – both dominant caste and Dalit – raise allegations against her that she is going outside the social rules and traditions."

Discrimination rooted in intersecting caste and gender identities was further enmeshed in gendered identities and negative stereotypes attached to widows and separated women. For example, in Ahmedabad district in Gujarat, Shantiben, a village panchayat president and benami for the dominant castes, felt she was treated differently because she was a Dalit and a widow. The panchayat letter pad and stamp, for instance, were kept at the vice president's house because people said that it would be inauspicious to see a widow's face in the morning. Likewise, Kamachi, a single woman from Coimbatore district in Tamil Nadu, recalled the following treatment by dominant caste members and even some Dalit male members and villagers: "I was derogatorily called in the singular 'avan (he) and aval (she)'. They would say 'any Tom, Dick and Harry comes to her house'... 'there is no one to question her'... 'she comes and goes as she likes'." In other words, alongside gender abuse were aspersions cast on her morality for not following traditional gender norms that circumscribe women's freedom of movement and speech.

This discrimination can be contrasted with the much smaller role of class distinctions due to the women's economically poorer backgrounds (mentioned only by 29 women or 19.5 per cent). This said, caste and class often converged in the case of many poor Dalit women, with caste being perceived as the stronger factor generating differential treatment. Another factor stemming from the women's low caste and gender status and underlying discrimination was their lack of education (34 women or 22.8 per cent).

A range of overt practices of discrimination were evidenced in the panchayats. Six women were not allowed entry into the panchayat office itself. As seen in the previous section on panchayat meetings, many women were called to the panchayat offices only when government officials visited. Otherwise, they were overtly or subtly discouraged from entering the panchayat office.

For most Dalit women elected representatives allowed to enter panchayat offices, discriminatory socio-cultural practices outside the panchayat offices were replicated within. A group of Dalit women elected representatives in Madurai district in Tamil Nadu observed, "In our panchayats the untouchability practices such as not being allowed to wear sandals, the two-tumbler system and not being allowed to sit on chairs, and so on still exist inside and outside the panchayats." Thus, 12.0 per cent of women (20 women), unlike other elected representatives, had to leave their sandals outside the office and enter with bare feet. The dominant castes made it a condition for their electoral support of Annammal during the village panchayat elections in Madurai district in Tamil Nadu that she should not wear sandals inside the panchayat office once elected. This mirrors untouchability practices in many villages where the wearing of shoes or any kind of footwear symbolises 'higher' caste status.

Complex segregation methods surrounded seating arrangements in the panchayats. For 38.0 per cent of the women (63 women), sitting on chairs on par with other elected representatives in the panchayat office was forbidden. On the one hand, a group of Dalit women elected representatives from Cuddalore district in Tamil Nadu noted, "When a Dalit woman wins the election and occupies her seat in the panchayat office, one of the dominant caste men derides her by saying, 'You are of a lower caste; how can you sit on the chair in front of us?' and simultaneously uses her caste name to scold her." On the other hand, Dalit women elected representatives in Ahmedabad district in Gujarat noted that Dalit women presidents rarely sit on chairs in the panchayat because of ingrained social norms that they should not sit in front of elders or dominant castes and that they should observe purdah. The strength of such norms is such that Archana, a district panchayat member in Tamil Nadu, would sit on a chair only when other panchayat representatives told her to sit. In the case of union panchayat president Sangeetha from Thirunelveli district in the same state, she never attempted to sit on the president's chair in the panchayat office. For Lalitaben, village panchayat president in Anand district in Gujarat, an inadequate number of chairs in the panchayat meant that she felt the need to leave the chairs for dominant castes and men. As with entry into the panchayat office, these norms were often dispensed with only when officials visited the offices. Thus, Thilagam from Coimbatore district in Tamil Nadu stated that, "For a long time I never sat on the chair reserved for the [village] panchayat president. I would stand or sit on the floor of the panchayat office. Only when any officials came to the office, I would be told [by the dominant castes] to sit on the chair."

Other studies have revealed how Dalit elected representatives are not allowed to sit with dominant caste elected representatives in meetings. They must either sit on the floor of the office or they must sit separately.[8] Many women would also be seated behind their husbands or otherwise physically excluded from being equal participants in panchayat meetings. The following newspaper excerpt illustrates this overall trend:

> As many as 17 Dalit panchayat presidents in Madurai district admit that caste-based discrimination, including the 'two-tumbler' system, still exists in their villages. A few of them even allege that the Vice Presidents, mostly caste Hindus, occupy chairs at official meetings while they sit on the floor as 'mute spectators'. The presidents have signed a statement attesting to this fact to a non-governmental organisation that surveyed villages in Madurai. In the Keeripatti reserved panchayat, where elections could not be held for a decade following stiff resistance from caste Hindus, the newly elected panchayat President M. Balusamy, admits to the prevalence of caste discrimination. 'The two-tumbler system still prevails in our village. Even a small boy, belonging to the dominant community, calls a senior Dalit by his name. In the nearby Poothipuram reserved panchayat, the president sits on the floor while the others occupy chairs and conduct official proceedings.'[9]

Similar practices were noted in the present research. Enforced segregation in seating was clear in the village panchayat where Rajniben from Ahmedabad district in Gujarat was a member. There were two chairs for the president and vice president, two mattresses to sit on for other panchayat members, and a sack on the floor reserved for Dalits to sit on. Sitting at a level lower than dominant castes has social meaning as a physical manifestation of caste hierarchy that emphasises the 'lower' caste status of Dalits. Even where separate chairs were kept for panchayat presidents, at times it was other panchayat members, especially dominant caste male vice presidents, who would occupy these chairs. Dalit women villagers in Surendranagar district in Gujarat mentioned this practice, as did Amarben, a village panchayat president from Anand district. Her chair was always occupied by the dominant caste vice president for whom she was a benami.

Still in many villages across India today, caste norms demand that Dalits stand as a sign of respect when dominant castes pass by, regardless of who is more senior in age or other status. Similarly, a sign of respect for elders and men is for women to stand in their presence. Hence, not surprisingly, 67.5 per cent of Dalit women elected representatives (112 women) stood up whenever a dominant caste person entered the panchayat office. Kamachi from Coimbatore district in Tamil Nadu mentioned how at the start of her first term as village panchayat president, the dominant caste vice president insisted that she stand up whenever he entered the panchayat office. Denied any respect or acceptance as leader of the panchayat, she allowed this situation to continue for only a few months.

Discriminatory practices related to water, tea and food in the panchayat offices present an interesting picture in terms of the number of ways in which these practices manifested and situations signifying equality were circumvented. The core issue is the strict prohibition on inter-dining imposed by the caste system, especially the sharing of vessels for food or drink with 'untouchable' castes. Openly admitting such practices, a dominant caste vice president from Anand district in Gujarat said, "Dalit women can't speak freely in front of anyone in the village and cannot drink water or tea in the panchayat. There are more limitations imposed on the Dalit community: they have to follow all the social rules within and outside their homes." While 64.5 per cent of Dalit women (107 women) reported that they were not able to drink water from the same container used by other elected representatives, 53.6 per cent (89 women) mentioned that they could not drink tea from the cups used by other representatives. Furthermore, 38.0 per cent (63 women) averred that they could not eat food served on the plates or with the utensils used by the others. Note that the latter figure was as small as this because 60 women (36.1 per cent) reported that food was not served in their panchayat offices.

As with seating arrangements, two trends again emerge from the statements of women reporting discrimination regarding water, tea or food. The first is that from the start of their term in office Dalit women were supplied with, told or made to bring separate utensils or water to show unequivocally that social norms would continue within the panchayat office. Kamlaben from Surendranagar district in Gujarat, for instance, was told by the panchayat peon that she and other Dalits needed to bring their own cups to enjoy tea in the panchayat office. The peon of the village panchayat in Kheda district in Gujarat where Chanchalben was president kept separate glasses for drinking water for Dalits as he knew the rules of the village. In contrast, Shardaben from Vadodara district in Gujarat, like all Dalit Valmikis, was not allowed to drink water in the panchayat at all.

A second trend is that several Dalit women had internalised these social norms so much so that they did not attempt to drink water or tea or take snacks in the panchayat office alongside others. Instead, they brought their own water, or refrained from drinking water or taking snacks. Preenaben from Surendranagar district never took tea or water in the panchayat, arguing that there was a limit for Dalit women doing these (prohibited) activities. Similarly, Pooncholai from Thirunelveli district in Tamil Nadu would not drink water or tea in the panchayat office in deference to social norms. Lakshmiben from Kheda district mentioned how snacks were served in sub-groups among the panchayat members. Dalit members were served on a separate plate. In the case of village panchayat members Chandraben and Dhanuben from Anand and Kheda districts respectively in Gujarat, they had separate glasses kept for them to take water in the panchayat office. Chandraben also had snacks served on a separate plate for her.

Considering water, tea and food/snacks trends together, roughly one-third of women said they were *not* discriminated against in terms of water, tea or food. Given the prevalence of the two-tumbler system in villages and proscriptions against inter-dining, an easy method to circumvent untouchability norms was to serve tea in disposable plastic cups and snacks on disposable plates. Another method in the village panchayat in Anand district in Gujarat where Pravinaben was president was to stop the practice of serving tea and food/snacks in the office when she assumed office. Village panchayat president Indiraben from Kheda district in Gujarat and union panchayat member Deepa from Cuddalore district in Tamil Nadu were among the five women who reported that no water pot was kept inside the panchayat office. Instead, most panchayat members brought water from their own houses to avoid any need to share water. Preetikaben, a village panchayat president from Anand district, stated that whenever there were community functions or festivals celebrated in the panchayat office, the dominant caste members would have their food served on leaves while sitting separately.

The case of Madhuben also illustrates the lengths to which other caste members would go to avoid sharing water, tea or food/snacks with Dalits. Madhuben, as a village panchayat member from Surendranagar district in Gujarat, was not allowed to sit on a chair but tried to do so. If the dominant castes entered the panchayat office, then Dalits were supposed to stand up, and again she tried not to do so. The panchayat peon was a Dalit Valmiki and so only the Dalit members would drink water served by him. Tea was brought from a tea stall and served in plastic cups. Given the peon's 'low' caste status, if the dominant caste members wanted a drink, they would order cool (soft) drinks to escape being 'defiled' by the peon. Snacks were also served on paper plates to avoid 'defilement'.

Given the extent of discriminatory practices evident in the panchayat offices, the small number of women who were able to successfully challenge and change these practices warrant separate mention. In the case of Preetikaben, president of a village panchayat in Anand district in Gujarat, she sat on a chair and remained seated when elders or dominant castes entered the panchayat office despite being explicitly told to follow social norms by dominant caste members. Sonaliben recounted how when she, as a village panchayat member from Ahmedabad district in Gujarat, went to the panchayat office for the first time, she was not offered a seat and had to sit on the floor. She objected and threatened the dominant caste members to allow her to be seated equally. From the next meeting onwards, she was given a chair. Sunitaben, a village panchayat president from Anand district, demanded the removal of all the mattresses put inside the panchayat office under dominant caste direction to ensure that she, as a Dalit woman, would not sit on a chair equally with others. Instead, she insisted, despite all the verbal abuse she faced, on the return of all the chairs to the office.

The long-term impact of challenging such discriminatory practices can be gauged by how women like Anjali, a village panchayat president from Madurai district in Tamil Nadu, removed practices such as those of dominant castes not touching Dalits, Dalits removing shoes and drinking from separate glasses in the panchayat office. The positive impact would be felt by the next Dalit woman in office. For example, Champaben, a president, did not face any overt untouchability practices in her village panchayat in Anand district in Gujarat because the previous Dalit woman president had fought for her rights and abolished such practices. This, however, did not stop Champaben from facing gender discrimination. Another example is that of Tejuben, a village panchayat president from Kheda district in Gujarat:

> There were some forms of untouchability that existed in the old panchayat council, but when I took charge, I tried my level best to remove all such obstructions. I put one common pot for drinking water and one glass for all. I told the other panchayat members that I would not tolerate [the two-tumbler system]. While formerly

the food packets for Dalits and non-Dalits were kept separately, I ensured they were all opened and put on a plate together so that all members had to take food from the same common plate. Also, while formerly the dominant castes used to distribute tea in different glasses, I ensured that all members, including Dalits, took turns to distribute the tea in any glass. Members grew afraid of committing atrocities like these because I was so vocal and firm on these issues. But I knew these were atrocities by law and I would have acted accordingly against anyone perpetrating such practices.

Finally, 51.8 per cent of the women (86 women) were not allowed to participate in the panchayat's public programmes. Participation here was taken to mean more than mere presence. For instance, Jasodaben, a village panchayat president from Surendranagar district in Gujarat, allowed her husband to attend public programmes in her stead. Because of her lack of education and observance of purdah, she felt ashamed to attend. Women were side-lined in public programmes at the higher panchayat levels as well. Archana, a district panchayat member in Tamil Nadu, was often not given invitations to public programmes. If she attended any programme, her husband spoke on her behalf. In the case of panchayat presidents Annammal from Madurai district in Tamil Nadu and Kalaben from Vadodara district in Gujarat, on Republic Day a dominant caste village elder was asked to hoist the national flag instead of them. Their examples highlight how informal leadership frequently supersedes Dalit women's formal leadership. Moreover, discrimination in food distribution at public programmes further underlines the difference between Dalit women elected representatives and dominant castes. All this re-emphasises the hierarchical social structure in which dominant caste men hold social status and authority.

In conclusion, the discrimination noted by most Dalit women elected representatives was rooted in their 'low' caste, class and gender status and the disadvantages attached to this status; that is, illiteracy, poverty, lack of information, and so on. As Dalits, they were expected to observe all untouchability rules which prohibited their equal interaction with others in terms of occupying the same physical public space, being treated as equals, or sharing food and drinks. As women, gender rules circumscribed their ability to interact with men of any caste, particularly at the level of seating and discussion. What underlay most of these practices were subtle forms of authority, expressions of who has power and who does not. The basic element of discrimination is to enforce the idea that the person discriminated against does not have any authority and power, and must accept this situation without question. Hence, discriminatory practices existing both inside and outside the panchayat sought to drive home the message that attempts to equalise formal authority structures through reservations did not confer power, authority and respect to Dalit women in political and public spaces. Instead, the patriarchal caste system was legitimised as the overriding structure conferring power, authority and respect. This replication of power relations and discrimination within the panchayats arguably signifies the co-option of the formal panchayat system into the wider social structure.

To overcome this discrimination, a group of Dalit women elected representatives from Cuddalore district in Tamil Nadu suggested two key measures. First, Dalit women and the Dalit community must receive support to become economically on par with the dominant castes. Second, when Dalits file complaints against discrimination or obstructions in the panchayats or villages, government officials and the police must take immediate action as per the law instead of making compromises with the dominant castes. This perspective can be contrasted with the statements by government officials covered in Chapter 8.

Right to Enjoy Full Term in Office

Given the above challenges to Dalit women's political participation, did the 166 elected representatives, especially the 119 presidents, enjoy a full term in office? The encouraging answer is that 151 women (91.6 per cent) did so. However, this must be weighed against the number of women who were proxy or benami representatives, and those who faced obstructions in the panchayats. While several women elected representatives in

Tamil Nadu noted false allegations filed against them, no one went so far as to threaten the women's term in office. By contrast, 10 women presidents in Gujarat (6.0 per cent) faced (unsuccessful) no confidence motion bids or, in one case, obstructions leading to a woman being temporarily suspended. A further five Dalit women presidents in Gujarat, however, were unable to enjoy the full length of their term in office due to successful no confidence motions or forced resignations.

NO CONFIDENCE MOTIONS

Ramilaben, a taluka panchayat president from Vadodara district in Gujarat and Congress party member, recalled how panchayat members affiliated with the Congress party accused her of not conducting general meetings properly and on time, and being unable to manage these meetings. She was also accused of corruption: using the official vehicle for her own purposes; and only giving contracts to her relatives or her own caste. The BJP party affiliated panchayat members opposed her due to party enmity, while the Congress members did so because she was an active and independent Dalit woman entering the panchayat on a reserved quota. She therefore had to thwart two no confidence motion attempts during her panchayat term with the help of higher-level Congress party leaders. She believed that, "as a Dalit woman president, I was discriminated against... The attempts to bring a no confidence motion against me and the regular opposition happened because a Dalit woman had occupied the president's chair."

Ramilaben's case illustrates perhaps the most direct violation of Dalit women's right to political participation, the motion of no confidence. Setting aside the number of benami presidents in the present research, among the smaller, remaining pool of women presidents who attempted to assert their right to political participation, the number of attempted no confidence motions becomes significant. This mirrors other research, which has shown that Dalit presidents face an alarmingly high number of no confidence motions whenever they have tried to assert their leadership.[10] The most common allegation levelled against the women was that of corruption. Another allegation was that the women were benamis allowing the misappropriation of their powers.

Given the minority status of Dalit women and men in the panchayat, dominant castes could often push through no confidence motions alone, or by bribing other panchayat members. These motions, therefore, emerge as important tools for dominant castes to retain political power and control over the panchayats. Indeed, the very possibility of these motions, let alone their actual use, aimed to instil fear in Dalit women elected representatives and encourage low levels of engagement and decision-making in the panchayats. No confidence motions also operated to warn future Dalit women representatives that political participation through reservations does not equate to the exercise of autonomous political power. The women who remained in power did so because of their ability to gain the support of government officials, by recourse to the courts, or by strategising their responses to defeat these no confidence motions.

Two village panchayat presidents – Shiviben from Kheda district and Jasodaben from Surendranagar district – were pushed out of office through successful no confidence motions engineered by dominant caste panchayat members. The example of Jasodaben illustrates how women benami candidates who attempted to assert their right to political participation were vulnerable to no confidence motions. Moreover, the dominant caste man instigating the no confidence motion went further to insinuate that because a Dalit woman had become president such things were happening. He thus reinforced the idea that Dalit women are incapable of handling panchayat administration.

Jasodaben was chosen for the post of panchayat president by a consensus engineered by one dominant caste who controlled the village panchayat. The dominant caste suggested that the villagers reach a consensus on the SC women reserved seat in order to collect the consensus award from the state government. Because she was poor, illiterate and not outspoken, the dominant castes chose her thinking she would make a good benami. Other villagers felt that development works would take place through her as her husband had previously been in the panchayat. Once elected, as expected, she functioned primarily through her husband, who in turn did only as directed by the dominant caste vice president.

Jasodaben, however, began to oppose the dominant castes regarding the distribution of development funds. The dominant castes wanted the money given as the consensus award to go towards building an entrance gate to the village. Jasodaben, however, wanted it to go towards constructing much needed drinking water and road facilities. Consequently, all the dominant caste members brought a no confidence motion against her two-and-a-half years into her term. The person who instigated the motion was a dominant caste man outside the panchayat. Jasodaben said, "He dominates the entire village and everything happens on his direction only. I was running the administration and that is why a no confidence was brought against me with the help of the other members. Only his rules prevail and he pushed me out from the panchayat. He said that a Dalit woman has tried to run the administration and that's why this [no confidence motion] was happening."

A meeting was called without her knowledge and in the absence of the only other Dalit woman member Jasodaben was accused of misappropriating money from a government scheme, the Swarna Jayanti Shahari Rozgar Yojana (SJSRY), and the no confidence motion was passed. While Jasodaben appealed to the TDO, she received no support and was removed from office two months later. She recounted the vice president's response to her appeal against the no confidence motion: "He told me to ask for forgiveness and that I should prostrate myself at his feet. When he said this, I decided that it's better to resign now instead of lying at his feet. All these [dominant caste] elders asked why I didn't ask for their forgiveness, but I didn't want to do that."

FORCED RESIGNATIONS

A related method was forcing Dalit women presidents to resign from their posts, as seen in the case of village panchayat president Shardaben from Vadodara district in Gujarat. Shardaben was initially a benami for the dominant castes. However, she gradually started to function independently. She opposed two development proposals with negative ramifications for the Dalit community: one was the attempt to construct an anganwadi which would block the path to a Dalit locality; the second was a plan by dominant castes to build their community hall on common land shared with Dalits and used for social and religious functions. After this, the panchayat members stopped telling her anything about the panchayat. On her husband's advice, Shardaben then filed a complaint with the previous dominant caste president, who had political contacts. He agreed to help her and informed the talati that if Shardaben gave a complaint against anyone in the panchayat, from then onwards no one would be spared.

Once the dominant caste vice president and panchayat members came to know of Shardaben's complaint, however, they reacted. She narrated, "Ten months later [after the election], the talati came to me for my signature on a blank piece of paper. To avoid any argument, I signed the paper. Later I came to know from the talati and vice president that I was no longer president because I had voluntarily given a resignation letter." Her signature had been used to write a false letter of resignation on her behalf, and the members also accused her of never attending the panchayat meetings. In response, Shardaben asked for help from the TDO. "The TDO, however, told me that I could not continue as president because I was not attending the panchayat meetings and had not been able to do anything in the panchayat. He said that all members were against me, and there was no need for him to inquire further. I lost hope then and stopped protesting [against the forced resignation]."

Finally, in Bhavnaben's case in Vadodara district, towards the end of her term in office the talati misappropriated half the money meant as cash relief for people affected by floods. As head of the panchayat, she was then accused by the dominant caste panchayat members and another talati of misappropriating the money. She was suspended. As she only had 15 days left to her term in office, she did not challenge the suspension order and let her term end that way.

Conclusion

The last three narratives of Jasodaben, Shardaben and Bhavnaben illustrate the high costs some Dalit women elected representatives have to pay when they assert their right to free and independent participation in panchayat governance. Bhavnaben's entire panchayat career was marked by this assertion. Jasodaben and Shardaben started their political career as benamis but eventually joined the same path as Bhavnaben. What is significant about the three women, though placed in different situations, is their common stand to assert their right to function as elected representatives. This was unacceptable to the dominant castes, who then put in place steps to remove them from office.

From the various aspects of Dalit women's right to political participation presented in this chapter, the extent to which a large majority of these women have not been able to exercise their right is clear. They faced serious limitations primarily from the dominant castes in the exercise of their authority. As attested by a group of Dalit women elected representatives in Cuddalore district in Tamil Nadu, dominant castes elected representatives "have man-power, money-power and caste-power…" Examining all the obstructions Dalit women elected representatives faced holistically, their significance lies in the message sent out regarding Dalit women's political participation. One set of obstructions involved dominant caste person/s utilising their political power to more directly impede Dalit women presidents' decision-making powers. Another set of obstructions combined dominant castes' social and political power to directly attack the women, in most cases, by portraying the women as politically inept, incapable of handling their panchayat responsibilities, or out to make personal gains. Although aimed at the individual woman, complaints regarding the quality of Dalit women's participation served to disparage their political capabilities and dissuade other Dalit women from active participation.

Four factors potentially determined negative responses from the dominant castes to Dalit women's assertions of their right to political participation. First, the assertions meant that a Dalit woman was visibly assuming a leadership position in a society entrenched in caste and gender hierarchies. Second, the women challenged the hitherto uncontested leadership and authority of the dominant castes. Third, the assertions opened up new political spaces for the future collective empowerment of Dalit community, which posed a threat to dominant caste interests. Fourth, the assertions vindicated the prerogative of Dalit women presidents to decide on the distribution of development resources for the welfare of the panchayat and particularly the Dalit community.

The fact that the above is what the Dalit electorate, both women and men, expect from their elected women is made clear in interviews with villagers. To the question on the positive points of Dalit women's participation in Panchayati Raj, a group of Dalit women in Vadodara district in Gujarat said, "Our President has done good management of the panchayat in comparison to women of other castes. She had performed her duties independently. She was opposed by the dominant castes, but they could do nothing against her... They opposed tooth and nail our President's pro-Dalit stand, but she was firm in her decision." Similarly, recognising the significance of Dalit women holding panchayat positions, another group of Dalit women in Cuddalore district in Tamil Nadu stated, "If a Dalit woman participates in panchayat politics, it is a rare opportunity for the growth of the community of Dalit women. Besides, from being an unidentified individual, she gets transformed into a public figure."

The underlying message that comes across from the Dalit women elected representatives is that to realise the objective of inclusive democracy via reservations, it is essential to recognise the agency of Dalit women. It is in proportion to their effective agency that the livelihood development, social status and political empowerment of Dalits will be ensured and enhanced. Noting the importance of Dalit women's participation in panchayat governance, a group of Dalit elders and male villagers in Surendranagar district in Gujarat said, "Dalit women's participation in the panchayat is necessary for the development of the community. The reservation policy should continue and with that our woman should be educated. For the Dalit community will support and elect unanimously only those of our women who are intelligent and active enough to participate in the panchayat administration. Even a little education and knowledge would be sufficient to start enabling their effective participation and serve our community." A group of Dalit women villagers in the same district added, "If a [Dalit] woman becomes aware of her rights, at least she can raise her voice against any kind of domination over her. And the dominant castes then wouldn't dare to oppress or disrespect her, as they would know that she, too, can raise her voice and take up issues at any level."

Heeding the voices of Dalit women and men, reservations alone are not sufficient to ensure the full enjoyment of these women's right to freely and independently participate in the conduct of public affairs. The obligations of the state also extend to monitoring how the wider social environment enables the women to exercise this right. Almost all government functionaries interviewed mentioned that apart from individual officials periodically visiting the panchayats or receiving reports on the panchayats from the clerks/talatis, no separate mechanism exists for post-election effective monitoring and accountability regarding the functioning of panchayat institutions.

At one extreme, a TDO from Surendranagar district in Gujarat did not visit the panchayats when meetings took place: "I have not gone to panchayat meetings because of less staff. A lot of meetings happen in the panchayat, and generally I do not go to these meetings. The talati reports to the TDO's office about meetings and resolutions taken by the elected representatives in every meeting. That helps us to do the monitoring." At another extreme an assistant director of panchayats in Tamil Nadu denied the very existence of benami politics in any panchayats in the state and negated the need to monitor the panchayats: "There is no need for us to monitor at all and neither is it our duty. The panchayat is created to bring about a free and independent administration. In such situation, why should we monitor or inspect it? This goes against its very nature." Linked to this kind of thinking is that of a BDO in Coimbatore district in Tamil Nadu, who spoke of the government having solved the issue of benami representation through certain interventions: "We know about Dalit women benamis. However, at present, due to the training programmes and interaction taking place, the people's elected representatives are very much aware of the situation, and they have started functioning independently."

Despite these denials and negations by state actors, Dalit women's voices as presented in this chapter provide ample evidence that emphasises the need to institutionalise state monitoring. The result should be the equal social status, economic development and political empowerment of the Dalit community, and especially Dalit women.

Notes

1. 'Good governance' definition in OHCHR, "Rights-based Approach: Human Rights in Development", <<www.unhchr.ch/development/approaches-04.htm>>, last accessed on 10.06.2004, p. 1.
2. See UN Human Rights Commission Resolution 2000/64: *The Role of Good Governance in the Promotion of Human Rights*, reaffirmed by Resolution 2001/72; see also OHCHR, supra note 1.
3. Human Rights Committee, 'General Comment No. 25/5-7: The Right to Participate in Public Affairs, Voting Rights and the Right to Equal Access to Public Service', UN Doc. CCPR/C/21/Rev.1/Add.7, 12/07/96.
4. 'What is a Rights-based Approach to Development?' in OHCHR, supra note 1, p. 3.
5. Human Rights Committee, supra note 3, para. 25.
6. *Purdah* refers to a gender norm prevalent in Gujarat wherein women are supposed to cover their heads with their saris when they move in public spaces, or interact with community members, even in their homes in front of male family members.
7. See Palanithurai, G., *Process and Performance of Gram Panchayat Women and Dalit Presidents* (New Delhi: Concept Publishing Co, 2005) in which all Dalit panchayat presidents reported caste discrimination in their villages, which often spilled over into the panchayats. A similar finding is seen in the EVIDENCE report at the Regional Roundtable Discussion on the functioning of the reserved panchayat presidents held in Madurai, Tamil Nadu on 16.05.2007,

which presents the preliminary findings of a state-wide study on untouchability practices prevailing in reserved panchayats.

8. See Unnati, *Status of Panchayati Raj Institutions in Gujarat 1995–2000* (Ahmedabad: Unnati, 2000).

9. *The Hindu*, "Caste Bias Unchecked Here", <<www.thehindu. com/2007/04/16/stories/2007041608530100.htm>>, last accessed on 16.04.2007.

10. Unnati, supra note 8, commenting on the number of no confidence motions against Dalit presidents in Gujarat between 1995 and 2000. While the present study did not record any cases of no confidence motions against Dalit women elected representatives in Tamil Nadu, Dalit organisations in this state suggest that a similar pattern also prevails in Tamil Nadu.

6

IMPACTING DEVELOPMENT

Whatever the types of discrimination I noticed, I did not take them to heart. In the midst of all these problems, my objective was to go beyond them and devote myself to providing developmental works for the welfare of the people. I confronted the dominant castes and fought for the rightful amenities of the Dalits... I did all this without the direct help of anyone.

                         – Annammal, village panchayat president,
                               Madurai district, Tamil Nadu

Annammal was speaking of her experience as a village panchayat president in Madurai district in Tamil Nadu. Encouraged by a relative to file a nomination for the SC women reserved post in her panchayat, she gained the support of her Dalit Arunthathiyar community as well as dominant backward castes. Conditions were attached, however, for the latter's support:

> They chose me because I am educated and would do whatever they wanted. They dictated that when I went for campaigning I should not wear shoes. When I was elected president, I was not to enter the panchayat office with my shoes on. Whatever responsibilities I undertook, I was to do so only after consulting them. Nothing was to happen without their knowledge... I was told not to enter the panchayat office and undertake any developmental activity without consulting them. At the time, I gave in to all their demands.

Once elected, Annammal's initial political participation was as a benami for the dominant castes. She did not take any decisions in the panchayat, did not wear her shoes inside the panchayat office, and on Republic Day a village elder was asked to hoist the national flag instead of her, despite it being the president's responsibility. No one showed her any respect and some dominant caste male members abused her using her caste name and sexual language. Later, however, she chose to function independently for the welfare of her Dalit community. According to her, "I learnt from the many training programmes and meetings I attended about my responsibilities as panchayat president, about the developmental works of the panchayat, as well as how to function. Then I was able to realise my potential and worked independently." She performed her duties despite the opposition and verbal abuse she faced from the dominant caste vice president, clerk and a few members in panchayat meetings.

Annammal was able to accomplish a number of developmental works such as the provision of drainage facilities, drinking water connections, tiled roofing for houses, construction of new houses and public toilets for Dalits, and similar facilities for needy backward caste families. She looked after all the accounts and personally supervised the panchayat's development works, thereby minimising corruption. At the same time, she faced a lot of obstructions to her development efforts. For example, the dominant caste vice president and clerk blocked her move to lay roads in the Dalit locality of her village. She took this matter to the BDO, who had been informed of her good performance, and got the road constructed. Throughout her term a dominant caste panchayat member harassed her through anonymous and false complaints. All this was done to remove her from power because she would not submit to the dictates of the dominant castes.

Another dominant caste panchayat member illegally occupied 3 cents of panchayat land and built a toilet for his family there. Annammal lodged a complaint about this with the union panchayat council. When the council did not arrive at a solution, she gave a written complaint to the police. The police acted immediately, and the BDO ordered that the toilet be demolished and a drainage system for the village built in its place. Before this could happen, however, the panchayat member again occupied the land. Annammal then made a complaint to the tahsildar. Having been bribed, the tahsildar spoke in favour of the dominant caste panchayat member. Next, another dominant caste panchayat member filed a case against her in the Madurai District Court, saying that the disputed land belonged to him. Only when the court confirmed that the land belonged to the panchayat was Annammal finally able to construct the drainage system.

Later, in retaliation, another five dominant caste panchayat members lodged a complaint with the BDO against Annammal, claiming that she had given excess water connections that led to a shortage of water in the panchayat. She said, "This time I decided to tackle the issue myself directly. I threatened that I would initiate court proceedings against them for insulting a Dalit woman. This threat gave them enough fear that they withdrew their complaint."

In accomplishing all these development works, Annammal related well with government officials at all levels, and many officials encouraged her proposals and gave their support. She also had her husband's support and that of the local youth and Arunthathiyar women's movements to counter the opposition coming from the dominant castes and some Dalits. Finally, she had the courage and capability to counter her opponents individually. This enabled her good performance in the panchayat and her ability, in her own words, to "go beyond them and devote myself to providing developmental works for the welfare of the people."

As a result of her exercise of the right to political participation, Annammal is convinced that "more and more Dalit women should contest the elections and become elected to the panchayat, and help the Dalit community become liberated from their bondage." At the same time, continuing threats from the dominant castes meant that she and her family live in constant fear.

Annammal's experience highlights three key points. One is the potential for a positive developmental impact on the Dalit community consequent to realising Dalit women's right to political participation. Second is the types of caste-class-gender obstructions Dalit women must deal with in responding to the needs of their constituencies, especially the needs of Dalits. Third is how factors such as education, local governance capacity building, a supportive husband and networks among local movements, as well as self-confidence and an ability to strategise interventions, enable Dalit women to deliver development outcomes.

The right of every citizen to take direct part in the conduct of public affairs confers on elected panchayat representatives an entitlement to exercise executive and administrative powers without discrimination or unreasonable restrictions, and to direct development programmes towards fulfilling the needs of their constituencies. The premise behind different social groups realising this right is to ensure that the interests and rights of all groups, particularly marginalised social groups, are equally represented and equally secured. Moreover, participation becomes a political resource to change the social norms and values governing the distribution of material resources, to ensure greater social justice and realise other rights.[1]

Given the factors that hinder Dalit women elected panchayat representatives from active, empowered participation in local governance, few evaluations exist of the developmental and social impact of Dalits, women, specifically Dalit women entering the panchayats through reservations. Measuring their impact in terms of representing the needs of their constituencies and bringing about positive development outputs for Dalits and women is also difficult. This is due to the inadequate political and financial autonomy granted to panchayats. As a result, they tend to be controlled by the bureaucracy and function merely as implementers of state government development programmes. This aside, as panchayats deliver social and economic programmes, Dalit women's empowered participation in governance should arguably lead to greater equity: equity in terms of the choices the women have, and equity resulting from the caste and gender-responsive policy and programme decisions made.[2]

In other words, in theory Dalit women elected representatives should be directly motivated to take up both women's *practical and strategic gender needs,*[3] and Dalits' *practical and strategic caste-class needs.*[4] These needs can be measured at three levels. The first level is positive development outcomes for individual Dalits and women through supporting resolutions for and monitoring the implementation of development schemes specifically targeting these two social groups to ensure benefits reach the appropriate beneficiaries. This level also ensures that other general development schemes do not bypass needy Dalits and women in their implementation. The second level is changing institutional rules and resource allocations in favour of Dalits and women to ensure their specific needs are met. The third level would see the restructuring of gender and caste relations to achieve social equality and justice.[5]

While being *responsive* to development and social justice needs through the panchayats, elected representatives must also be *effective*. Indicators of effectiveness include adequate knowledge about developmental issues; ensuring panchayat programmes meet their objectives; taking an interest in the planning and implementation of development projects; strengthening panchayat institutions through (presidents) conducting or (members) participating in panchayat and gram sabha meetings regularly; taking specific action against corruption; and visiting government officials for panchayat related matters.[6]

In addition, elected panchayat representatives must be *efficient* in terms of using the resources available to them to maximise development outputs. They must also be *accountable* to their constituencies: that is, they must represent the interests of the people, allowing for deliberation and consultation on development decisions, and ensure transparency by keeping the public informed of development programmes and budgets. This includes the duty to prevent the misappropriation of government resources meant for citizens in general or for special groups such as Dalits.[7] All state agents have an obligation to monitor the functioning of the panchayats and distribution of resources by virtue of Article 46 of the Constitution of India, which enjoins the state to promote with special care the educational and economic interests of Dalits, and protect them from social injustice and all forms of exploitation.

This chapter examines two issues. First is the extent to which Dalit women elected representatives were responsive to the practical caste-class-gender needs of Dalit women, Dalits and women. In other words, were they able to increase resources to address the critical livelihood needs of these groups and support the realisation of their social, economic and cultural rights?

Second is the extent to which these elected representatives were effective, efficient and accountable in delivering development outcomes to both marginalised groups and the wider panchayat constituency.

Development Impact

The expectation that Dalit women's political participation in the panchayats would ensure greater development benefits reached Dalits was common among Dalit women elected representatives and other Dalit villagers. The growing political awareness brought about through reservations, increased political participation and greater access to information has slowly increased Dalits' knowledge of panchayat development schemes. This is especially the case for those schemes earmarked for them. There is also an understanding of how these schemes are being diverted to serve others' interests. Jasodaben, a village panchayat president from Surendranagar district in Gujarat, summed it up as follows: "[Dalit women's political participation] is necessary for the Dalit community and its development because if a Dalit woman is elected, then she will work for the Dalit community and Dalit women. Other castes will never work for the Dalit community. Moreover, they will eat the money that comes under Dalit grants."

As seen in Chapter 4, while the majority of Dalit women elected representatives contested elections at the suggestion of others, a motive for at least some families or Dalit community members was to ensure the representation of their interests in the panchayat and greater development benefits for the community or area. For example, the villagers supported Gandhimathi for the post of union panchayat president in Coimbatore district in Tamil Nadu. She was seen to be an influential and bold woman who could bring development to their area. In a few instances, women villagers also indicated their support for Dalit women entering the panchayats to cater to the specific needs of women, like village panchayat president Lakshmiben from Vadodara district in Gujarat.

SOCIAL ACCOUNTABILITY: RESPONSIVENESS

Once in the panchayats, just under half of the Dalit women elected representatives indicated that their main target group for development schemes was the Dalit community, while around one quarter mentioned the poorest people and another quarter all people in the panchayat. Evidence of Dalit women's greater understanding and responsiveness to Dalit development needs can be seen in the words of village panchayat president Kamachi from Coimbatore district in Tamil Nadu: "I tried to ensure that development works reached all the people who needed it. My focus was particularly the Dalits. There were one thousand Dalit families in my panchayat. Most of them had no basic facilities. I had experienced their struggles myself... The atrocities, discrimination and the sufferings that my people endure inspired me to work for them, to fight for them."

Distribution of Panchayat Development Benefits: Dalit women elected representatives were asked which groups primarily benefited from a number of panchayat schemes and services. These answers were later cross-checked in many instances with villagers in the concerned panchayats. The 36 women elected in the 2006 panchayats did not answer this question as it was too soon after their election to state conclusively who the development schemes would be implemented for. Of the remaining 130 women elected representatives, the overwhelming majority (121 women or 93.1 per cent) felt that the dominant caste community – backward castes and/or forward castes – obtained sizeable development benefits from the panchayats. This mirrored their generally larger population size and socio-political control over the panchayats.

By contrast, 79 women (60.8 per cent) felt that the Dalit community received a good number of development benefits. This percentage appears high given evidence from other research that Dalits were often marginalised by or even left out of the distribution of panchayat development benefits.[8] Three qualifications, however, may explain this data. One is that a number of services such as roads or health facilities would have benefitted the entire village or area, not just Dalits. Second is that as a number of development schemes are specifically earmarked for Dalits, the panchayats would have given them at least some, though often not all, of the allocated grants. Third is that where Dalits had previously received no development benefits from the panchayats, even the allocation of small benefits to them may have registered as major gains for Dalit women elected representatives.

The veracity of these qualifications is seen from the number of Dalit women elected representatives who mentioned how dominant castes controlled the allocation of development schemes and contracts so that Dalits were completely left out of allocations, or allocated minimal or fewer benefits. The practice of skimming some part of the development grants earmarked for Dalits to benefit other communities was common, according to Dalit women elected representatives in Cuddalore district in Tamil Nadu. Dalit women elected representatives from Surendranagar district in Gujarat noted, "Where dominant castes put up a benami candidate or the Dalit woman elected representative gets no support from other panchayat members, work will happen in the village generally, but nothing much will happen in our Dalit localities." Dutiful benamis for dominant castes who did not assert their rights sometimes received development schemes for their community. For instance, Vimalaben, a village panchayat member from Anand district in Gujarat and benami for the dominant castes through her husband, mentioned that the vice president's dominant caste gained the most in terms of panchayat development schemes. However, through her husband, she was able to ensure the construction of five houses for Dalits, as well as electricity connections and a road through one Dalit sub-caste locality.

The dynamics of the power relations at work when it came to the distribution of development schemes was explained by a dominant caste union panchayat president from Coimbatore district in Tamil Nadu:

> To be able to function in a way that ensured the distribution of resources to all sections of the panchayat community; as president, I saw to it that development projects were distributed to each section. However, to prevent disaffection from the dominant castes, prior allotment went to them, and only then to the Dalits.

It also happened sometimes that one section of the dominant castes returned for another allotment or wanted to enjoy the allotment meant for the Dalits, thereby making the latter forego its due share... Compared to the village panchayat, the situation at the union or district panchayat levels is more complex due to the powerful roles played by political personalities and their parties. Although as president I took efforts to help all communities benefit, a lot of accommodation had to be made for such political forces in the distribution of development funds in terms of the quantum of money and the kind and quality of development projects.

In sum, caste and political party pressures were two factors that had an overriding presence in the development decisions made by the panchayat councils at all panchayat tiers. This limited the responsiveness of Dalit women elected representatives to the development needs of their constituencies.

Another significant beneficiary of panchayat schemes and funds were the families of the mostly dominant caste panchayat vice presidents. One-third of the women (42 women or 32.3 per cent), especially in Tamil Nadu, noted the diversion of funds towards the vice presidents. This indicates both the influence and control vice presidents exerted over the panchayat administration as well as the extent of corruption in development schemes. To a much lesser extent the women noted their families receiving a number of benefits from panchayat schemes (15 women or 11.5 per cent), particularly where they were panchayat presidents. Similarly, the families of mostly dominant caste panchayat presidents where Dalit women were panchayat members also gained benefits to a slightly smaller extent (noted by 14 women or 10.8 per cent). Other beneficiary groups such as panchayat clerks/talatis, Muslims and Adivasis were mentioned by less than 10 per cent of the women. Overall, therefore, dominant castes – villagers, vice presidents and presidents – benefitted the most from government development schemes and resources.

Influence over Distribution of Panchayat Development Benefits: When it came to whose influence ensured that the above groups or individuals benefited from panchayat development schemes, the

36 women who had been just elected did not answer this question for the same reason as before. Of the remaining 130 Dalit women elected representatives, just under half (60 women or 46.2 per cent) felt that the panchayat council decided according to the interests of the panchayat constituency as a whole, or which people were most in need. This percentage is encouraging because it indicates the women's perceptions of the democratic process at work as allowing elected representatives to collectively decide the allocation of resources bearing in mind the needs of their constituencies.

In contrast, more disturbing trends in influences over the direction of services and development projects were noted by the remaining women elected representatives. Discussions with the women elected representatives unearthed a political party influence at the taluka/union and districts levels, but also in a number of village panchayats. However, given the link between party power holders and dominant caste status, caste becomes a more significant marker of influence. Hence, over one-third of women (46 women or 35.4 per cent) recorded the influence of the mostly dominant caste vice presidents, another one-third (45 women or 34.6 per cent) that of dominant caste persons both inside and outside the panchayat, and another 14 women members (10.8 per cent) that of mostly dominant caste presidents. Women from Tamil Nadu recorded these influences in particular, while Gujarat – with higher numbers of Dalit women panchayat members – mentioned the invariably dominant caste presidents more frequently. This reinforces the link between decision-making power, discussed in the previous chapter, and those who wield power in the panchayats: in many cases the power lay in the hands of dominant caste vice presidents or presidents, resulting in their own economic interests being served through diverting panchayat funds to their families. An extreme example is of Madurai district in Tamil Nadu, where village panchayat president Vijaya was a semi-bonded labourer under the control of her employer. She was thus unable to help five Dalit families when they applied to her for house sites. Instead, her employer placed pressure on these families to vacate their village and ensured no development works took place for Dalits in the panchayat.

In comparison, a smaller percentage of women panchayat presidents (24 women or 18.5 per cent) felt that they had a significant say in the distribution of development schemes, or that their husbands exercised such influence (nine women or 6.9 per cent). In other words, dominant caste control of the panchayats and influence over development schemes remained almost as common as collective decision-making in the panchayat. No women mentioned Dalits influencing development decisions, and only a few mentioned their own influence. This indicates a significant gap between the actual political powers wielded by Dalits and Dalit women.

Regarding the distribution of development scheme benefits, Dalit women elected representatives have dual responsibilities; they have to look after the section of society they represent through reservations in addition to the general constituency. As a group of Dalit women elected representatives Ahmedabad district stated,

> Dalit women should not work for Dalits only. It is necessary to work for each section of the village in order to maintain peace and support, but we should especially keep the needy in mind... It is very necessary to work for poor people, because they never receive the benefits that they are supposed to. The panchayat politics of the dominant castes mostly stops the poor from benefiting from any schemes. For example, Dalit names are not listed in the BPL lists; only those economically well-off and with land are listed. These [dominant caste] people are getting all the benefits of government schemes.

What also has to be borne in mind at the same time are the narrowly demarcated and limited state government funds and schemes disbursed to the panchayats, which circumscribe the women's ability to do more than merely secure development schemes targeted towards Dalits. Nonetheless, women like Kamachi show that some Dalit women were able to fulfil both responsibilities. A village panchayat president from 1996–2001 and 2001–2006 in Coimbatore district in Tamil Nadu, Kamachi said:

> In 2001, my second term in office, I contested as an independent candidate. My five years' experience in the panchayats helped

me a lot. For the second term, I handled my responsibilities independently, holding general meetings, discussing issues and coming to consensus decisions. My struggles in the initial days were short-lived as I joined hands with the opponents of my opponents. I was quite successful in the way I managed the administration and benefited people of all castes. I handled everything with a sense of equality. I met villagers personally, discussed their needs with them and subsequently worked towards fulfilling their needs.

The Dalits received housing, water, street lights, electricity, roads, expansion of the school, a midday meals centre and a building for SHGs. Some families, for example, had to walk many miles to collect water. Some of them did not have electricity connections or land/house documents. I worked towards getting these facilities for my people. I used all my knowledge, picked up information regarding available schemes, knocked on the doors of officials and brought in funds to the panchayat. Though I have done well in the panchayat administration, I am a bit disappointed because I was not able to do much for the welfare of Dalit women... Even with my experience, education, my training and knowledge on panchayat issues, I still needed the cooperation of government officials and the local [dominant castes] to accomplish my work. Only then can a Dalit woman serve well. It is not enough that the government gives political power to a Dalit woman. It should continuously monitor how the power is being executed.

Turning to the types of development schemes implemented, it should be noted that most central and state government rural development schemes are implemented through the panchayats. Given the existing evidence of dominant caste controlled panchayats generally neglecting Dalit colonies, this research focused on which socio-economic rights were fulfilled for Dalits during the panchayat terms of Dalit women elected representatives. The development schemes extended to Dalit colonies are primarily micro-level infrastructural projects for basic amenities,[9] which contribute to Dalits' enjoyment of their right to an adequate standard of living. By far the most common of development benefits, mentioned by over half the women, were roads (121 women or 72.9 per cent), housing (100 women or 60.2 per cent) and drinking water (96 women or 57.8 per cent). A substantial number of women also mentioned electricity connections (79 women or 47.6 per cent) and sanitation facilities (59 women or 35.5 per cent) as important gains for the Dalit community. In terms of the basic services vital to building human resources, health facilities (50 women or 30.1 per cent) and, to a lesser extent, education facilities (29 women or 17.5 per cent) saw less improvement. Meanwhile, a small number of women (23 women or 13.9 per cent) catered to gender needs through the provision of maternal and child welfare services. Less common as well, though very important in terms of income generation and potential economic mobility for Dalits, were the smaller number of women reporting distribution of employment benefits (31 women or 18.7 per cent), agriculture-related benefits (31 women or 18.7 per cent) and loans (30 women or 18.0 per cent).

This data has to be interpreted in the context of the limited decision-making powers many Dalit women elected representatives actually enjoyed, as discussed in the previous chapter. A number of elected representatives who were benamis for either dominant castes and/or their husbands tended to conflate their achievements with that of their husbands or other male family members. Moreover, as previously mentioned, some women, though benamis, were still able to attain limited benefits for their community in return for relinquishing their official duties to others.

These women aside, Dalit women elected representatives accomplished the above development gains for their communities either individually amidst frequent opposition, or in several cases, with the help of others. The latter included the support of Dalit panchayat members, political parties and a support base in the panchayat, or through negotiations with other caste panchayat members. Setting aside for now the obstructions placed in the path of efforts to implement development schemes for Dalits, the following cases illustrate the different types of factors which aided Dalit women in achieving the aforementioned development outcomes. A few women, like village panchayat president Neelamben from Anand district in Gujarat, used their previous political experience in the panchayats to push through development projects for Dalits. In Neelamben's case, she also held a hunger strike in front of the district collector's office until she received road and transportation facilities for her panchayat. Another village panchayat president, Aarthi from Cuddalore district in Tamil Nadu, used her past experience in an SHG, support from a political party of which she was a member, and knowledge gained through her membership of the state-wide Women Panchayat President's Federation to gain development benefits for Dalits. She likewise organised a protest gathering in front of the district collector's office and succeeded in removing encroachments on panchayat common property lands used by all villagers. Active networking with a political party, previous experience in a taluka committee, economic independence and joining hands with another Dalit panchayat member also aided Ushaben from Kheda district in Gujarat in accomplishing a number of development works for Dalits in her village panchayat. The potential of Dalit women's active political participation is perhaps best illustrated by the case of three-time village panchayat president Jayashree from Thirunelveli district in Tamil Nadu: her efforts to develop the four villages in her panchayat earned it the title 'Best Panchayat' from the union and district panchayats in her district.

At the higher panchayat tiers, especially the district panchayats, several Dalit women were able to negotiate to some extent with political parties and other key interest groups and direct funds to the lower panchayats for development works. In general, district panchayat representatives, who formed part of the majority political party in the panchayats, tended to have fewer problems directing funds towards Dalit development projects. In Tamil Nadu, for instance, district panchayat president Malar made efforts to channel funds toward Dalit reserved village panchayats. Similarly, in Gujarat, Dinaben, though lacking formal education, was able to use her 35 years of experience as a political party worker to influence funding for Dalit projects while she was a district panchayat president. Even the few district panchayat members who functioned as benamis for their husbands faced no significant problems as their husbands usually worked for the main political party and, therefore, were able to influence development funding. At the taluka/union panchayat levels, the same pattern emerged in some instances. However, the stronger influence of socio-politically powerful actors at this lower tier tended towards a greater degree of control over Dalit women elected representatives' ability to direct development funds and schemes towards Dalit areas.

Most Dalit women, except for complete benamis who had no knowledge of development schemes, thus fulfilled a number of practical development needs for the Dalit community. It was much rarer for them to address gender needs such as maternity welfare, widow's pensions or anganwadi activities, indicating the precedence of caste/community identity over gender identity in shaping the women's responsiveness. This was in part due to three factors. One was the caste-based divisions among women and the caste discrimination which served to emphasise community identity over gender identity, and thereby community needs over gender-based needs. Second was the greater availability of specific schemes targeting the Dalit community as compared to schemes targeting women's needs. Third was the gender-based obstructions to women's political participation by men in the panchayats.

Furthermore, following the *73rd (Rural Panchayats) Constitutional Amendment Act 1992*, panchayats have been given a key role to play in public service delivery, which has a small impact on unequal development power relations. There was a predominance of provisioning basic amenities – roads, electricity, sanitation, and so on – over projects aimed at economic development with great significance for economically marginalised Dalits – loans, employment, agricultural services, land, and so on. Dalit women thus lacked the power to negotiate in the panchayats and, possibly, the funds required to achieve this wider goal. The overall result was to limit gender gains through the panchayats as well as reduce the potential of the panchayats to deliver socio-economic justice. Dalits, with their poor capital resource base (land, financial capital, and so on), were unable to access more substantive development projects (employment, agricultural inputs, loans, livestock, and so on) through their Dalit women elected representatives. Consequently, whatever state resources were channelled through the panchayats for such purposes tended to instead be seized by the propertied class of dominant castes to augment their economic base. Panchayati Raj is yet to transform the fundamental structural inequalities preventing Dalits' access to and control over capital resources.

The state governments, for their part, have a duty to monitor the implementation of panchayat development schemes through their block/taluka and district development officers to ensure that development benefits reach the neediest in the panchayat, such as Dalits and other poor people. However, as one TDO from Gujarat admitted, they rely on the talati or panchayat president to inform them whether benefits reach the poor, without any independent verification. Their failure to perform their supervisory duty lowers accountability for the allocation of development funds, allowing disbursement of Dalit specific grants to benefit other less needy communities, or for such funds to be distributed among panchayat members as commissions. It is for this reason that Dalit women elected representatives from Cuddalore district in Tamil Nadu recommended that "government officials should supervise the panchayats and audit panchayat funds once a month. Then they will understand how much the Dalits are suffering, whether the funds reach the people and how they are actually utilised."

SOCIAL ACCOUNTABILITY: GRAM SABHAS

Another key aspect of social accountability is how Dalit women relate to their constituencies in terms of communicating information on panchayat development schemes, consulting their constituencies on development priorities, identifying the most deserving recipients of panchayat development schemes, and running a transparent administration by sharing information on panchayat budgets and expenditures. The primary mechanism for this downward accountability at the village panchayat level, where the majority of Dalit women respondents in this research were located, is through the gram sabhas, or village assemblies. According to the Government of India:

[The *gram sabha*] has a key role in bringing about transparency in the functioning of *gram (village) panchayats*, in ensuring equitable distribution of benefits, in creation of community assets and in bringing about social cohesion. It is envisaged to plan and prioritise development works to be taken up in the village, approve the annual plan for the *panchayat*, seek active participation of women and other marginalized groups, ensure transparency in the working of the *panchayat*, select beneficiaries under various schemes of the Central Government undertaken for rural development, and move towards full control over management over natural resources. In brief, the *gram sabha* is a forum where the marginalized can influence decisions affecting their lives.[10]

The limitations of gram sabhas as effective formal mechanisms to promote grassroots participation in development, however, were spelt out by Dalit villagers. Dalit elders and men from Surendranagar district in Gujarat mentioned that, "most of the time, the talati and panchayat members try to conduct the gram sabhas on paper only. If a Dalit member proposes to conduct a gram sabha, the other panchayat members ignore him/her. Only if some district government officials come to the village, then we are informed of a meeting. There also we are generally scared to say anything." A group of Dalit women villagers from the same district likewise confirmed that the gram sabhas often only happen on paper, or the villagers are not told the date and time of the gram sabha and which issues are to be raised there. Only the families of panchayat members know and participate in the gram sabha. Similarly, as per Dalit elders and men from Vadodara district in the same state, "Most people attend the first gram sabha of the year, then they do not attend any more. If the talati feels that there will be some nuisance in the gram sabha, then he does not call for it. He makes all the people sign resolutions without holding the gram sabha." Dalit elders and male villagers in Thirunelveli district in Tamil Nadu alluded to bureaucratic control and discrepancies in holding gram sabhas. In their case, "All the villages do not get the invitation for the village panchayat meetings: [government officials] don't send any invitation to the [Dalit] Paraiyars of Anna Nagar, for example. Despite this, one or two persons from there attend regularly. When information [of a gram sabha to be held] comes from the BDO, only people from Kuppam come and participate in the meeting."

Participation by Dalit Women Elected Representatives and Villagers: As with responsiveness to development needs, interviews regarding the functioning of the gram sabhas present a mixed picture as far as Dalit women elected representatives are concerned. Lines of accountability were disrupted most clearly in the case of benamis, where women elected representatives played no major role in convening these meetings and directing discussions. For example, Chanchalben, a village panchayat president from Kheda district in Gujarat, attended the eight or nine gram sabhas held during her five-year term, all chaired by her husband and at which development issues were discussed. At no point, however, did she speak. In the case of Vimalaben, a village panchayat member from Anand district in the same state, her husband always attended the gram sabhas in her stead.

Dalit women elected representatives from Ahmedabad district in Gujarat highlighted how gender norms inhibited women's involvement in the gram sabhas: "Men are always more in number [in gram sabhas], especially dominant caste men. What can a woman say among a large number of men?" The women further referred to well established village norms dictating that most women, except elderly women, should observe purdah and generally not speak in front of men; to do otherwise would result in their being considered uncultured and immoral. The internalisation of gender norms was strongly evidenced in some women's belief that their husbands were their first priority and that they had a greater responsibility to these men than to the villagers who elected them to the panchayats.

At the other end of the spectrum, active Dalit women elected representatives stated that they were able to convene and preside over gram sabhas. In addition, they tried to respond to the needs people raised in the meetings by following up with government officials and allocating development schemes accordingly. At these meetings, for example, village panchayat president Pushpa from

Thirunelveli district in Tamil Nadu noted that, "the immediate plans and future plans are discussed there, based on people's needs. The accounts for the funds received are presented for the people to see." Likewise, village panchayat president Jayashree from the same district noted how gram sabhas allowed the panchayat body to review people's petitions. In the case of Sunitaben, a village panchayat president from Anand district in Gujarat, "the most important question raised was regarding benefits for those below the poverty line. In this regard, considering the large number of poor people, I got many benefits like housing and widow and old age pensions for them. I also helped them in getting their names onto the BPL list." The gram sabhas thus served to identify beneficiaries and share panchayat benefits, rather than to work out an overall panchayat development plan.

When examining the role of Dalit women villagers in the gram sabhas, however, the picture is not so positive. Dalit elders and male villagers from Surendranagar district in Gujarat mentioned, "women in general and Dalit women in particular don't come to the gram sabhas... If they attend, it is to fulfil the quorum only. There will be a lot of dominant caste village elders and so [the women] sit in purdah and never speak." Dalit women villagers separately confirmed that they have to be in purdah and are not allowed to speak directly to any man, especially not in front of any dominant caste person. If they want to raise anything in the gram sabha, they often tell their husbands prior to the meetings. Dalit women villagers interviewed in Vadodara district in the same state and in Madurai district in Tamil Nadu revealed that they did not attend gram sabhas, in the latter case to avoid caste tensions with the dominant castes. In contrast, Dalit women villagers in Thirunelveli district in Tamil Nadu explained that because their husbands did not want them to participate in the gram sabhas, they stayed at home. Dalit elders and male villagers added further reasons of women's household duties, their inability to express themselves in public, and a lack of knowledge of village needs. Other gender and caste limitations in the gram sabhas, as per Dalit women elected representatives in Cuddalore district in the same state, were: "In the village meetings generally Dalits participate well only when there is a question of basic needs such as drinking water, road or electricity facilities. The annual income and expenses of the panchayat are what dominant castes solely look after. The village meetings are not viewed as a forum for the participation of Dalit women. Mostly our husbands speak in such meetings."

Gender and caste discriminatory norms, therefore, emerged as the strongest reasons for both Dalit women elected representatives' lack of participation in gram sabhas, as well as Dalit women villagers' constraints regarding active participation and voice in these meetings. These norms particularly denied women their rights to freedom of movement outside the house and freedom of speech in public meetings. The denial of women's right to non-discrimination became a critical factor in preventing Dalit women elected representatives from building up the close relationships required to improve their responsiveness to villagers' needs, as well as accountability between them and their constituencies. It also denied Dalit women villagers their right to an equal say in how panchayat schemes were implemented and funds were spent, which ensured that Dalit women's priorities were not considered by the development schemes of the panchayats.

FINANCIAL ACCOUNTABILITY

Intrinsically linked to social accountability is financial accountability for funds received and disbursed for panchayat schemes. Financial accountability requires Dalit women elected representatives to exercise control over panchayat revenue, development and welfare funds, monitor the effective and efficient use of funds, and effectively deal with corruption. However, over half of the women (99 women or 59.6 per cent), primarily benami panchayat presidents and members, did not review how funds were spent, whether by monitoring the accounts or checking the implementation of development works. A further seven women (4.2 per cent) were not permitted to review accounts when they asked for them, indicating financial control exercised by either talatis/ clerks or vice presidents. All this hampered accountability between these elected representatives and their constituencies.

The roughly one-third of women elected representatives remaining mainly undertook three courses of action: most commonly, they personally monitored development works (53 women or 31.9 per cent); over one-quarter (45 women or 27.1 per cent) checked the accounts to ensure that receipts reflected the funds paid out for actual work done; and 21 women (12.7 percent) took concrete action when they saw people misusing funds. Two other women also set up monitoring systems to ensure that development work was done properly.

To be borne in mind, however, is the commonly acknowledged fact of corruption in the form of the commissions often taken from development schemes and paid to panchayat members. This open system of corruption, according to a dominant caste vice president in Anand district in Gujarat, functioned as follows: "The percentage [of commission money] is fixed everywhere for all contracts and development schemes that come through the panchayat. The talati in my panchayat always asks for his commission, though he always tells the Dalit woman [president] that he is not getting any commission. And he always gives it to me." Moreover, panchayat members often vied for panchayat contracts, seen as a lucrative means of either receiving commissions from contractors or utilising lower grade building materials and pocketing the balance of money allotted for projects. The latter method applied particularly to Dalit development schemes, as noted by Dalit women elected representatives in Kheda district in Gujarat. Contractor selection was often influenced by bribes as well. The end result of this corruption were two-fold economic gains for dominant castes; that is, seizing the majority of commissions as well as ensuring that their communities received most of the panchayat development benefits.

Thus, while only 96 of the 166 Dalit women elected representatives (57.8 per cent) acknowledged that corruption took place during their terms in office, this percentage is likely higher. Most women who admitted to corruption taking place in their panchayats (75 women or 78.1 per cent) did nothing, or felt they could not do anything when everyone, from government officials to panchayat representatives to contractors, was involved.

This fits with suggestions by some authors that women's ability to reduce corruption and caste-based patronage politics depends on a number of political and institutional factors. These factors include their level of political experience, social networks, participation and power in political parties and networks, as well as the implementation of state sanctions against corruption. In particular, the higher the presence of benami or *de facto* politics, the greater the probability of corruption.[11] In the present research, concrete action against corruption primarily consisted of women elected representatives taking the matter to the BDO/TDO or DDO, or raising the issue in panchayat meetings. Kamachi, a village panchayat president from Coimbatore district in Tamil Nadu, however, took a more pragmatic approach: she campaigned to increase the travel allowance of panchayat members in order to combat corruption, for "what can one do in the panchayat with ₹330 as a monthly allowance?"

Dalit women who were active in the panchayats tended to take on the responsibility of checking corruption through regularly inspecting the accounts, monitoring the implementation of development works, and visiting panchayat services such as primary schools, anganwadi centres and healthcare centres. Specifically, village panchayat presidents like Lakshiben from Vadodara district in Gujarat signed all bills only after checking them first and reviewed all the accounts periodically, while Preetikaben from Anand district and Tejuben from Kheda district made it a point to review all vouchers and expenditure sheets regularly, either by themselves or with the talati. Similarly, village panchayat president Kamachi from Coimbatore district in Tamil Nadu ensured financial transparency by verifying all development works as per government guidelines and checking all the accounts. Consequently, with the help of other panchayat members, she dismissed a corrupt vice president. Jayashree, village panchayat president from Thirunelveli district in Tamil Nadu, made it her business to supervise all panchayat works. Hence, "the contractors in my panchayat are frightened of me, because I have always been personally present when panchayat development works take place. There is no possibility for corruption. So, they always think too many times before getting any contracts from my panchayat." Sunitaben's case is yet another example of good financial practices by a Dalit woman panchayat representative. Sunitaben, a village panchayat president from Anand district in Gujarat, faced opposition from the vice president, dominant caste and Dalit panchayat members, who said she should undertake her panchayat duties as directed by them and that they should 'get something out of the panchayat'. Sunitaben's reply was as follows:

> I told them that I would not indulge in any corruption and would ensure that no one was involved in corruption. I often visited the village school and looked into the children's scholarship forms, and used to discuss how the children's education was progressing with the teachers. I used to plan with women in the primary healthcare centre and discuss children's vaccinations and improvements to their health. I visited most of the panchayat projects to check if they were proceeding in an organised manner. Whatever funds came to the panchayat, in meetings I reviewed their appropriate usage. I checked the records, revenue and account books in the meetings every month, and used to discuss the accounts with the Talati. Often, I would review the accounts page by page.

Sunitaben gave an example of the opposition she faced: for a road construction project, the other panchayat members told her to use low cost materials and distribute the remaining money among the members, which she refused to do. In retaliation, the members opposed her and gave the contract to another contractor, and later made a false complaint of corruption against her to the TDO over another contract. The complaint was found to be false.

By contrast, where Dalit women elected representatives were benamis for male family members, these men often reviewed the accounts and supervised panchayat development works instead. The gendered perception that women are not capable of understanding and checking accounts was prevalent in both states. This was particularly the case where the women lacked formal education. As mentioned by Dalit women elected representatives in Ahmedabad district in Gujarat, "[vice presidents and talatis] only contact our husbands in relation to any work or to give any information... We don't monitor or check accounts, development works or welfare funds. This is done by our husbands only because it is they who interact with contractors and deal with money-related matters." In one instance, the husband of benami village panchayat president Ratanben from Kheda district in Gujarat, who undertook all her panchayat duties as directed by the dominant castes, confronted the vice president over misuse of funds and from then onwards got to check all the accounts.

Tackling corruption by others through concrete action proved to be harder for the women, with sometimes adverse consequences. For instance, when benami village panchayat president Thilagam from Coimbatore district in Tamil Nadu complained about the clerk's misappropriation of funds to the vice president, he advised her not to file a complaint. Fearing she might ultimately face corruption charges as the head of the panchayat, she informed the BDO, but was merely advised to tell the vice president and, failing that, the police. When the vice president found out that she had approached the BDO, he warned her not to approach government officials again. No further action was taken against the clerk. A fearful Thilagam, while not allowed to see any of the accounts, started to secretly check the receipts through her son. A stronger adverse consequence, noted by Dalit women elected representatives in Ahmedabad district in Gujarat, is that if Dalit women did not allow corruption, they would often be removed quickly through no confidence motions. Even at higher levels, corruption seems to be taken for granted. For example, when Ramilaben, taluka panchayat president from Vadodara district in Gujarat, approached the development commissioner to complain about the TDO's corruption, she was told by the commissioner that everybody received a fixed commission at each level. He did not take any action, and she gave up, thinking nothing further could be done.

OBSTRUCTIONS TO DALIT WOMEN'S RESPONSIVENESS

Finally, any assessment of Dalit women's development impact in the panchayats must encompass the types of political rights violations they faced. These violations determined the extent to which the women were able to create any substantial impact.

Caste-class-gender obstructions weighed against the assertiveness of Dalit women elected representatives and their free political participation. Consequently, while development schemes may have reached the Dalit community, it is likely that the majority of potential benefits were siphoned off elsewhere.

Summarising the main reasons why Dalit women felt unable to influence development outcomes, especially those in favour of their community, the strongest obstacle by far was their proxy political participation as benamis, mainly for the dominant castes, but also in some cases their husbands (mentioned by 91 women or 54.8 per cent). Aside from the link between benami participation, corruption and the lack of development for Dalits, another link lies between benami participation, the lack of development for Dalits and the reinforcement of caste norms. This can extend beyond the caste norms that dictate Dalits' submission to other castes, to more concrete acts of discrimination. An example is the case of Lalitaben from Anand district in Gujarat, who as panchayat president supported whatever the dominant FCs in her village panchayat told her to support. This went to the extent that she agreed to a separation wall between this dominant caste community and the Dalit localities, thus reinforcing Dalits' alleged inequality and 'polluted' presence. She also passed a panchayat resolution that all village conflicts should be resolved within the village itself in an attempt to remove the right of villagers to a legal remedy for any caste discrimination and violence.

Another quarter of Dalit women elected representatives (41 women or 24.7 per cent) felt that their lack of knowledge regarding development issues and panchayat schemes hindered their responsiveness to Dalit development needs. A significant gap exists in the government's fulfilment of its duty to provide adequate information and training for elected representatives on panchayat administration. Moreover, Dalit women elected representatives consistently quoted a lower level of education as a handicap. This handicap often negatively impacted their ability to understand panchayat schemes and accounts, and their self-confidence and ability to interact with government officials and other panchayat members. As pointed out by a dominant caste village panchayat vice president in Nagapattinam district in Tamil Nadu, Dalit women, to some extent, functioned better at higher panchayat tiers than they did at the village level. This was because they were able to gain information directly from government officials such as the BDO/DDO or panchayat commissioners who participated in union or district panchayat meetings.

A lack of self-confidence (noted by 34 women or 20.5 per cent) was particularly the case for many first-time elected representatives with little knowledge of and exposure to the public sphere, let alone political life. As Dalit women villagers in Madurai district further pointed out:

> Only just now have Dalit men and women started participating more in the panchayats. Though they have power, there is no marked development for the community. The dominant castes take away even the basic facilities of Dalits while reporting to government officials that they have done everything for Dalits. The main reason for this is that the Dalit panchayat president and members do not go to the meetings regularly. Out of fear, they also do not speak boldly against the dominant castes. Another reason is that almost all Dalits are working in the agricultural fields of the dominant castes and depend on them for their livelihood. Hence no change has taken place in the Dalit community.

Therefore, continued economic dependence on the dominant castes, as well as caste norms of submission to these castes reinforced by 'untouchability' practices and violence together constitute psychological barriers to Dalit women's active political influence regarding development issues.

Aside from benamis or women for whom the aforementioned internal reasons reduced their development impact, Dalit women elected representatives also raised external reasons primarily linked to obstructions created by others. As far as 35 Dalit women elected representatives (21.1 per cent) were concerned, no one in the panchayat prioritised Dalit development needs. A further 14 women (8.4 per cent) stated that development schemes or projects that would benefit the Dalit community were not approved. For another seven women (4.2 per cent), development projects/ schemes and funds for Dalits existed but were not implemented by the panchayats; while for 21 women (12.7 per cent), it was the lack of funds under Dalit development schemes made available to their panchayats. A further 15 women (9.0 per cent), mainly in Gujarat, mentioned the lack of support from their families, the Dalit community, or the wider community to implement development schemes for Dalits. Examining all these related reasons together, a pattern appears in which, whether women took initiative to raise issues pertinent to their community or not, other panchayat members generally failed to respond to or prioritise Dalit development needs.

Finally, around a third of Dalit women elected representatives (49 women or 29.5 per cent) reported the active blocking of their development efforts in the panchayats. The main perpetrators were dominant castes – primarily vice presidents, presidents or panchayat members, and to a lesser extent talatis/clerks (mostly dominant caste) or dominant caste villagers. These different dominant caste actors often joined together in their efforts to control how development resources were distributed, evidencing how caste loyalties and interests remain a strong basis for political organisation and control. Any moves that challenged this control and appropriation of resources, such as the independent behaviour of some Dalit women benamis or Dalit women elected representatives directing development work towards the Dalit community, then triggered obstructions. At the same time, obstructions, especially those rooted in discriminatory behaviour, served to reinforce social norms of submissiveness and the lack of political voice and power among 'low' caste women. In contrast, BDO/TDO/DDOs, Dalit panchayat members or Dalit villagers were far less likely to oppose the women's development efforts.

By far the most common experience of almost half these women was to be silenced or ignored in panchayat discussions (reported by 24 women). Often utilised against Dalit women who were seen as too vocal in articulating their community's interests, the use of this tactic was aided by Dalit women's lack of information on panchayat funds and schemes. In the case of Tejuben, a village panchayat president from Kheda district in Gujarat, when she raised the issue of a dominant FC community encroaching on government grazing lands, other caste members ignored her and would not respond to her queries for information. This, along with the refusal of the concerned dominant castes to vacate the village common lands, led her to take the issue up with local government and police officials, and finally tell the Dalits to drive their cattle onto the encroached land for grazing.

Dalit women panchayat members revealed that members often did not get the opportunity to speak in meetings on development issues, even at the taluka/union levels. At the higher panchayat tiers, political party affiliations also delineated the extent to which members could influence discussions on development schemes. Political party interests, moreover, often intermingled with caste interests. In Thirunelveli district in Tamil Nadu, union panchayat vice president Jayalakshmi faced a complete lack of respect from the dominant caste president and members, who disliked her affiliation to a Dalit political party. They would ignore and even verbally abuse her in meetings, refuse to tell her about the schemes being implemented in the panchayat, and block her attempts to direct development schemes towards her community.

Reshmaben's case below highlights how active elected representatives who threatened dominant caste interests were often silenced or ignored in one way or the other. A village panchayat member from Ahmedabad district in Gujarat, Reshmaben raised questions in panchayat meetings regarding issues Dalits prioritised, like building a boundary around the Dalits' cremation ground, common land encroachments and repairing a water pipeline leading to the Dalit locality. However, no one in the dominant caste controlled panchayat listened to her. She said, "I have raised these issues again and again, but I have not succeeded. The president in the panchayat is a benami, supported by and acting upon the wishes of the two influential [dominant backward castes] outside the panchayat." Unlike other women panchayat members, who were allowed to speak in the panchayat, Reshmaben was deliberately ignored. Nonetheless, she succeeded in seeing the removal of rubbish from the Dalit locality as well as an encroachment blocking the Dalits' pathway. She said, "No funds have come to the panchayat yet. But once

they do, the dominant backward caste members will start blocking
all efforts to get development benefits for Dalits... I am trying
for the development of my community because no one acts on
Dalit issues. Until now, most of the benefits have gone only to the
dominant backward castes because everybody is scared of them."

Another common tactic 15 women reported was to block the
passage of any resolution or approval of development projects
Dalit women supported. Other panchayat members often refused
to agree to resolutions that would distribute development projects
to Dalits. In some cases, the dominant caste vice presidents would
refuse to sign such resolutions in an attempt to derail them.
Caste-class-gender prejudices and vested interests were often
apparent. Village panchayat president Kannagi from Cuddalore
district in Tamil Nadu, for example, had to contend with constant
arguments and hindrances by dominant caste members that even
prevented a resolution allowing Dalits to access drinking water
from the common village tap. Dominant castes also manipulated
Dalit members to thwart the development efforts of Dalit women
elected representatives. Thus, Dalit community members,
instigated by the Dalit women who had lost the elections and some
dominant castes, created problems for Kannagi over her removal
of huts on panchayat land. A desire to misappropriate funds
also drove some of the opposition to Dalit women's proposals.
When village panchayat president Tejuben from Kheda district
in Gujarat favoured a pucca RCC road construction project,
dominant caste members argued for a cheaper stone road. This
was because they wanted to embezzle funds allocated for the
RCC road construction. When she used her executive authority
as president to push through the resolution for an RCC road, the
panchayat members pressurised her into giving the contract to a
dominant caste person of their choice.

More frequently mentioned as a reason for the inability of Dalit
women elected representatives to respond to Dalit development
needs was the oppositional party politics evident in the panchayats.
If the women belonged to the minority opposing party, they
were often side-lined or opposed in panchayat discussions on
development schemes and funds. District panchayat member

Indurani from Tamil Nadu made complaints to the vice president, district collector and local MLA regarding the oppositional politics in her panchayat that resulted in all her development requests being side-lined. However, they did nothing to resolve her grievances.

A third category of obstructions just over a quarter of the women (14 women) referred to was the delay, or misappropriation, of development funds, particularly those meant for Dalit development. As seen in the previous section, misappropriation of development funds was a common experience in many panchayats. Even funds targeted at Dalits often illegally ended up in the hands of other castes. If the funds weren't misappropriated, then delaying the release of funds aimed at a similar result. In the case of taluka panchayat member Sumeetaben from Kheda district in Gujarat, the dominant caste panchayat members, an influential dominant caste contractor and the local MLA belonging to an opposition political party used their contacts with state government officials to delay the release of funds for Dalit development. Moreover, elected representatives who were unable to cultivate good relations with higher panchayats tiers and government officials who controlled a certain amount of funding grants also witnessed a reduced or delayed release of funds. For instance, the district and union panchayats refused to release funds allotted to the village panchayat headed by Kalaimani from Nagapattinam district in Tamil Nadu. A dominant caste union panchayat member in particular made sure that all the funds and developmental works meant for her area were siphoned off to his dominant backward caste instead.

While attempting to pass resolutions on or implement panchayat development schemes, 11 Dalit women elected representatives were offered or faced demands for bribes, commissions, or panchayat contracts. For instance, dominant caste panchayat members, the vice president and clerk all offered bribes from development funds to village panchayat member Rukmini from Nagapattinam district in Tamil Nadu in order to prevent the passage of resolutions on Dalit development. Where women refused to indulge in any corrupt practices, the opposition they faced became more pronounced as a result. In Anand district in Gujarat, village panchayat president Preetikaben stated, "Dominant caste members never opposed me on these development projects, but they constantly told me to siphon money from the projects and distribute it to all the panchayat members. I refused to do so. My opponents in the panchayat constantly opposed me on all financial matters; they accused me of corruption and alleged in front of other panchayat members and villagers that I used all the money for my own interests."

If not obstructed at the stage of passing development resolutions, 13 Dalit women elected representatives witnessed various people preventing the implementation of approved development projects, especially those meant for Dalits, or other panchayat resolutions supported by the women. An example relates to encroachments by dominant castes on panchayat or other village common lands, a widespread practice across both Gujarat and Tamil Nadu. In rural areas where land aggregations often correspond with socio-economic and political power, and where the majority of Dalits are landless daily wage labourers dependent on the landed dominant castes for their livelihood, the removal of land encroachments was often a highly politically charged issue. This is clearly seen in the case of village panchayat member Reshmaben from Ahmedabad district in Gujarat, who was attacked following the announcement of the election results due to her husband, the former president, having taken up the issue of land encroachments by one dominant caste community. When Reshmaben likewise raised this issue in the panchayat meetings, she received no support to remove these encroachments. This was so even after she negotiated to shift encroachments by Dalits in a bid to pressurise the dominant castes to move off village common grazing lands in return. A hunger strike before district government offices similarly yielded little in terms of pressurising the dominant castes to vacate the public land, or sparking concrete action from government officials.

Moreover, the sub-divisions created by dominant castes during the panchayat elections occasionally lingered, affecting relations in the panchayats and thereby hindering Dalit development efforts while maintaining dominant caste interests. A clear example is the case of Sunitaben from Anand district in Gujarat. In the village panchayat where Sunitaben contested elections for the president's post, one dominant sub-caste had tied up with another Dalit sub-caste by promising to support their Dalit candidate for vice president if that sub-caste supported the dominant caste candidate for president. When Sunitaben won the president's post instead, the dominant castes used the Dalit vice president, who was their benami, to obstruct the implementation of development projects. Sunitaben said,

> In any discussions of development works or in any issues, the [Dalit] vice president always used to say 'yes' in the meetings, but later he opposed me and created obstacles for me in implementing the resolutions. Everyone in the panchayat body – the members, vice president and the talati – created obstacles for me... [For example], I passed the resolution to lay the pipeline that would have benefited both Dalit sub-castes, but the vice president opposed it and tried to dig the pipeline in such a way, going uphill, so that only dominant castes and his community would get the water. Later, a resolution was passed for installing a water pump for my sub-caste, which the vice president agreed to, but when the pipeline was put in place he opposed it arguing that it should pass through a dominant caste colony. I argued that the pipeline should be laid as had been passed in the resolution, but as the dominant castes now opposed it, the completion of this project was delayed.

While the afore-mentioned obstructions concerned panchayat decisions and funds, eight women faced personal attacks on their character – particularly caste or gender-based verbal abuse – and their performance in the panchayats. As seen in the case that commenced this chapter, that of village panchayat president Annammal from Madurai district in Tamil Nadu, this abuse was targeted towards women who were seen to be too independent in their decision making, who thereby overstepped the caste and gender norms governing their public roles. Another example, which also provides evidence of how caste cuts across political party affiliation, is the case of Alamelu from Nagapattinam district in Tamil Nadu: Alamelu, an active political party member, won the election to the post of union panchayat member on her political party ticket. But once the election results were announced, the opposing party candidate who had lost the elections and her supporters attempted to assault Alamelu. She escaped with the help of Dalit political party members, who then helped her file a police case regarding this incident. As a result, however, both her political party members as well as the opposing political party members in the panchayat caused problems for her in the panchayat itself; they abused her, harassed her and silenced her when she spoke on development issues, all due to caste prejudices against her and the Dalit party which supported her. It was only three years later, when she supported the president from the opposing political party to overthrow a no confidence motion against him, that she was able to get any development schemes implemented for Dalits through the panchayat.

Other women also reported varying forms of harassment centred around their duties or their physical person: for example, false complaints stating that they were not doing development work properly; accusations of working solely to secure development benefits for certain communities; damage or destruction of panchayat infrastructure projects sanctioned by the women or the women's homes; harassment or assaults on the women and/or their families; passing or attempts to pass no confidence motions to remove the women from office, or false complaints to get the women temporarily suspended from office or forced to resign from their posts. For example, in Nagapattinam district in Tamil Nadu, a dominant caste panchayat member and his supporters demolished the health centre that village panchayat president Asha had built. His reason was that she had not informed him before building this centre and not given him any commission from this project. Village panchayat president Preenaben from Surendranagar district in Gujarat was suspended for one month by the DDO due to her panchayat council failing to pass its budget. The truth of the matter was that the dominant caste talati and panchayat members blocked the passage of the budget as they felt it favoured the Dalit community too much.

Overall, therefore, the women were either personally attacked or had their development efforts directly obstructed. In both cases, the aim was to prevent Dalit women's political participation from translating into concrete gains for their community. The result was to maintain the development status quo in the panchayat areas, with Dalits receiving little benefits and dominant castes receiving maximum benefits. The significance lay in the disincentives to Dalit women's active participation in the panchayats, in terms of minimising their ability to create any impact and, therefore, seeking to deter other Dalit women from attempting the same in the future.

Conclusion

It has been globally recognised that "without the active participation of women and the incorporation of women's perspective at all levels of decision-making, the goals of equality, development and peace cannot be achieved."[12] In India it can be further stated that these goals, by virtue of the predominance of a social system based on caste hierarchy, cannot be achieved without the integration of those traditionally excluded from political life into governance institutions. While reservations in panchayat institutions have facilitated the integration of Dalit women into political life, the extent of their successful political participation and institutional performance can be measured in two ways, as indicated at the start of this chapter: first is the responsiveness to Dalit and women's needs in terms of development impact; second is the effective, efficient and accountable performance of political duties. How far did guaranteeing Dalit women's right to political participation through reservations accomplish these two goals?

The answer to this question, as the above analysis reveals, is mixed. In a broad sense, it was the type of political participation – benami or proxy participation, participation hindered by a number of obstructions impacting on responsiveness, and active participation where obstructions were overcome to a great degree – that largely determined whether these goals were met. The following conclusions, therefore, represent only the broader trends

without trying to minimise the experiences of individual Dalit
women elected representatives.

In terms of development impact, few Dalit women elected
representatives were able to exert any substantial influence in the
panchayats to ensure development benefits for their communities,
though more did articulate the interests of Dalits or attempted to
do so. The net result, particularly at the village panchayat level
where most women in the present research were located and where
caste and patriarchal norms are more entrenched, was still that
the majority of resources and development schemes – even those
allocated for Dalits – went to local dominant caste elites instead
of socially marginalised Dalits. That is, the village panchayats
still did not function as decentralised political-administrative
units of governance. Instead, they remained primarily under
the control of dominant caste male local elites. The presence of
special development schemes for Dalits, particularly the provision
of basic amenities and housing, did mean that Dalits received
some of these benefits in a number of panchayats. However,
they derived fewer benefits from panchayat schemes linked to
economic development, such as land distribution, employment or
loan schemes. The result was to enhance their standard of living to
some extent, without touching upon the economic power relations
that circumscribe Dalits' economic mobility and independence
in the first place. As such, democratic decentralisation and the
inclusion of marginalised communities in local governance
seems to have only a marginal impact on existing patterns of
inequitable development.

Moreover, the types of development benefits Dalits received
during the women's terms in office reveal that while a number
of the practical caste-class needs of Dalits were fulfilled to some
extent, Dalit women were by and large unable to fulfil strategic
caste-class needs. Entrenched caste interests, linked to a dominant
caste exercise of socio-political power and control over resources,
prevented these needs from being realised. Nor were women able
to fulfil any practical or strategic gender needs. An explanation
for this is that many Dalit women were forced to forgo pursuing
caste-class or gender needs in order to gain cooperation from

other dominant caste panchayat members. Another explanation lies in the large number of benamis who did not function independently in relation to decision-making on development schemes. Furthermore, taking up more strategic caste and gender needs, such as alternative employment or land-related schemes for Dalits or combating untouchability practices, often brought Dalit women elected representatives up against more overt opposition from dominant caste men in particular.

Circumscriptions on these women's participation and voice in the Gujarat and Tamil Nadu panchayats, therefore, had a direct bearing on their inability to successfully tackle development or social justice issues. This points to a hostile socio-political context and the adverse influence of caste-class-gender structures on development. A further hindering factor was the lack of capacity-building programmes for Dalit women representatives to enhance their human capital – in terms of education and information, confidence and the ability to articulate Dalits' and women's development needs. Resource constraints and the kind of politico-administrative features and functioning of Panchayati Raj in both states also played a role. Disrupted lines of accountability through non-functioning gram sabhas or Dalit women's lack of voice in these meetings was another determinant of these women's inability to respond to the needs of their constituencies. Indications then are that Dalit women representatives have not yet gained political power adequate enough to face these multiple constraints, despite reservations in the panchayats.

A number of barriers reduced the ability of a majority of Dalit women to effectively and efficiently discharge their panchayat responsibilities and be accountable to their constituencies. The major barrier is benami participation, but other barriers include inadequate levels of knowledge on development schemes and programmes; other panchayat members not prioritising Dalit development needs; and multiple obstacles created by others, ranging from hindering Dalit women's participation and voice; misusing funds meant for Dalit development; to personal attacks on the women. Dominant castes both inside and outside the panchayat, and Dalits to a lesser extent, constantly sought to

manoeuvre panchayat development schemes in order to secure
their own social, economic and political interests. Reinforcing this
process, gender and caste norms were often strategically utilised,
highlighting both the expediency of these social norms as well as
how formal political power patterns sought to replicate and even
consolidate social and informal political power patterns.

Deficiencies in accountability practices were observed in many
panchayats. Two-thirds of Dalit women elected representatives
did not review how panchayat funds were spent, or monitor the
implementation of development works, while most were unable to
take specific action against corruption. The lack of transparent,
consensus decisions on panchayat contracts and dominant
caste pressures to secure contracts for their caste contractors, in
particular, allowed for the practice of commission-taking from
panchayat schemes to flourish. Transparency and accountability
in governance were further weakened by the general inability of
Dalit women elected representatives to participate equally in gram
sabhas. Gender norms, and to a lesser extent, intermeshed caste
norms, played important roles in silencing Dalit women's voices in
gram sabhas, reducing their interaction with their constituencies
and, therefore, their ability to gauge development needs and
transparently discuss development schemes and budgets.

Given the aforementioned hurdles to Dalit women's political
participation, the small numbers of women who were successful
in effectively delivering a number of development benefits for
their community, who monitored accounts and development
projects and who sought to curb corrupt practices in the
panchayats deserve separate mention. As discussed in the previous
chapter, a number of factors facilitated their responsiveness,
effectiveness, efficiency and accountability in political life. These
include personal factors such as education; relative economic
well-being and independence; knowledge of panchayat schemes
and programmes; previous panchayat experience; social capital
in the form of active membership in political parties or social
organisations; previous experiences of active participation in
social issues; and finally self-confidence and the ability to express
their opinions in panchayat meetings and strategise to overcome

obstructions to their development efforts. Additionally, a number of external factors also added to the equation, including supportive husbands and/or other family members; supportive vice presidents and talatis/clerks in the panchayats; collaboration with other Dalit panchayat members; and good working relationships with government officials and members of higher panchayat tiers.

Not all these factors needed to be present, but their accumulative presence made it easier for Dalit women to exercise their political rights and overcome any obstacles encountered in the panchayats. Even then, as noted by village panchayat president Kamachi from Coimbatore district in Tamil Nadu, strong caste interests in the panchayats had to be accommodated. She noted:

> Though I had enough knowledge, experience, self-confidence, training from NGOs and very good guidance, I still had to give up many initiatives and make some adjustments. Though the district collector had enough information [about the obstacles I was facing in my panchayat], he could not do anything. The caste system is so strong. Hence, the government should not stop with saying that the Dalits, too, have political power and rights; it should help them to execute their political power. Only then can obstacles from political parties and the caste system be removed.

What is apparent is that while Dalit women's representation in Panchayati Raj through reservations led to a limited attainment of positive development outcomes for individual Dalits and women, the impact on resource allocations and institutional rules in favour of Dalits and women was much lower. In other words, increasing these women's representation in governance may contribute to enhancing the process of political learning and the actual political capabilities and voice of Dalit women. Their representation does not, however, guarantee that the institutional power and resources acquired by them will be translated into greater social justice and qualitatively better representations of Dalit women's, Dalits' or women's interests.

It is for these reasons that greater state and civil society attention needs to be placed on equalising the social structures and power relations which, to a large extent, control the quantity and quality of the development impact Dalit women are able to produce through accessing their right to political participation in local governance. This is, of course, in addition to the political and administrative reforms required to truly make the panchayats institutions of self-government. At the same time, building on the enabling factors that enhance these elected representatives' impact is essential, above all by extending specific support to these women. Moreover, the small number of Dalit women elected representatives who have made dents in caste, class and patriarchal structures through their development impact become important examples that highlight the potential of Dalit women's political participation and exercise of equal political power for their communities.

Notes

1. Human Development Resource Centre, *Decentralisation in India: Challenges and Opportunities,* Discussion Paper Series 1 (New Delhi: UNDP, 2001), p. 78.
2. Kabeer, N., "Resources, Agency, Achievements: Reflections on the Measurement of Women's Empowerment", in Kabeer et al, *Discussing Women's Empowerment: Theory and Practice,* Sida Studies 3 (Stockholm: Swedish International Development Cooperation Agency, 2002).
3. Strategic gender needs challenge gender relations and roles, such as the division of labour or gender violence, and demand substantive equality in all spheres of life. By contrast, practical gender needs derive from ascribed women's roles within the sexual division of labour and enable them to meet basic needs such as healthcare, water and income: see Molyneux, M., "Mobilization without Emancipation? Women's Interests, the State, and Revolution in Nicaragua", *Feminist Studies,* vol. 11, no. 2 (1985), pp. 227-254.
4. Strategic caste-class needs can be said to challenge caste and class relations and norms such as 'untouchability' and demand substantive equality in all spheres of life, while practical caste-class needs can be said to stem from Dalits' ascribed occupations, resource deprivation and consequent poverty, and address basic livelihood concerns.

5. Kabeer et al, supra note 2, p. 27.
6. See 'Indices of Successful Leaders' developed by the Institute of Social Sciences, New Delhi: Bose, A., "Empowerment of Women: How and When?", *Economic and Political Weekly*, vol. 34 (August 2000), pp. 3005-3007.
7. Mathew and Mathew, "India: Decentralisation and Local Governance – How Clientelism and Accountability Work", in Hadenius, A. (ed.), *Decentralisation and Democratic Governance: Experiences from India, Bolivia and South Africa* (Stockholm: Almqvist and Wiksell International, 2003).
8. For example, see Crook, R.C. and Manor, J., *Democratic Decentralisation in South Asia and West Africa: Participation, Accountability and Performance* (Cambridge: Cambridge University Press, 1998); Vijayalakshmi V. and Chandrashekar, B.K, "Authority, Powerlessness and Dependence: Women and Political Participation", *ISEC Working Paper 106* (Bangalore: Institute for Social and Economic Change, 2002).
9. A limitation of this data is that it does not quantify the extent to which these development services and schemes were extended to Dalits, and hence the gap in terms of fulfilling Dalits' needs for each service or development scheme, or the gap between grants available for Dalit development and how much actually reached the Dalit community. Collecting this data would require detailed cross-checking and verification with a number of actors, which was beyond the scope of this research. That said, however, the data serves as an indication of the general areas in which development benefits were distributed to Dalits.
10. Government of India, *XV, XVI, XVII, XVIII and XIX Periodic Reports to the Committee on the Elimination of Racial Discrimination 2006*, UN Doc. CERD/C/IND/19.
11. V. Vijayalakshmi, "Rent-Seeking and Gender in Local Governance", *ISEC* Working Paper 164 (Bangalore: Institute for Social and Economic Change, 2005), pp. 2, 20.
12. Beijing Platform of Action 1995, para. 181.

7

IMPACTING SOCIAL RELATIONS

Despite some social change taking place, no real changes have happened in terms of women's positions in decision-making processes at the village or higher panchayat level. Still today if a woman is president, her husband will run the panchayat administration. Women still do things only after asking others – their husbands or family. The vice president still controls the administration, but women do not say anything. The savarna (twice-born 'upper' castes) still are saying that Dalits can't do administrative work and project only their (dominant caste) people as capable… A woman can come into the panchayat only through reservations because men won't allow them in general seats. The 33 per cent reservation is good, but there should also be protection for illiterate village women. In addition to the party ticket, back up support, training, education and protection also should be given.

— Ramilaben, taluka panchayat president,
Vadodara district, Gujarat

Ramilaben was elected on a Congress party ticket to an SC women reserved seat in a taluka panchayat in Vadodara district in Gujarat. As the president's post was also reserved for SC women, Ramilaben was then elected president. She fulfilled her panchayat responsibilities, but experienced obstructions from both dominant caste Congress and BJP party members, who were not happy that a Dalit woman had become the president. At first, Congress party members felt that they would at least be able to fulfil their interests through her. Later, however, they turned against her for being an active and independent president. Dominant caste panchayat members planned a no confidence motion against her two times, but she prevented this move with the support of higher Congress party representatives.

Panchayat members also always opposed her and accused her of not conducting meetings properly, not being able to manage these meetings, or being involved in corruption – for example, using the official vehicle for her own purposes, or giving contracts only to her own people. The BJP members were a minority in the panchayat, but still opposed her resolutions due to political party enmity. According to Ramilaben, "I feel that as a Dalit woman president I was discriminated against. The attempts to bring a no confidence motion against me as well as the regular opposition happened because I, a Dalit woman, had occupied the president's post."

Despite this opposition, Ramilaben managed to ensure the distribution of development works to all villages in the taluka. She discussed the villagers' development needs with them. She considered favourably issues such as housing, roads and electricity that Dalit and women village panchayat members brought to her notice. The only limitation was that the Congress party directed her to only grant the smaller development sub-contracts for Dalits. She stated, "Until now an FC man occupied the president's post, and [Dalits] did not have access to it. Now, as we have the opportunity to do this work, we should do it well... I brought in grants from every government source, properly utilised SC funds and implemented government schemes. I also actively encouraged inter-caste marriages between Dalits and other castes, as well as between [Dalit] sub-castes."

Whenever Ramilaben attended public programmes in schools, she spoke against caste discrimination, saying that it was illegal and should not be promoted. She said, "I gave priority to the development issues of my community. I never allowed anyone else to sit on my [the president's] chair." In performing her panchayat duties, her self-confidence was supported by her education, trainings on the panchayat system, her family and husband's support, and some support from higher Congress party officials and the Gujarat president of the Dalit Panthers Movement.

She also felt that her participation in the panchayats resulted in some positive social changes. While she didn't feel valued by her family earlier, she now experienced greater respect: her husband's elder brother asked for her views on any question, and the young men and other family members said that they did not have to worry because their aunt was the taluka president.

Village elders also now called her to caste panchayat meetings and village social, religious and cultural programmes, of which women were traditionally not part. She noted, "Now they consult me on all matters and provide me with the president's chair. They call me on the stage every time." Even though she is no longer in the panchayat today, she is still known as the first woman who dared to enter taluka politics and succeeded in finishing her term in office. Both Dalits and some dominant castes respect her because she was very active and did many good things for the taluka.

Another important change was that more women villagers, inspired by her, participated in party politics. Women also spoke more in public places and were ready to contest the elections.

Dominant castes also addressed her with respect now and called her 'president' or 'madam'. Further, she said, "If I went to the dominant castes' houses, they immediately gave me a chair to sit on." However, overall, she felt that there has been no substantial change to social norms because of her political participation.

At the same time, she was convinced that, "women's political participation, Dalit women's in particular, is necessary so that society can develop. Only women will think about women's issues. Only Dalit women can take a stand on Dalit issues and particularly Dalit women's issues... Nothing is attainable without exercising authority, and my desire is to increase the confidence of Dalits to fight and gain authority and power in society for their development."

Ramilaben's case provides a good starting point for exploring whether Dalit women's political participation in local governance institutions has brought about wider social change at the family and societal level. Despite the positive developments her political participation in the taluka panchayat brought about, and the positive changes in social relations between herself and others, her statement at the start of this chapter on the extent to which structural changes have occurred is more cautionary.

Aside from securing socio-economic rights for Dalits through development schemes, guaranteeing Dalit women's right to political participation in the panchayats could potentially disrupt and ultimately restructure social (caste and gender), economic (class) and political power relations. Opening the political arena to socially excluded communities through affirmative action aims at two fundamental power changes. One is the equitable distribution of resources to create a more level economic playing field. This is significant given that Dalits have traditionally been denied access to resources under the caste system. Restructuring the economic base of the caste system would spell Dalit independence from dominant castes. Complementing this is a second change in social attitudes towards Dalits and women through their integration into public life. Greater social interaction and the eradication of 'untouchability' practices and gendered practices that confine women to the private sphere aim at enabling Dalits and women to challenge caste-class-gender discriminatory norms and assert their right to equality. Concurrently, dominant castes and men are encouraged towards a greater recognition of the equal social and political rights of Dalits and women. Key to ensuring substantive equality and broader, sustainable social change is to transform both these power relations.

This chapter explores whether Dalit women elected representatives in the panchayats were able to challenge and transform inequitable caste and gender norms. That is, was their political participation in the panchayats an effective tool to transform power relations? Answering this question involves examining what changes in caste and gender perceptions, behaviours and norms occurred because of the political participation of the 166 Dalit women elected panchayat representatives. This is measured by shifts in the support bases of these Dalit women; whether they were approached to resolve conflicts; their perceptions of greater respect shown to them; and changes in social interactions resulting from the women's political participation. Flowing from this are the various effects of political participation on the 200 Dalit women at the personal, family and community level, leading to their willingness or otherwise to contest elections once again.

Shifts in Support Base

Both in Gujarat and Tamil Nadu, shifts in power relations and support bases occurred while the Dalit women elected representatives were in office. On the one hand, 47 women lost the support of certain social groups. For almost half of them, this loss of support came from Dalits for several key reasons, including the Dalits feeling that the women did not ensure that development benefits reached the community, allowed sub-standard development work to take place, allegedly earned money through the panchayats, or were benamis for others. In sum, the perceived failure of Dalit women elected representatives to respond to the Dalit community's development needs changed support patterns. Village panchayat president Saroja from Nagapattinam district in Tamil Nadu, for example, was the only Dalit woman in her panchayat. She faced opposition from all the other members, including the Dalit male members who supported the vice president in return for financial benefits from the panchayat. In this situation, her husband performed most of her panchayat duties, and they managed to push through some development schemes for Dalits. However, Saroja was forced to apologise in her last gram sabha meeting for allegedly not implementing adequate development schemes for one section of Dalits.

Dominant castes withdrew their support for over two-thirds of these Dalit women elected representatives primarily because the women were not submissive enough to dominant caste interests or functioned in opposition to the dominant castes. This loss of support was particularly noted where Dalit women or husbands of benamis pushed through development schemes for Dalits or prevented corruption in development contracts. Dominant castes thus viewed Dalit independent participation as a threat to be countered through the simultaneous withdrawal of support and obstruction of the women's political functioning. For example, dominant castes withdrew support for village panchayat president Tejuben from Kheda district in Gujarat, and she faced obstructions when she initiated action to remove dominant caste encroachments on panchayat common lands. Similarly, political parties withdrew their support where Dalit women or the husbands of benamis were perceived to act too independently in the panchayats.

On the other hand, 45 Dalit women elected representatives earned the support of social groups from which they previously had little or no support base. For three-quarters of these women, mainly from Gujarat, they gained support from Dalits due to their pushing through development schemes for Dalits or with the expectation that they would do so. A positive sign was where Dalit women overcame sub-caste differences within the Dalit community to ensure all benefited from panchayat schemes. Jayashree, a village panchayat president from Thirunelveli district in Tamil Nadu, stated, "My husband, family and the Dalit community have stood with me and supported me in all my efforts. Even though the Dalit Paraiyars opposed me initially, later they offered their support once I fulfilled their needs such as roads, water connection, electricity supply and cremation ground. Today they collaborate with me."

Just under a third of these women mentioned that dominant castes also expressed their support for them as their term in office progressed gradually. The main basis for this change was the delivery of development benefits for the dominant castes or to ensure that development benefits accrued to them. Otherwise, submission to dominant caste interests in the panchayat, whether as benamis or otherwise, won some measure of support as a reward for foregoing the right to active political participation.

In terms of actors outside the panchayats, a few women mentioned support from political parties and local MPs/MLAs arising from perceptions of the women's active and independent leadership in the panchayat or the fulfilment of party interests. In the case of union panchayat member Alamelu from Nagapattinam district in Tamil Nadu, she eventually won the support of the opposing political party after she backed the president from that party in defeating a no confidence bid against him.

Shifts in political support to Dalit women elected representatives, therefore, depended on the extent of the women's active participation and whose interests they guaranteed through their development decisions in the panchayats. Whether this changing support base meant a longer-term change in power relations, however, is examined later in this chapter.

Leadership in Conflict Resolution

One measure of Dalit women's growing status as public leaders is that 51 of the 166 women (30.7 per cent) were sought out to intervene in conflicts in the community – personal and family conflicts mostly, but also intra and inter-communal violence and development related conflicts. A few were already known leaders due to their previous involvement in public life through social organisations, anganwadis, or independent involvement in local social issues. For the majority, however, the panchayats were their first opportunity to step into the public sphere outside of waged work. Not surprisingly, the overwhelming majority of these 51 women were approached by members of their own community to resolve problems. More surprising was the fact that just under half of these women were approached by dominant castes, mostly those just above them in the caste hierarchy; that is, 'lower backward castes'. Though remaining spatially and socially segregated from Dalits, these communities often share the same class status as Dalits. One explanation for their approaching Dalit women elected representatives might be to harness the positional status of these women to arbitrate conflicts.

In over 80 per cent of these conflicts Dalit women elected representatives personally intervened to try and resolve matters. For the remaining conflicts, the women either chose not to get involved, or another family member, usually their husband, intervened on their behalf. The positive flow on effects of Dalit women having gained or consolidated their social status as leaders through political participation were the opportunities presented to further involve themselves in community affairs and build their social networks. This thereby created future spaces for their public participation outside of the panchayats with greater freedom of expression.

Social Changes for Dalit Women

Social changes in attitudes towards Dalit women elected representatives manifested in the respect accorded to them at different levels and to different degrees. Over half of the Dalit women (97 women or 58.4 per cent) felt more respected because of their panchayat position. For almost all these women (93 women), this respect came from Dalit women in their immediate social milieu, while three-quarters of the women (73 women) felt they had gained greater respect from Dalit men. Not surprising, given caste exclusion and social segregation, less than half of the Dalit women felt they received greater respect from dominant caste women or men (42 women each). It would therefore appear that gender barriers to respect, as a precursor to equality, were more easily breached than caste barriers. This may stem in part from three factors. One is the small number of Dalit women who did bring development benefits to their Dalit communities. Second is the Dalit men's feelings of pride on the election of someone from their community. Third is the inability of Dalit women elected representatives to bring about significant shifts away from traditional Dalit occupations or to overcome caste barriers, discrimination and 'untouchability' practices.

What Dalit women viewed as respect, however, needs to be examined further. Several researchers mention how Dalit women elected representatives sometimes perceive a formal elected position, and the authority associated with it, as social mobility. That is, as compared to their earlier status as socially excluded Dalit women, the position of panchayat president or member increases their prestige.[1] Many women in the present research confirmed this trend. This respect was manifested in acts that might appear insignificant to others, but were important for the women as they were new experiences: for example, being greeted by everyone in the village, respectfully called 'president', invited to people's houses, offered chairs to sit on, offered tea or cool (soft) drinks, and so on. For example, Chanchalben, a village panchayat president from Kheda district in Gujarat, felt she received more respect from all Dalit and dominant caste villagers as they now greeted her and asked how she was doing, whereas before they would not speak to her. The women panchayat presidents were also often called for public or social functions that happened in the villages, particularly in the Dalit community.

This perceived increase in respect or status, however, must be seen in light of the fact that at least three-quarters of Dalit women elected representatives in this research were either benamis or faced strong opposition to their political participation and working for Dalit development. The difference between the enhancement of status or 'positional respect' gained through simply holding a formal position of authority, and 'personal respect' signalling transformational change based on equality and dignity is then apparent. Personal respect is underpinned by personal capacities and a more equitable distribution of economic resources, political power and social status. While a good number of women achieved the former, few achieved the latter. Village panchayat president Jasodaben from Surendranagar district in Gujarat was forthright in stating the instrumentality and limits of this respect: "Because I was president and useful to them, both Dalits and non-Dalits respected me, but they never supported me as an individual. That is also because of panchayat reservations; otherwise who respects Dalits?" An example of how positional respect can be confused with structural changes in social relations and social status is the case of Thilagam from Coimbatore district in Tamil Nadu. During her term as a benami president for the dominant castes, they called her 'president' and 'leader', and came to her house. Thus, she felt she was being treated equally and respected by the dominant castes. At the end of her term, she planned a marriage for her daughter outside the village in a big hall, spending lavishly on the arrangements and catering. She expected 2000 people to attend, but not even 200 came. It was then that she realised that she had been used by the dominant castes and that their seeming respect for her was not real. Social relations between them had not changed at all.

However, where the women manifested their political authority by being outspoken on social issues or active in panchayat administration and bringing benefits to their communities, this respect was more likely to reflect actual rising social status. Take the example of taluka panchayat president Ramilaben from Vadodara district in Gujarat, noted at the start of this chapter. She felt that outside the panchayat she was increasingly respected by some dominant sub-castes due to her active political participation and responsiveness to the villagers' needs. Likewise, the Dalits respected her for this, and also because she was the first Dalit woman to become taluka panchayat president. Similarly, Gujarati village panchayat president Preetikaben from Anand district mentioned, "Dalits also call me with respect and come to me for any issues or suggestions. They ask about things like whom to contact or what procedure to go through to get different pension or housing schemes... This is happening even now when I am no longer president."

Further verification of whether this respect corresponded to a substantial shift in terms of recognising Dalit women's right to equality and dignity in political participation can be gauged from the changes in attitudes from different sections of society in their panchayats, as laid out in the following sections.

CHANGES IN ATTITUDES TOWARDS DALIT WOMEN FROM THEIR FAMILIES

The greatest changes in attitudes towards Dalit women elected representatives occurred in their families, though only 66 women or 39.8 per cent of women indicated these changes. A qualification to this low number is that a few women expressed that they already enjoyed freedoms within their families; and, therefore, nothing changed for them. The most common change, shared by around half of these women (37 women), was that their families looked after the children while the women were at the panchayat office or fulfilling other official duties. In the case of village panchayat president Preetikaben from Anand district in Gujarat:

> My husband supported and accepted me throughout my tenure in the panchayat. He gave me courage and never stopped me from taking initiatives and going out of the home... My mother-in-law and brother-in-law took care of my children when I

attended meetings or other panchayat related activities outside the home... My family members respect me in my house as well. They ask me certain questions related to government or administrative matters.

More significant indicators of transformational change mentioned by around half of the women were that their families and relatives increasingly consulted them or took their advice on important family and other matters (35 women), and that they also enjoyed greater decision-making powers on family matters (31 women). Given prevailing gender norms that emphasise women's duties over their rights, and submission to the male patriarchal head of the family, these changes in the sharing of caring responsibilities towards children and the inclusion in family decision-making can be viewed as the fulfilment of strategic gender needs. The rise in women's decision-making powers in the family, in particular, signals a step towards realising equal rights in marital and family life.

An explanation for these changes in advisory and decision-making powers is that women who became active panchayat participants to some degree acquired ideas and information to which they never previously had access. This knowledge, as well as the ability to take decisions outside of the family, brought increased self-confidence to speak up more in their homes. They were now no longer an ordinary daughter or wife, but a panchayat president or member who commanded at least positional respect in the community. Moreover, the fact that panchayat posts often brought economic benefits for panchayat members and their families meant that women were sometimes accorded greater status as substantial income generators. As active women also expanded their contacts with the outside world and knowledge on social affairs, their families began to value them more, and their opinions started to count. This can be contrasted with the situation of benamis, especially benamis for husbands, where the opposite impact occurred: that is, a reinforcement of the women's dependence on male family members and the reinforcement of gender norms in family life.

Twenty-eight women also mentioned that in critical situations such as obstructions or harassment from other panchayat members, their families supported them completely. As previously noted, family support is one key factor that enabled Dalit women to enjoy their right to political participation and aided them in overcoming any opposition to their participation. Most of the women in this research who were widely viewed as successful elected representatives cited family support for their participation. According to Lakshmiben, a village panchayat president from Vadodara district in Gujarat, because patriarchal society is not ready to accept social changes among women, "focus must be on a woman's freedom within the family for things to change. I have so much freedom in my family, because I am a working woman, and my family is economically well off." Family support was an important factor in Lakshmiben's strong participation and ability to ensure development outcomes for Dalits.

Other research has stated that the greatest potential for transformation flowing from women's participation in the panchayats is the recognition of the handicap of a lack of education and illiteracy. The potential impact on the family could include securing girls' right to education.[2] Many Dalit women elected representatives recognised the disadvantages of illiteracy: as per village panchayat president Jasodaben from Surendranagar district in Gujarat, "Because of my age, illiteracy and lack of information, I could not do anything... I faced lots of problems [in the panchayat] because of my illiteracy." Village panchayat president Anjali from Madurai district in Tami Nadu felt that education is *the* priority, if Dalit women are to be more efficient and effective in the panchayats. Education was prioritised equally with information/trainings on panchayat administration by Dalit women villagers interviewed across both states. Its emphasis highlights the need to secure other rights as enabling factors to enjoying the right to political participation – especially the rights to education and information, alongside the right to equality within the family and in society.

CHANGES FOR WOMEN DUE TO DALIT WOMEN'S
POLITICAL PARTICIPATION

Did gender norms change because of Dalit women's political participation in the panchayats, so that they and other women could now do things that they could not do before? Just over one-third of Dalit women elected representatives (57 women or 34.3 per cent) believed that change had occurred.

Over two-thirds of these women (39 women) felt that some women now spoke up more freely in their households. Just less than one-half (27 women) felt that women could speak up in gram sabhas more than previously. Tamil Nadu village panchayat presidents Jayashree from Thirunelveli district and Kowsalya from Coimbatore district specifically mentioned how they encouraged more women to attend and speak in the gram sabhas. Greater freedom of speech in both the family as well as public spaces, therefore, emerged as one of the most significant influences of Dalit women's active political participation. The importance of this gain should be viewed in the context of the aforementioned caste and gender norms that inhibit and seek to control this freedom. Freedom of speech, moreover, brings with it the possibility for women to attain other social and economic rights: equal rights in family life in terms of an equal say in decisions on household income and educating their children, in work and economic independence, and in building up social networks as they engage more in public life.

A second important consequence of Dalit women's political participation in the panchayats was the number of other women, particularly in Gujarat, who now indicated their interest in panchayat politics. A caveat, however, applies here. Increasing interest, while in some cases attributable to Dalit women's political participation, also stemmed from the perceived increase in Dalit women's social status (that is, 'positional respect' in many cases), as well as economic benefits flowing in from holding a panchayat post. Just over half of the women (29 women) mentioned that other women were more willing to contest panchayat elections after witnessing these women's political participation. Village panchayat president Lakshmiben from Vadodara district in Gujarat believed that "more women are now inspired to contest elections and believe they can do things. I support these women, for example, by accompanying them to government departments and teaching them and giving them space to get on with their lives. As the SHG leader, I also sit with them and discuss many issues surrounding the panchayat system and its functioning... So, in 2006 three women contested for the president's post." According to a group of Dalit women elected representatives from Thirunelveli district in Tamil Nadu, reservations were necessary for them to gain self-confidence and learn about panchayat administration, which then inspired other women to follow the same path. This change attests to the positive, multiplying effect of reservations for furthering the realisation of the right to political participation of Dalit women. It also confirms that Dalit women panchayat representatives have the potential to create both development and social impacts.

Another encouraging shift for 18 women was that more women were participating in demonstrations and other forms of public gathering organised by local women's groups. For instance, village panchayat president Pushpa from Thirunelveli district in Tamil Nadu was involved in a struggle to shut down a liquor shop that was ruining their families. She achieved this through complaints to the police and union and district panchayat members, and was proud to state that, "Dalit women have grown in their struggle against systemic oppression." Linked to this, a few village panchayat presidents believed that more women were moving or were interested in moving into public spaces through their involvement in the activities of women's groups, SHGs, or village employment. As per Lakshmiben from Vadodara district in Gujarat, "More women today are thinking about their position and representation in every field. For instance, now Dalit women are involved as anganwadi workers and *gram mitras*, whereas earlier I was the only woman from my village working outside my home with the government and in the panchayats." Preetikaben from Anand district in the same state mentioned her role as panchayat president and SHG leader in encouraging women to speak out on their issues in the panchayats and gram sabhas. As a result, women had more confidence and were becoming involved in different SHGs and public programmes, including the gram sabhas, and were even going to higher authorities regarding village issues.

By contrast, only three women elected representatives felt that during their panchayat term women had become more knowledgeable about social issues, rights or panchayat functions. This low number must be interpreted in a social context where knowledge has traditionally been denied to women (as with Dalits), and their education levels are still lower than men's. Dalit women's political participation, therefore, has not yet filled this important gap.

While one-third of Dalit women elected representatives signalled that their political participation had resulted in tangible benefits for women, the remaining two-thirds saw no changes in gender relations. As can be expected, women benamis witnessed no change. Instead, several village panchayat presidents from Surendranagar district in Gujarat underlined the strength of gender norms in women's lives. As far as Banuben was concerned, she was a 'daughter-in-law'[3] of the village, and thus felt it was not good for her to appear and speak in front of so many village members in the panchayat. Sareekaben further pointed out the continuing inhibitions created by gendered perceptions of women's lack of political capabilities, the sexual division of labour, and the immorality linked with women's freedom of movement. According to her, women sometimes upheld gendered practices in order to operate in newly opened public spaces outside their homes:

> In relation to sitting on a chair in the panchayat, women think that if someone 'higher' than them is present, then it is not good for them to sit on a chair in front of that person. If there is an elder brother-in-law or dominant caste elder and a woman wears purdah in their presence, then the woman is considered good. Women also think that within purdah they are 'safe' from men in such a public space as the panchayat, and hence give importance to the practice... Moreover, women who travel outside their villages for administrative work are still called 'bad characters' and accused of neglecting their household duties by the villagers.

The gender norms operative in family life were generally even more invisible to Dalit women due to the internalisation of these norms. Thus, benamis for husbands often did not feel that it was wrong that their husbands took over their panchayat posts and performed all their duties, and did not feel that they faced any discrimination from their husbands. The rigidity of these norms was evidenced in a statement by village panchayat president Chanchalben from Kheda district in Gujarat: "Here everybody follows the traditional gender norms. No change has taken place in this and no change has ever taken place for any women of the village. I know for sure that, till now, not a single woman has been able to do any work without asking their husbands or families."

The extent of this internalisation is perhaps most apparent in the case of Vasantha, a union panchayat member from Cuddalore district in Tamil Nadu:

> As far as I am concerned, my husband is *the* person for me. I cannot look at myself as separate from my husband... I do not like to do anything by myself. That's why I have handed over all my [panchayat] responsibilities to him. And he gives me my freedom and that's why I'm happy... I took part in public functions very rarely and that, too, only with my husband by my side. Besides, if there were any problems in the village, people used to approach only my husband. I simply look after domestic works like bathing the children, sending them to school, purchasing needed household items. I never do anything without asking my husband. I will not do anything that would hurt his feelings. I do what he likes, and what he likes I like. I do not know what happens in this village. My husband also does not share with me, nor do I ever ask him. He manages by himself whatever must be done or faced. That's why I am not interested in knowing about anything that happens.

Dalit women's political participation did not lead to the fulfilment of other strategic gender needs, such as the lessening of gendered restrictions on women's freedom of movement and their political participation, or the removal of purdah in Gujarat. Both villagers and family members still accused the women of immorality for exceeding caste-and-gender limits on their freedom of interaction with others, especially men, and freedom of movement in public. Moreover, several women mentioned that while some small socio-cultural changes have taken place over time in their areas – for example, in terms of dress, purdah or women's mobility outside the home (at least in the case of vocal or assertive women) – no real change has occurred in women's positions in decision-making processes at the village level or higher. Sunitaben, village panchayat president from Anand district in Gujarat, pointed out that, "a woman, be she Dalit or non-Dalit, looks after the household administration and no one opposes her. But if she wants to enter into the panchayat administration, then people say that she doesn't have the skills for administration and hence cannot handle it." A group of Dalit women elected representatives in Ahmedabad district in Gujarat likewise candidly stated, "There have been no changes in gender norms and traditional beliefs... Their husbands are known as the president in the village, and no one gives value to women."

CHANGES IN ATTITUDES TOWARDS DALIT WOMEN FROM THE DALIT COMMUNITY

One envisaged outcome of greater responsiveness by Dalit women elected representatives to the development needs of their Dalit community is that attitudes towards them, particularly gendered attitudes among Dalit men, would change. However, less than one-third of Dalit women elected representatives (48 women or 28.9 per cent) indicated this change.

The most significant shift which 38 of the women mentioned was that Dalits now approached them to represent their developmental problems to government officials. In other words, political participation by a member of the community was linked with an enhanced possibility of their development rights being fulfilled. Village panchayat president Tejuben from Kheda district in Gujarat, for example, felt that it was especially due to her political participation that the Dalit Valmikis were increasingly raising their voices on issues of concern to them. She mentioned how, after receiving requests from the Valmiki community, she regularised the salary of the Dalit Valmiki safai karamchari in the panchayat and added some increments. Exactly half the women (24 women) indicated that Dalits or Dalit women now settled disputes among themselves under the elected women's leadership, or abided by their verdict on conflict issues. As previously mentioned, approaching Dalit women elected representatives for conflict resolution indicated a rise in the recognition of these women's emerging leadership and status in the community. This leadership role was further apparent for five women who specifically mentioned that Dalits have approached them to file their complaints against dominant castes with the police. Finally, the positive example set by 23 women elected representatives had inspired other Dalits to contemplate stepping into the political arena. The significance of these changes can be appreciated in contrast to the gender biases existing in traditional village leadership structures which generally exclude women.

The broader indications, however, are that the Dalit community did *not* recognise the significant role played by Dalit women elected representatives in the panchayats. That is, Dalit women, for all the reasons laid out in the preceding sections, have not yet been able to create an image of positive leadership among the Dalit community despite the past decade or more of reservations. This can partially be explained by the number of benami elected representatives, whose lack of participation meant that there was little impact on the development or social justice concerns of Dalits. Another explanation lies in the continuing economic dependence of Dalits on dominant castes, which sometimes precluded open support for Dalit women elected representatives. As explained by village panchayat president Sunitaben from Anand district in Gujarat, "I speak to people about women's participation in the panchayat, but it has no effect on the Dalit community. If the Dalit community supports me positively, then the dominant caste community opposes me. Moreover, Dalits work on dominant castes' land, and hence they are scared to speak or support me. It is very difficult to bring changes as the Dalit community is dependent upon labour work provided by the dominant castes. So, they have to accept whatever the latter say or else be denied employment."

A third explanation is the continuing patriarchal attitudes among Dalit men: in the words of Dalit elders and male villagers from Thirunelveli district in Tamil Nadu, "The attitude that only men can do anything and that women should not appear in public as their presence is an insult to men is still prevalent in the minds of Dalit men." The absence of changes to gender norms, particularly those limiting Dalit women's freedom of movement, speech and rights within the family, further confirms this attitude. Only a few of these men felt that things were slowly changing and that in future more Dalit women making decisions and functioning independently could be expected. Finally, a fourth point is the lack of awareness raised among Dalit women of their rights: again, in village panchayat president Sunitaben's words, "If we look at the Dalit community, Dalit women's participation can bring change. However, in our area there is no such change happening because Dalit women need to be educated so that they become aware. Along with this, there is a need to set examples to show that other women can also move towards change."

CHANGES IN ATTITUDES TOWARDS DALIT WOMEN FROM DOMINANT CASTES

Finally, Dalit women elected representatives were asked whether their political participation had produced any changes in attitudes from dominant castes in their panchayats that might signal the transformation of 'untouchability' practices or caste norms. Not surprisingly, the least attitudinal changes were registered with dominant castes. Given the socio-economic power they hold over their villages and, by extension, their political power over the panchayats, any significant change in attitudes from dominant castes would signal the greatest shift in caste-class-gender power relations towards equality and respect for Dalit women. Only just over one-fifth of Dalit women elected representatives (35 women or 21.1 per cent) felt that some change in attitudes among dominant castes had occurred.

Three-quarters of these women (26 women) felt that they could interact with dominant castes more because of their holding public office. This is an inevitable change that came from entering a mixed-caste space in the panchayats, given caste segregated living arrangements and the discouragement of social interaction between these two social groups. A little under half of the women mentioned their ability to walk freely along dominant caste streets in the village now (17 women) and being able to wear their shoes while performing official panchayat duties (17 women). The latter two gains are linked to the loosening of untouchability norms which prevent Dalits from 'polluting' dominant caste residential areas with their presence and violating norms accorded to their 'low' caste status by wearing shoes in the presence of dominant castes. A smaller number of Dalit women further noted that dominant caste men did not address them with degrading caste epithets now (11 women), pointing to an increase in the women's social status. Similarly, respect for Dalit women elected representatives' position and status made dominant castes respond positively to invitations sent by 10 women to discuss matters concerning the panchayat administration or village development. And finally, six women mentioned how dominant caste women no longer harassed them when they drew water from the common well/tap.

To what degree were these attitudinal changes long-term and not dependent on the women holding office? And to what degree were these changes directed solely at individual Dalit woman elected representatives, without significantly changing social power relations between dominant castes and Dalits as a whole?

Only a few Dalit women village panchayat presidents such as Tejuben from Kheda district in Gujarat and Anjali from Madurai district in Tamil Nadu mentioned changes to untouchability practices in the panchayats due to their insistence. These types of changes could possibly be longer term, having an impact on successive tenures of Dalit elected representatives. Anjali mentioned, "Before my entrance into the office there was discrimination; for example, Dalits could not wear their shoes nor touch a dominant backward caste person. The two-tumbler system also existed both inside and outside the panchayat office. After my assuming charge as panchayat president, I took special efforts to rectify the untouchability practised by the dominant castes and today we don't experience such discriminatory practices." In a similar manner, Tejuben stated,

> Earlier there was discrimination in the panchayat regarding drinking water, but nobody opposed this practice. Now there is one pot for all and one glass for all to drink water. Even tea is taken in common saucers and refreshments are taken together. I took active initiative in the first panchayat meeting and told everyone

that I am a Dalit and any kind of discrimination would not be tolerated. I replaced the system of separate cups, water pots or glasses with common pots, glasses and cups. And now everybody is using these common items. I raised this concern then because I knew that it has existed for many years in the panchayat and needed to be resolved in the first meeting.

The dominant caste members did not like it, but they knew that they would not be able to oppose her actions as untouchability is illegal, and they feared Tejuben might disclose these practices to government officials.

Most indications, however, show that many of the attitudinal changes in dominant castes were short-term – that is, occurred solely during the women's terms in office – and didn't result in any wider transformations of caste prejudices or a reduction in discriminatory practices against the Dalit community. This is clear from the case of Ramilaben, taluka panchayat president from Vadodara district in Gujarat: despite her speaking out against caste discrimination in public programmes, dominant caste perceptions that Dalits are incapable of panchayat administration still remain. The temporary nature of changes in relations between dominant castes and Dalit women elected representatives is no clearer than in the case of Kamachi, twice village panchayat president from Coimbatore district in Tamil Nadu. She said:

> Because of my participation in the panchayat, a lot of changes have taken place. However, in terms of gender nothing has changed. Likewise, in terms of caste nothing really has improved. For instance, in 2006, this post was declared a general constituency. At that time when I contested, all the dominant caste people came together and voted against me. Already in the 1996-2001 and 2001-2006 panchayat periods, the dominant castes joined together and worked against me. One could see how strong these dominant castes were about aligning with other dominant castes... Ultimately, I could not rectify this caste problem.

While she was initially not allowed to sit on a chair in the panchayat office and function as panchayat president, she asserted her rights and eventually achieved both. However, after her defeat in the 2006 election, she came to know that her chair was removed from the office and that the dominant castes performed a pooja in the office to 'purify' it. Only after this did the next dominant caste president come and sit on the president's chair.

What the above examples reveal is that in most cases dominant castes accorded Dalit women elected representatives positional respect as a means of fulfilling their own economic and political interests. This respect was either temporary or (less commonly) long-term, depending on the extent to which these women fulfilled dominant caste interests. It also depended on the personality of the women and whether they could continue to influence village affairs and maintain relationships with government officials after their panchayat terms ended. In other words, the greater the social capital accumulated by Dalit women through the panchayats, the greater the chance that changes in attitude from dominant castes lingered, though this was only for the woman herself. Even as far as untouchability practices were concerned, the aforementioned changes in attitude indicate how the dominant castes employ 'untouchability' as a strategy of convenience; it is either used to keep Dalits submissive under their control, or discarded when there are gains for them from Dalits' political participation, thereby manipulating it to their advantage both ways.

Moreover, most Dalit women elected representatives in Gujarat and Tamil Nadu confirmed the lack of change in caste relations either towards themselves or towards their community, despite their presence in the panchayats. At most, some active women elected representatives in Madurai district in Tamil Nadu mentioned how, due to their efforts, some untouchability practices in their panchayats had decreased while they were in office. Furthermore, for some women, personal confidence and the economic gains made through the panchayats helped them shift from daily wage labour under others to small-scale self-employment, such as small goods vending or cattle rearing. However, a group of women elected representatives in Surendranagar district in Gujarat elaborated how the lack of socio-economic change among Dalits continued to be reflected in prejudicial attitudes towards Dalit women's political participation:

Other castes never support [Dalit women], even other caste women. Because of the lack of competency and information about the panchayat system, dominant castes always pass snide comments on the [Dalit] women like 'now Dalits will run Gujarat on their labour'. Actually, the dominant castes control all employment and land, and that is why Dalits are always living in fear and behind them... There is no change in this situation of the Dalits. This is because first, the caste system is strong; and second, Dalits are economically poor and have to depend on the dominant castes for labour. The Dalits also depend on them for emergency monetary help [loans].

In Vadodara district in Gujarat and Madurai and Thirunelveli districts in Tamil Nadu, Dalit women villagers equally discounted any major changes to caste norms resulting from Dalit women's political participation in the panchayats. Women in Madurai district noted that, "the discrimination that existed ten years ago still exists today. No change has taken place. It is only the dominant castes who rule the roost." Even in districts such as Thirunelveli with a high Dalit population, and in the village panchayats where dominant castes are a minority, such as where Priya was president, caste discrimination still prevails. In Priya's case, the following attitude held by dominant caste men remained throughout her term: "How can we work under a Dalit woman?" They would just sign the panchayat register and leave the office, refusing to participate in any panchayat meetings, support her in any decision-making processes, or sign panchayat resolutions. In such a situation, she was forced to depend on her husband to execute her panchayat duties. Moreover, when the constituency was declared a general constituency in 2006, the dominant castes pitted the different Dalit sub-castes against each other and, in the end, coerced the majority of Dalits into supporting a dominant caste man for the president's post.

By contrast, Dalit elders and male villagers from Vadodara district in Gujarat and Thirunelveli district in Tamil Nadu were more optimistic about small changes resulting from Dalit women's political participation. Dalit men in Thirunelveli district recounted how "ten years ago women could not even dream of coming out of their houses. Now, though there is still a lot of caste discrimination, the fact that Dalit women are able to face it and go ahead in their [panchayat] duties is indeed a big change." This change, however, was not evenly spread across the Dalit community. Dalit male villagers in Vadodara district noted how change was more noticeable among the more socio-economically 'forward' Dalit sub-castes, while others trailed behind in politics.

What emerged from Dalit women and men as a requirement for any substantial changes to caste norms and practices was the need for changes in the traditional occupations of Dalits in order to ensure economic independence from other castes, as well as greater education, information, knowledge of the laws protecting their rights, social networks and political experience. In addition, women villagers in Thirunelveli district in Tamil Nadu believed, "If women want they can remove untouchability practices from the village, but they need support from society. In particular, support from their husbands and family members is important because most of the time it is they who stop the women from challenging the existing social norms in the village."

Effects on Dalit Women, Their Families and Community

Moving beyond social relations, the political participation of all 200 Dalit women, both those who failed to access as well as those who accessed and participated in panchayat institutions, should ideally result in some positive effects on themselves, their families and their Dalit community. At the very least, it should propel more Dalit women into the political arena, widening the possibilities for social and economic justice.

EFFECTS ON THE WOMEN

Political participation was closely linked with the realisation of these women's 'power within' or ability to participate in and manage public affairs. This was evidenced by over half the women who felt they had gained self-confidence in the process (110 women or 55.0 per cent), while around one-third believed they had improved their leadership skills (62 women or 31.0 per cent). In particular, successfully overcoming obstructions to their participation contributed to the women's realisation of their strength and capacity to deal with matters outside the family. Even for less active women, the opportunity political participation afforded to move outside their homes and enter public spaces to interact with other villagers was an important means of boosting their ability to operate beyond the sphere of the family. The positive effects even extended to two women who contested but lost the panchayat elections: they mentioned feelings of pride for having contested the elections and having received so many votes, thereby recognising their first foray into public life as an achievement in itself.

Greater freedom of movement, greater knowledge and social awareness point to the potential for 'power within', in terms of enabling these women to build social capital, access information and potentially organise to assert and claim further rights. Around one-third of the women felt that they now had more social contacts (75 women or 37.5 per cent), greater freedom to move around in public without accompaniment (63 women or 31.5 per cent), and an increased awareness of the social and political problems in society (59 women or 29.5 per cent). The number of benamis and women who faced caste-class-gender obstructions that effectively curtailed their free political participation explains why these figures are not higher. Dalit women elected representatives in Gujarat highlighted the opportunities participation in the panchayats gave women in terms of acquiring greater knowledge about politics, government departments, government schemes and how to access such schemes, which could help them in terms of securing livelihood-related rights in the future. The women emphasised the rarity of Dalit women having access to such knowledge outside of political participation.

In contrast, the negative effects political participation wrought on the Dalit women were more varied. For 37 women (18.5 per cent), their panchayat experience had brought with it increased fear, while for 30 women (15.0 per cent), it had diminished their self-confidence. This was particularly the case where women lost the elections due to political manipulation by others, or won the elections but faced obstructions and/or derogatory comments as

Dalit women panchayat representatives. The link between the fear attached to political participation and its potentially adverse economic consequences is seen in the case of village panchayat president Leela from Madurai district in Tamil Nadu. Having had her panchayat powers auctioned off and then functioning as a mere benami for the dominant castes, she felt more under the power and control of the dominant castes than previously. She was afraid of attracting any adverse reaction from the dominant castes and yet was forced into this situation because her work in the fields of a dominant caste landlord was at stake. Another example is Urvashi from Madurai district in Tamil Nadu, who after filing her panchayat nomination against the wishes of the dominant castes received threats and saw the attempted murder of her husband. Though forced to withdraw her nomination, she and her family continued to live in constant fear. Their livelihood also suffered, with the family not daring to step outside their home to work for many days. As seen in this case, experiences of harassment or obstructions to participation also led to reduced freedom for 13 women (6.5 per cent) to move around in public, as well as having a detrimental impact on their livelihood.

The remaining effects, all experienced by less than 5.0 per cent of women, encompassed psychological issues such as depression (9 women), feeling they had lost the respect and good will of their families (5 women) and community (7 women). In the words of Kamachi, a village panchayat president from Coimbatore district in Tamil Nadu from 2001 to 2006, "I have faced so many problems, opposition and protests, especially from my family, that resulted in plenty of physical and mental consequences. I have spent quite a few sleepless nights and spoiled my health, leading to mental agony and discouragement. My defeat in the 2006 election by the dominant castes as well as my own Dalits, especially the clerk whom I appointed, has made an awful impact on me." For the six months following the 2006 election, she was unable to participate in any meetings outside and had to remain inside her home due to ill-health.

The loss of employment or threat of the same, as experienced by six women, was a serious concern for daily wage earners who could not afford to reject paid work to fulfil their panchayat responsibilities. In the case of Lakshmiben from Vadodara district in Gujarat, she had to resign from her job as anganwadi worker and lose her regular government salary to become village panchayat president. She did so, feeling she would be able to work more for Dalits in the panchayats, but ended up facing a lot of opposition and two no confidence motions during her term. Now she works as an agricultural labourer. A conflict, therefore, arises between active political participation and more immediate livelihood needs such as waged employment for Dalit women. It is perhaps for this reason that this research shows a fair percentage of housewives entering the panchayats, who would have the time to actively participate, potentially due to less immediate economic exigencies. This suggests that economic stability is another enabling factor in active political participation.

EFFECTS ON THE WOMEN'S FAMILIES

Political participation also had positive effects on the women's families. When compared to the increased respect and social status Dalit women experienced themselves, around double the number of women indicated the same for their families, both from Dalits (109 women or 54.5 per cent) and the broader community (84 women or 42.2 per cent). A probable explanation for this lies in the number of benamis for husbands or male relatives. With their husbands or male relatives adopting a more public role in the panchayat and with government officials, overshadowing the women, and in some cases even coming to be known as 'president' in lieu of the women, their family's social status was enhanced. Even where Dalit women's husbands worked for the dominant castes in the panchayat to ensure the latter's interests, this raised their social status and resulted in at least token respect from dominant castes. This can be seen clearly in the case of village panchayat member Vimalaben from Anand district in Gujarat, who was a benami for the dominant castes through her husband. Consequently, "My husband's representation through me has increased his respect in my family. The [dominant castes] are also happy with my husband because he does what they want."

As far as increased social status among the Dalit community is concerned, the example of village panchayat president Kalaimani from Nagapattinam district in Tamil Nadu illustrates the changing status of even some benamis and their families:

> The Dalit community treats me with respect. They give me and my husband great importance in their family functions. They ask me, for example, to take the marriage *thali* and give it to the groom to tie the knot. Those who arrange the marriage celebration say that the new couple should also live a good married life like my husband and I. Whenever there are any family problems among the Dalits, they seek out my husband or me for advice and guidance. On such occasions, my husband or I call for the concerned persons and reprimand those at fault and help the family to be together... All my relatives also consult my husband on any family matter... Even those Dalits who did not support us in the election now abide by whatever my husband tells them. Last year, it was my husband who kept the accounts of the village festival, submitted the accounts in public and handed them over to the village temple priest. Previously, this would be done only by those appointed by [our dominant caste opponents].

As previously mentioned, in several cases, including benamis, Dalit women's political participation provided a means of increasing family income or employment opportunities (42 women or 21.0 per cent). Granted that, when interviewed, some women might not have revealed information on these economic gains, the fact that only one-fifth of women reported these gains suggests two things: one is that the remaining four-fifths of women were accountable to their constituencies in terms of not receiving economic gains through the panchayat administration; the second is that they lacked power over the allocation of panchayat resources and funds. The types of gains for their families were either material or financial, the former particularly from the allocation of development schemes. From her husband's activities in the panchayat, for instance, village panchayat president Anandhi from Cuddalore district in Tamil Nadu noted that her family could enjoy a newly constructed house. Likewise, village panchayat president Thilagam from Coimbatore district in the same state ensured the allotment of house sites, water pipes and electricity for her children. These trends, although small among the elected women, are still worrying in so far as they indicate the pervasive mindset among all communities, even Dalits as relatively new entrants into the panchayats, regarding the use of political participation as means to economic gain for oneself or one's family and relatives.

As with the personal effects on Dalit women, their political participation also produced several negative effects for their families. Balancing what has been said above regarding economic gains for Dalit women's families, over one-quarter of women (52 women or 26.0 per cent) indicated how their families had suffered economic losses arising out of their political participation: losses in terms of money spent on elections which the women lost, in fighting no confidence motions or other cases foisted against them, or income losses arising from the reduced time spent on paid work due to performing panchayat duties. The financial situation of Jasodaben, a village panchayat president from Surendranagar district in Gujarat, for example, became more difficult after she incurred debts in fighting the no confidence motion mounted against her by dominant castes. Kalaimani, village panchayat president from Nagapattinam district in Tamil Nadu, explained how, to tackle every opposing force in the panchayat, "we had to spend a lot of money from our own savings. We even had to sell our land and house as well, and now we are living in a small hut on government *poromboke* land. After my husband was attacked, we were so frightened that the dominant castes might harm us again that we finally decided to leave our village."

Kalaimani's case also indicates another negative effect on the women's families: fear, as noted by 30 women (15.0 per cent). Tensions and fear arising out of Dalit women's political participation can be seen in the case of village panchayat president Sagunthala from Cuddalore district in Tamil Nadu, who was a benami for her husband, the panchayat clerk. The Dalit candidate who had lost the elections and her supporters continued to create problems for Sagunthala's husband in the implementation of development schemes. In the ensuing conflicts, her husband and father-in-law were attacked and her husband's hand was cut off. A further six women pointed to destruction or damage done to their property during the course of their panchayat term. For instance, when the TV news reported that Rajakumari from Madurai district in Tamil Nadu was prevented from filing her panchayat nomination by three dominant caste men in 2001, these men gathered with their caste men at her house. They pelted stones at the roof of her house, breaking the tiles and damaging the walls with sticks and rods.

In a pattern similar to that of individual women, five Dalit women indicated a decrease in the respect Dalits directed towards their families. Women's families were blamed for the women being benamis for the dominant castes either alone or through their husbands. In one case in Tamil Nadu, some Dalits boycotted a women's family due to a lack of agreement on a common election candidate. In another case in Gujarat, it was the losing candidate and her family who continued to socially boycott the elected Dalit woman's family. A further three women mentioned that their families had been forced to leave their villages: in one case due to threats and harassment from dominant castes arising from the woman's political participation, and in the other two cases due to soured relationships between the women's families and the Dalit community caused by the women being benamis.

EFFECTS ON THE DALIT COMMUNITY

Moving beyond the personal level of the women and their families, and comparable to data on the social impact of Dalit women's participation, the least positive effects of Dalit women's political participation were felt by the Dalit community. That is, while political participation had personal effects, its relative inability to shift power relations is reflected in the smaller effects on Dalits. Hence, just under one-third of women gauged an increase in confidence levels among Dalits (65 women or 32.5 per cent), which was linked in part to the one-fifth of women (44 women or 22.0 per cent) mentioning increased unity among the Dalit community. This was particularly the case where Dalit women had been active panchayat members, thereby bringing development benefits to the Dalit community, including ensuring their distribution to the different Dalit sub-castes. Successful political participation, therefore, tended to promote feelings of community pride and more importantly, a greater confidence in Dalits' abilities to overcome political exclusion and generate change for the betterment of their community.

Specific gender benefits were evidenced by less than one-fifth of the women, who felt more Dalit women now wanted to participate in the panchayats (34 women or 17.0 per cent), and spoke out more in their communities (29 women or 14.5 per cent). When viewed against changes in confidence levels and unity among the Dalit community, Dalit women's greater response to community needs over gender needs is again apparent. Given the extent of patriarchal attitudes among men in general, and emphasis of community over gender, this data is not surprising and reflects overall trends regarding social impact.

When compared to the women who felt their participation had increasingly unified the Dalit community, an almost equal number of women (45 women or 22.5 per cent) stated that their political participation had increased factionalism instead. This is an important point to examine in detail, as only in a few instances did Dalit women mention that jealousy of the women's success or development initiatives caused divisions within the community. Much more common were divisions along Dalit sub-caste lines. Sociologically and during the democratic process, Dalit sub-caste politics manifest as different sub-castes assert their identity and vie for the political power to claim their rights. In this sense, these politics are the first stage in a process by which political power is accessed by those traditionally excluded from such power. Ideally, the next stage would be the creation or consolidation of alliances between different Dalit sub-castes, which is required to collectively and effectively demand social change and economic resources. This does not diminish the challenges of uniting the Dalit community: village panchayat president Kamachi from Coimbatore district in Tamil Nadu stated, "I tried to bring together the Arunthathiyar and Pallar communities to my house or to the office and treated them equally. However, I could not succeed in bringing both communities together... Still, I tried to ensure that balanced benefits went to both groups."

What must be examined further, however, is *who* creates these sub-divisions and *how* these divisions impact the overall development of the Dalit community. Sub-caste politics arising from community assertions are not necessarily negative. What raises significant concern, however, is the number of instances of the dominant castes instigating sub-caste divisions among the Dalits, or exploiting sub-caste politics to indirectly wrest potential power from Dalits. This is because these manipulated divisions often strengthen a sense of caste difference among Dalits that prevents them from organising and exercising political power collectively. As Dalit elders and male villagers in Surendranagar district in Gujarat pointed out, "The Dalit community's influence over the elections has been limited just because they are not organised and don't understand the hidden divide-and-rule politics of the dominant castes. We need to work to reach consensus and overcome sub-caste divisions." In the case of village panchayat member Reshmaben from Ahmedabad district in Gujarat, for example, one dominant backward caste community instigated a Dalit sub-caste not to vote for the sub-caste to which Reshmaben belongs.

Dominant castes also used tactics like boycotts, harassment, threats and even violence against Dalits (mentioned by 13 women or 6.5 per cent) to punish those who supported the women's attempts at independent political participation, and/or to retain political control over the panchayats and resource allocations. The clearest example is again the case of Reshmaben. In addition to attacking her and other Dalits after she was elected as a village panchayat member, the main dominant backward castes also socially boycotted both Reshmaben's sub-caste and the other Dalit sub-caste they had told not to vote for her. Consequently, the Dalits had to travel to the nearest town for all purchases, thereby increasing their expenses. Similarly, village panchayat president Leela from Madurai district in Tamil Nadu, a benami for the dominant castes, reported how dominant castes socially ostracised the other Dalit candidates who contested the elections against her.

They were punished by being denied work in the dominant castes' fields, refused entry into the village streets where dominant castes resided, refused access to drinking water, prevented from buying anything from the village shops, prohibited from grazing their animals in the dominant castes' fields, and not permitted to speak with others.

Interlinked with the negative effects related to caste were those related to gender. Seven women witnessed increasing Dalit opposition to women's participation in the panchayats as an outcome of their political participation, particularly the types of caste and gender-based obstructions they faced. Connected to this, two women observed a decreased confidence among Dalit women on seeing the elected women face obstructions. In both instances, patriarchal norms restricting Dalit women's participation in the public sphere were reiterated. On the one hand, Sunitaben, a village panchayat president from Anand district in Gujarat said, "This is the first time that a woman has been elected on a reserved women's seat in the village. In fact, this is the first time that this is happening in my community." However, on the other hand, "I have been troubled a lot by the panchayat council. That is why other women also feel scared and are unable to think about entering the panchayat and doing the same as me. Also, other women are unsure of support from their families and hence are not ready." An opinion held by the Dalit women and men in the village panchayat where Kamachi was president in Coimbatore in Tamil Nadu was that while Kamachi was a good panchayat leader, "after all she is a single person and does not have any children. So, she could afford to confront the dominant castes in the panchayat". But in their case, they felt they could not do so.

All these negative effects help maintain the inequitable political status quo. 'Divide-and-rule' tactics, harassment and violence emphasise dominant caste male political power and control over the panchayats and punish any Dalit who challenges this. Hence, while active and effective Dalit women's political participation promotes confidence and unity among Dalits, benamis and women whose political experiences engendered negative effects for their communities serve to reinforce and perpetuate the caste hierarchy and patriarchy.

Future Political Participation

Given these social impacts, were the 200 Dalit women willing to contest panchayat elections once more? Significantly, almost three-quarters (145 women or 72.5 per cent) were willing. This is an encouraging sign of the process towards Dalit women's empowerment. At the very least, it signals a shift towards an interest in politics for many women who were new entrants to political life and who had filed nominations largely at the behest of others. This optimism about further political participation included women who had faced numerous obstructions in the panchayats, or had tried but failed to access panchayat institutions. For instance, two-time village panchayat president Kamachi from Coimbatore district in Tamil Nadu, while referring to the pain caused by losing the 2006 village panchayat elections, stated her willingness to serve her people despite the dominant caste opposition she faced. In her words, "The atrocities, discrimination and suffering that my people endure inspire me to work for them, to fight for them. It makes me think seriously and it gives me strength and courage. If I were given one more chance, I will be only too happy to do many things for the development and welfare of Dalit women." Likewise, Rajakumari from Madurai district in the same state, who was forced not to file her nomination in 2001, and contested and lost the 2006 elections, said, "I will continue to contest the coming elections as I want my community to progress in life. Now my community respects me more. Therefore, I am more confident that I will win the elections."

By far the most common reason was women's desire to do more development work for their Dalit community, women or the poor in general. Several women even went so far as to indicate that they would like to move to the higher panchayat tiers or begin a political career as a means to influence the development of their community. In other words, many women linked the exercise of political rights to the attainment of the resources and capacities required to realise a wide range of economic and social rights.

A small number of women also mentioned their wish to remove untouchability, caste discrimination and corruption from the panchayats as motivating factors.

Other Dalit women recognised the link between political participation and empowerment, dignity and respect. They worked to raise the awareness or confidence levels of Dalits, women or the poor, initiating women's leadership, or providing other Dalit women with examples of what they could achieve through the panchayats. For instance, Manguben, who contested but lost a village panchayat member's seat in 2001 in Kheda district in Gujarat, wanted "to show that Dalit women panchayat presidents or members can run the panchayat administration independently and do not always have to transfer authority to the dominant castes." Personal growth or empowerment was also a significant reason for the continuing interest in political participation. Women wanted to gain more leadership skills, political skills and knowledge of political life and development schemes. At the same time, perceptions of the greater respect and dignity they received as elected panchayat representatives drove Dalit women's continuing interest in political participation. As per Hiraben, a village panchayat president from Surendranagar district in Gujarat, "I get respect as a Dalit woman in the village now, and re-contesting elections will increase my dignity."

It was evident from the words of village panchayat president, Amarben of Anand district in Gujarat, that reservations have also created a recognition of Dalits' right to political participation: "I want to contest because it is our right and we should take an interest in [Panchayati Raj], and jump into it for the development of our community." Even a benami village panchayat president, Sagunthala from Cuddalore district in Tamil Nadu, now spoke of her wish to exercise her rights, expressing her slight dissatisfaction that her husband, as panchayat clerk, had appropriated her panchayat responsibilities. Only a few women indicated that they would contest elections once more if the dominant castes told them to do so. Overall, therefore, political participation was viewed as opening more opportunities for personal and community respect, awareness, growth and development.

By contrast, roughly one-quarter of Dalit women (55 women or 26.5 per cent) did not want to contest panchayat elections again, mainly because they were tired of being benamis under the control of others in the panchayats. Women likewise cited bad experiences of political life, including obstructions from dominant castes, their removal under no confidence motions, negative panchayat politics and a lack of support during their terms in office, as reasons for their disinterest in re-contesting. Only a few mentioned personal reasons linked to their capacity to carry out panchayat duties: illiteracy; lack of knowledge of panchayat administration; ill health; old age; being overburdened with household duties; and financial inability. Finally, a small number of women felt they had had their chance at political participation and that someone else should have the opportunity now.

The women's further political participation, however, also required changes. Both women willing and unwilling to re-contest panchayat elections expressed the need for better access to information and training on Panchayati Raj and related laws.[4] Alongside this was the need for training to help overcome caste-class-gender inhibitions to their involvement in the male dominated domain of public affairs. Training aside, Preetikaben from Anand district in Gujarat suggested the formation of a woman's rights forum. The forum could initiate women's leadership in the village on local issues and increase employment opportunities in order to build women's confidence to operate in public affairs and lower the economic constraints to their political participation. At the same time, external support, especially from government officials, was required to create an atmosphere in which they could function in the panchayats with freedom and independence. Kamachi from Coimbatore district in Tamil Nadu clearly specified four types of support: security for Dalit women panchayat presidents; increased salary or travel allowances to make panchayat presidents self-sufficient; government monitoring and support to ensure Dalit women elected representatives could effectively exercise political power without obstructions; and street-wise monitoring once panchayats were reserved to prevent electoral manipulation aimed at stopping active Dalit women from winning reserved posts.

In sum, the women's key priorities were to build their human and social capital, alongside government, non-government and community support to combat discrimination and obstructions in the panchayats. The fact that all these factors link to caste and gender constraining norms in the women's social contexts highlights the need to approach political participation for socially marginalised communities from a more holistic perspective. This would involve understanding the active hurdles posed by the social system to the realisation of the various rights of Dalit women – to education, information, free choice of employment and decent wages, free movement in public and free speech, freedom of association, equality and non-discrimination. Tackling these matters must become part of any government strategy to effectively implement the reservations policy in Panchayati Raj.

Conclusion

Aside from Dalit women's ability to create a development impact through the panchayats, another indicator of successful political participation is their wider social impact in terms of shifting gender and caste power relations towards a position of greater equality. Evidence shows that even active Dalit women elected representatives could challenge and transform power relations in their wider social milieu only to a limited extent. Few structural changes to gender and caste relations occurred as an outcome of Dalit women's political participation. The greatest changes were at the personal and family levels: higher levels of self-confidence, widening freedom of movement and social contacts, increasing recognition of the need for education and information for stronger political participation, and greater status and decision-making power within the family. Individual women who were assertive, independent and able to bring some development impact also noted positive changes in attitude and the respect they were granted. This included Dalit and dominant caste recognition of their leadership capabilities in areas such as conflict resolution. However, this did not lead to any similar gains for Dalits or women as a whole.

In particular, changes in support patterns, respect and dominant caste and male attitudes towards the women appeared to be more transitional. It was expedient for women to hold political positions for it allowed others to secure their own vested interests. Consequently, many women noted an accrual of positional respect as a result of their posts which did not last longer than their term in office. Moreover, positional respect has to be distinguished from the recognition of Dalit women's power and authority, especially as panchayat heads. The dynamics of the interests and power at play in the panchayats were further visible in the patterns of support by dominant castes. Where Dalit women served dominant caste interests in the panchayat by directing the majority of development benefits towards this community, the women were granted instrumental support. Where Dalit women supported Dalit development needs or asserted their right to freely and independently participate in the panchayat, dominant caste support was withdrawn and obstacles were placed in the women's paths instead.

The transformation of gender and caste biased attitudes towards Dalits and women, however, was minimal. The continuing prevalence of benamis and obstructed political participation, Dalits' economic dependence on dominant castes, the relative lack of socio-political awareness, and internalised gender and caste norms countered any social transformation. The direct link between Dalit women's representation in the panchayats and structural change, therefore, appears to be weak. In fact, some might argue that reservations in Panchayati Raj have resulted in new methods of reinforcing caste hierarchy and patriarchy at the social and institutional level. Some of the women's experiences detailed in this and previous chapters would seem to reinforce this argument. At the same time, in the absence of Dalit women's participation in local governance, it can also be argued that the divide between Dalits and others on key development and social indicators would be even wider.

All this can be contrasted with a statement made by former prime minister Manmohan Singh, where he said that reservations for women "constitutes a historic measure for gender equality. It has brought about a significant shift in public policy and in social attitudes towards women."[5] The experiences of Dalit women indicate that there is still a long way to go to attain gender and caste equality in India. Much more serious and substantive efforts are required before positive social attitudes towards women, Dalits and Dalit women become a reality. Political representation alone is not a sufficient enough empowering tool to eradicate caste-class-gender discrimination and promote social, economic and political equality. Wider systems of support and protection for Dalit women in local governance are vital: for example, education, economic development, promoting their social organisation, rights awareness, capacitation trainings, and zero tolerance leading to government action to remove caste-class-gender obstacles to these women's participation. This must be complemented by widespread government and non-government led education initiatives to openly discuss, condemn and transform discriminatory caste and gender norms. In other words, social transformation requires an altogether different level of engagement within the Panchayati Raj system not only for Dalit women, but also for all relevant government and non-government stakeholders.

Notes

1. Vijayalakshmi V., "Citizenship, Differences and Identity: Dalit Women and Political Inclusion", *ISEC Working Paper 147* (Bangalore: Institute for Social and Economic Change, 2004), p. 16; Inbanathan, A., "Affirmative Action and Dalits: Political Participation in Panchayats", *ISEC Working Paper 138* (Bangalore: Institute for Social and Economic Change, 2003), p. 14.
2. Tambiah, Y., "The Impact of Gender Inequality on Governance", Human Development Resource Centre, *Essays on Gender and Governance* (New Delhi: UNDP, 2003), p. 76.
3. Dalit women who marry men from other villages in Gujarat are considered 'daughters-in-law' of their husbands' villages and accordingly face several restrictions on social interaction, particularly with other male villagers. For example, they are not supposed to speak in front of their elder brothers-in-law or village elders, are expected to strictly observe purdah in public, should

not wear shoes in front of male villagers, should not sit with their husbands in the presence of villager elders, should not speak loudly in public, and so on.

4. Training sessions and information on panchayat administration, the roles and responsibilities of elected representatives, available development schemes, and so on. Other types of trainings mentioned, to a lesser degree, were laws related to the panchayats, elections and Dalit rights, how to handle politics, especially in the higher panchayat tiers, social awareness, public speaking and leadership skills.

5. Prime minister Manmohan Singh's speech at the East Asia Gender Quality Ministerial Meeting (New Delhi, 06.12.2007), reported in "We are Committed to Providing Quotas for Women in Governance", *The Hindu*, 07.12.2007.

8

ADDRESSING OBSTRUCTIONS IN THE PANCHAYATS

The police initially refused to accept my complaint. They only proceeded with it when I returned with legal representation through [an NGO]. My case is currently pending in court. I am determined to continue with the proceedings. In fact, I have been threatened again following my refusal to drop the complaint, and so I've filed a second legal complaint. This case is also pending.
                                             – Sunitaben, village panchayat president,
                                                             Anand district, Gujarat

Sunitaben used various tactics to overcome attempts to obstruct her work as a village panchayat president in Anand district in Gujarat. Several panchayat members from a powerful dominant caste or benamis for this caste, as well as dominant caste village leaders, tried to block her panchayat decisions, obstruct her work and take benefits for themselves throughout her tenure. She explained, "There is opposition to women from panchayat members because no one – non-Dalits, Dalit men, or husbands – likes to share power with a woman."

In panchayat meetings, she used her authority to override opposition and pass resolutions. "During discussions on any resolution, members gave their views and opinions, but opposed any resolution for village development…they never used to accept my decision on any issue." However, while she was able to push through resolutions, people, particularly the vice president, later created obstacles for the implementation of development works such as the laying of new water pipelines. The lack of support from her own community exacerbated this situation.

In response to development related problems, Sunitaben approached government officials such as the TDO and DDO, as well as the local MLA. The MLA promised to resolve the problems, but Sunitaben felt that he only helped the dominant castes causing delays in the development project. "[The local MLA] promised to help get electricity poles put up for the Dalit locality. He wrote a letter to the police, but side-stepped negotiations with [the dominant castes] who were refusing to allow electricity poles to be put in their fields. Without this, it was not physically possible to put up the poles... He told me that I had to work out the problem myself because it involved my community." The project was not completed.

Sunitaben faced two no confidence motions during her tenure, one due to alleged corruption and the second over allegations that she had cut and sold a protected forest tree. She approached government officials in both crises. She stated, "After the no confidence motion brought against me [over the alleged forest wood scam], I approached the district authorities and other government officials. Though I had to make repeated visits, the TDO and DDO finally came to investigate the issue." They found her innocent. From then onwards, officials knew and supported Sunitaben, but she still had to repeatedly visit government offices to get her work done. She also strategically sought advice from government officials to strengthen her political skills and overcome panchayat problems.

Sunitaben continually tried to engage those who opposed her. Her perspective was, "If I have to spend five years with them, I can't keep grudges and not talk to them." She sought practical solutions to remove obstacles. For instance, she removed the water pumps that a dominant caste group was improperly using for irrigation, and which were the reason for their opposition to a fishery contract in the village pond. However, she was also not afraid to take formal action. She filed a police complaint when two dominant caste individuals verbally abused, physically assaulted and threatened her with death in retaliation for her removal of the water pumps. As she explained in the quote at the start of this chapter, the police only filed her complaint on the insistence of a local NGO. Despite the threats to make her drop this compliant, she continued to persevere with the case.

When the opposition to development works or allegations of corruption troubled her too much, Sunitaben contacted the Congress party state president and asked him to intervene. He agreed to contact panchayat members, the TDO and the DDO. She later felt, however, that the NGO she approached for guidance had been more useful. Sunitaben's husband also played a strong role in her efforts to seek redress for obstructions or to overcome them and enable her effective political participation. He had been elected panchayat representative two times in the past, and gave Sunitaben support and guidance. Her confidence and skills also came from her experience in running an SHG, and her involvement with two Dalit oriented NGOs. While she and her husband cultivated their own marginal land holding (1.2 acres), their annual household income – ₹16,800 – remained very low.

Sunitaben's experience reflects many of the common struggles that Dalit women panchayat representatives face throughout their tenure. Her story highlights how independence and strength can induce obstructions. At the same time, women can engage with various actors to expand their influence in decision-making and development. Her persistence with government officials and their support proved crucial in surviving the no confidence motions. These factors also contributed to her empowerment, allowing her to gain the skills, knowledge and political allies needed to achieve development goals. Her awareness and creativity in using the resources around her, such as her reaching out to an NGO to ensure that her police complaints were registered, were essential. The power of knowledge is a striking insight in her case. Another insight is the link between caste and power that resulted in the MLA and police refraining from confronting dominant caste interests.

This chapter draws out key aspects of Dalit women's experiences in seeking justice for obstructions faced in local governance. Previous chapters have detailed their experiences in accessing and assuming their roles as equal leaders in the panchayats. Colouring these experiences have been a myriad of obstructions, including discrimination and violence, through which various individuals have sought to exclude Dalit women from decision-making power. In this chapter, the women's responses to these violations are examined. An assessment of the Indian state – particularly its law enforcement and district administration – is made with regard to the fulfilment of its duties to both prevent and respond to obstructions against Dalit women in the panchayats.

The Indian state is obliged to ensure that all persons are equal before the law and enjoy equal protection of the law. The state is also required to protect all persons against discrimination on grounds such as caste, colour, sex, religion, political or other opinions, national or social origin.[1] More specifically, per Article 46 of the Indian Constitution, state actors should monitor the functioning of the panchayats and distribution of resources in a way that promotes the educational and economic interests of Dalits, and protects them from social injustice and exploitation. Various state institutions are entrusted with these obligations, along with more general duties to protect human rights. Law enforcement agencies and district bodies with devolved powers and duties from state and national ministries hold primary responsibility for ensuring that Dalit women can freely exercise power within Panchayati Raj institutions.

The state has also established various institutions with specific human rights monitoring and advisory functions, such as the National Human Rights Commission (and corollary state commissions), the National Commission for Women and the National Commission for Scheduled Castes. These commissions are charged with safeguarding and protecting rights guaranteed under the Indian Constitution, as well as under various laws passed by the Parliament and international human rights laws enforceable by courts in India. They can investigate violations of human rights on their own initiative or on the basis of a complaint, and can summon and examine witnesses and documents through the civil courts. However, they lack the powers of a criminal court and thus cannot enforce their findings.

Civil society institutions, social networks and informal adjudication processes also require consideration. Those excluded and discriminated against by dominant culture and formal state institutions often resort to mechanisms and remedies outside of formal state structures. It has been noted that, "[l]ocal traditional systems of adjudication are commonly perceived to be far preferable to formal court systems. They are approachable, affordable, familiar and culturally relevant, led by community leaders and framed on principles acceptable to the community majority."[2] In this case, however, the community majority is often the dominant castes, whose decisions are likely to reinforce the inequality and oppression of Dalit women. On a smaller level, the women's family and Dalit community may provide social security, social control and operate as primary mechanisms that define and protect rights. Traditional support networks and systems, however, do have restrictions. While they often provide a major element of protection and security, they may also reinforce violations against women, rather than render justice for them.

This chapter examines the level of accountability demanded of actors who violate the political rights of Dalit women. The identification of effective channels for socio-political change requires an understanding of how Dalit women dealt with discrimination and exclusion while asserting their right to political participation, and how those obliged to protect the women's rights fulfilled their duties. Problems in relation to the provision of remedies to Dalit women for obstructions to their participation in local governance point to important areas for future support.

Most Dalit women (88.5 per cent) experienced at least one obstruction while accessing and/or participating in the panchayats. These obstructions occurred at different stages: 26.2 per cent at the pre-election stage right up until the announcement of election results; 27.9 per cent at the post-election stage when attending and participating in meetings, and fulfilling other panchayat duties; 17.4 per cent when women attempted to advance development initiatives in the panchayats; and 28.5 per cent as continual overt discrimination, including 'untouchability' practices, from other elected panchayat representatives. Notably, prevailing gender norms may have contributed to why some of the remaining 11.5 per cent of women did not view behaviour that prevented them from exercising political power as an obstruction.

The previous chapters have shown that at both the pre-election and post-election stages of political participation, systemic factors weigh against Dalit women's participation in local governance. Although the women acquire political authority upon their election, they are denied the right to exercise it. The underlying reasons become apparent when one examines the number of women elected representatives facing discrimination and untouchability, as well as the obstructions they face while trying to advance development, particularly for their communities and women. When the women's political authority is denied, it is not simply due to their lack of skills or education or sound economic base. The underlying reasons for obstructions are the women's 'low' caste and gender status and the high stakes other panchayat members have in acquiring the panchayat's economic resources. If obstructions at the pre-electoral stage are a pre-emptive strategy, those in the post-election stages are a protectionist strategy.

When obstructions to their political participation occurred, Dalit women were more likely to deal with the issues themselves or take no action. Consequently, those who violated the women's rights through these obstructions were not brought to account. Significantly, Dalit women reported only 28.7 per cent of obstructions to someone outside of their immediate family. In most cases, women preferred to approach state actors (24.4 per cent of obstructions) over non-state actors (4.2 per cent of obstructions) for redressal.

Reasons for Not Seeking Redress

Almost all the women who faced obstructions and did not approach external actors for redress pointed to personal limitations as the reason for not doing so. However, there is a clear structural dimension to these limitations. By far the most common reason why Dalit women approached no one about obstructions was uncontested social norms. Of the women who did not seek redress, in around a third of obstructions (124 obstructions) their reasons centred on a belief in their inability to oppose, or acceptance of, gender and caste-based discriminatory norms. Women felt that they had to accept obstructions because "I am a woman and unable to function independently", because "this is what happens to you when you are a Dalit", because "untouchability practices are part of life", because "I did not think it was possible to make a complaint against a government official". An illustration of this is the case of Reshmaben, village panchayat member in Ahmedabad district in Gujarat. She said, "I never had tea or water in the panchayat because I know that as a Dalit I am not allowed." Despite being vocal and strong in her political participation and willing to confront the aggressive dominant castes in her village to the extent of filing a FIR against them, she could not challenge these untouchability practices.

Similarly, as noted in a previous chapter, during the election process a woman's husband, political party representatives or dominant caste community members often canvassed for her in her stead. As 28 women did not view this as a problem, they did not take any action in response to this kind of obstruction. This reveals how the women perceived their role, both as candidates for the election and as elected representatives, seeing themselves as only the front for other actors to exercise the political power conferred through panchayat posts.

Patriarchal norms also influenced some women's desire to function in a 'peaceful' or subservient manner through compromising (in 15 obstructions) and a reluctance to bring dishonour on themselves or their families (11 obstructions). The prevailing culture was to blame women for caste or gender-based assaults and other obstructions committed against them, stigmatise women in public positions as immoral, or for the women to feel that their inadequacies had led to the obstructions or complaints against them. Their disadvantaged position in an unequal socio-economic system also influenced the women's silence. This manifested in the women's lack of awareness of the law and redressal mechanisms (4 obstructions), a lack of money to seek remedies (11 obstructions) or pressure from their supporters, family or husbands to do nothing (9 cases). For example, Jasodaben, a benami village panchayat president in Surendranagar district in Gujarat, approached the police after she was removed from her post through a no confidence motion. However, she was too scared to respond to their questions because the police personnel were too aggressive in asking questions and she did not know anything about the law.

A significant number of women (62 instances of obstructions) stayed quiet out of fear – for personal, family or community safety, for livelihood security or for fear of being removed from office. Leela, a village panchayat president in Madurai district in Tamil Nadu, was forced into inaction through a fear for her safety as well as her livelihood, after her dominant caste landlord employer forced her to sign away her land deeds to keep her under his control. In the case of Saraswathi, who contested a member's seat in a union panchayat in Coimbatore district in Tamil Nadu, dominant castes supported another Dalit woman nominee and threatened the Dalits on the election day, causing them to flee their village and abstain from voting. Fear of dominant caste retaliation prevented Saraswathi from making a complaint. Village panchayat president Gangaben from Anand district in Gujarat experienced complete control over her actions by a dominant caste man feared by all in the panchayat for his association with murder and kidnapping. She stated, "Because the Valmiki community are very much suppressed, Lakshmanbhai could use threats to cut off my husband's livelihood. We did not dare to speak against or without the permission of Lakshmanbhai. He knew this, and that is why he chose me... The entire village is so scared of Lakshmanbhai that they always say that if they do anything without his permission, he will burn down their houses."

Fear of retaliation for speaking out against obstructions was another factor. As seen in the previous chapter, Ramilaben, an active and independent taluka panchayat president in Vadodara district in Gujarat, limited her participation levels and remained quiet in the face of obstructions. This was not out of fear for her safety, but more a fear of being removed from office. The dominant caste panchayat members tried to bring a no confidence motion against her on two occasions, and used this as a constant threat. In her own words, "I could not do anything against the opposition because members used to pressurise me, and I always felt the threat of a no confidence motion."

Other Dalit women did not approach any external actors to counter obstructions because they felt that they would not receive justice or a remedy (56 obstructions). For some, this assessment stemmed from their lived experience as a Dalit woman. For others, this was reinforced through futile efforts to influence panchayat decisions or to receive redress for other problems. Pushpa in Thirunelveli district in Tamil Nadu repeatedly tried but failed to get the police to take her complaints of obstructions during the election period seriously. She therefore conceded defeat and did not approach the police with subsequent post-election obstructions to her functioning as the village panchayat president.

Perceptions that the obstruction could be either ignored or resolved by the women themselves, or with their husband's support, determined the actions of another set of women (45 obstructions). Dalit women's attitude of perseverance and accepting opposition is summed up by panchayat president Sunitaben from Anand district in Gujarat. She mentioned that as women are generally opposed in society, they are used to facing problems. Hence, Alamelu from Nagapattinam district in Tamil Nadu, contesting the union panchayat elections, ignored the verbal abuse and threats she faced on the election day from supporters of the opposing party candidate. Shyamala from Cuddalore district in the same state also ignored the demands of the dominant backward castes that she accept their choice of vice president in order to gain their votes in the village panchayat elections.

This reasoning is also evidenced by those who directly refused to comply with untouchability practices and ignored the resulting opposition. Preetikaben, a village panchayat president in Anand district in Gujarat, ignored dominant caste pressure and went against social norms. She said, "I was told by dominant caste members not to sit on a chair or remain seated when an elder or member of the dominant caste entered the panchayat office. However, I did not listen to them, and I did things that seemed proper to me." Sunitaben, mentioned above, acted in a similar vein:

> In the first meeting of the panchayat, two dominant caste elders and panchayat members said that from now onwards we would sit on the mattresses instead of chairs, and the panchayat peon then

removed all the chairs and spread the mattresses in the panchayat office. They decided this as they did not want to imply any equal status by sitting on a chair alongside a Dalit woman. After some time, when my husband came to drop me at the panchayat office, he saw the mattresses and told me to raise this question in the panchayat meeting and press the point to conduct all meetings while seated on a chair. First, I inquired about the whereabouts of the chairs owned by the panchayat and ordered the peon to remove all mattresses and put the chairs back in place. The peon responded that there are not enough chairs in the panchayat for everyone. I replied, 'Bring all the wooden chairs which are lying outside the panchayat room. From today onwards, all the members will sit on chairs.' Other women, both Dalit and non-Dalit, then said to me, 'How can we sit in front of dominant castes and elders?' I told them, 'We will be in purdah, but from now onwards we will sit only on chairs in every panchayat meeting.'

Some women took obstructions in their stride as emerging political actors. Instead of directly seeking redress, they built their political base and experience, and showed results to sustain their position and silence any opposition. They also considered practical action that served their community's interests more effectively than approaching state actors for remedies. As Annammal, a village panchayat president in Madurai district in Tamil Nadu, shared, "Whatever the types of discrimination I faced, I did not take them to heart. Amid all these problems, my objective was to go beyond them and devote myself to providing developmental works for the welfare of the people." Kamachi, a village panchayat president in Coimbatore district in Tamil Nadu, dealt with opposition to her political participation by equipping herself with knowledge, allies and skills, and by providing a counter-force. She shared, "My struggles in the initial days were short-lived. I joined hands with the opponents of my opponents. That helped a lot. I met villagers personally, discussed their needs with them and subsequently worked towards fulfilling their needs." She also confronted panchayat members and leaders within her panchayat and in other village panchayats when necessary. Other members, including the vice president, tried to block all her work and raised party pressure against her. The vice president abused her, refused to sign documents and used other delay tactics to inhibit her work. In response, she said, "I was very objective and very transparent about money matters and people saw that my hands were clean. I took immediate action when people brought problems to me. I was able to bring down the corrupt vice president with the help of other members [through a no confidence motion]."

In the case of Preetikaben, a village panchayat president in Anand district in Gujarat, she overcame opposition from the dominant caste panchayat members by directly confronting her opponents when they challenged her in meetings. She undertook development works to ensure the satisfaction of her constituency. She also took a more pragmatic approach to problems. For instance, when she saw the dominant castes encroaching on 75 acres of panchayat land, she pushed the Dalits to plough the land so that they could claim their share. While she repeatedly approached government officials in relation to implementing projects, she did not raise her mistreatment in the panchayat. Clearly then, many of the women who struggled with or overcame obstructions without recourse to redressal mechanisms had no belief in the ability of available mechanisms to afford them justice. Instead, they saw persistent action as the only means of achieving their goals, particularly that of their community's empowered participation and development. This indicates a great potential to secure political power, development outcomes and social change. At the same time, it also points to major deficits in the current political system: the lack of recognition of Dalit women's disadvantaged social status and its impacts on effective political participation; and following this, effective measures against obstructions and towards the enforcement of the law for Dalit women in the panchayats.

Remedies Sought for Obstructions

Dalit women sought redress from state actors for 24.4 per cent of the obstructions they faced. The focus on approaching state actors indicates the women's recognition of the fact that, as elected representatives, they are entitled to use state institutions to resolve conflicts. It also throws light on the greater importance placed by women on the formal legal-political system, as they preferred it over traditional power structures to protect their right to political participation. This suggests that as socio-political and legal awareness increases, more and more Dalit women may use available legal and political mechanisms to seek justice and claim their power and authority in local governance.

Of all the state actors approached, the women gave importance to local government officials dealing directly with the administration and developmental activities of the panchayats – block/taluka/district development officers, project officers (Tamil Nadu) or district development commissioner (Gujarat) for 36 obstructions, the police (26 obstructions) and the district collector (23 obstructions). These three sets of actors occupy important positions of authority in the executive arm of governance. By contrast, few women approached the taluka or district panchayat president or the District Social Justice Committee president for redress, and even fewer approached officials like the talati/clerk or other members of their own panchayats.

In addition, five cases of obstructions were taken to the tahsildar, election mamlatdar, State Election Commission or the National Commission for Scheduled Castes and Scheduled Tribes. Women directly approached the courts concerning only four obstructions.

Women clearly favoured formal complaint mechanisms over informal or traditional ones. Various explanations for this include a lack of faith in the responsiveness of the latter to their needs, or the realisation of the responsibility of state actors to remedy any violations faced. They, therefore, rarely approached Dalit elders or their community for redress (only for seven obstructions). More common was to appeal to political actors for support. The link between the panchayats and political parties was evidenced in 14 cases of obstructions where political party actors, largely party presidents or MLAs, were approached. NGOs received a remarkably small number of complaints (seven complaints of obstructions). One woman also approached a Women Panchayat President's Federation in Tamil Nadu. A potential gap thus exists in terms of current NGO outreach to rural Dalit women for awareness and support.

The Dalit women who did seek external support to remedy obstructions or violations of their right to political participation were largely driven by their sense of justice, their reputation, and desire for active and free participation. Over half of the women sought redress for this reason. The other major motive was linked to their awareness of their status and needs as Dalit women. They wanted to create precedents that recognised their leadership, demonstrated their presence in the political system, and inspired others. In other words, the women felt the need to prove themselves, to stand up to discrimination and oppression and to reclaim their position as equals in both the panchayat and society. These reasons provide further insight into how Dalit women approach not only participation in panchayat governance, but also the daily struggles and hardship they face as Dalit women in their social contexts. At the same time, the responses of both state and non-state actors approached by the Dalit women also impacted patterns of whether, and from whom, the women sought redress.

Responses by State Actors to Complaints of Obstructions

A positive trend is that a number of state actors approached by the women sought to help them overcome obstructions. Women received advice on ways to resolve the problem (8 obstructions); their cases were investigated and the problems resolved (24 obstructions); or the women's complaints were registered, investigated and a compromise or solution was reached (16 obstructions). For instance, the district collector helped Janaki, a village panchayat president in Cuddalore district in Tamil Nadu, overcome opposition from the vice president and ensure the construction of a road she had planned. On another occasion, the TDO upheld the disputed decision of Natya, a village panchayat president in Nagapattinam district in Tamil Nadu, to dismiss the village water supplier for poor performance. There were also several similar matters resolved after an FIR was registered through a complaint to the police. A further 13 cases of obstructions, half of which involved police investigations, resulted in judicial proceedings.

However, in most instances the responses Dalit women received from state actors were less positive. Pushpa's case illustrates how multiple state actors neglected their duties to address her complaints. The police refused to take any action against the husband of a Dalit candidate who prevented Pushpa from filing her nomination for the village panchayat president's post in Thirunelveli district in Tamil Nadu, forbade her from putting up election posters, and threatened her with murder and other crimes. She reported that, "the police showed no interest in helping me even though I was forced to go to the police station many times." Higher police officials filed the complaint and investigated, but took no further action. After the announcement of the election results, the husband of the unsuccessful Dalit candidate and his relatives assaulted Pushpa and her family. Further complaints to the police yielded no results.

As panchayat president, Pushpa also faced continual challenges from the dominant caste vice president and other panchayat members, who constantly opposed her every move and obstructed the fulfilment of her responsibilities. The vice president tried to take over the leadership of the panchayat by falsely accusing her of misappropriating panchayat funds, stopping the supply of electricity and water to Pushpa's house, forcing her to remove her son from school and pressurising her to resign from her post. After one serious incident, Pushpa filed a police complaint, and complained to the BDO and district collector as well. However, officials forced her to compromise. She made no further complaints after that, noting, "I did not take other problems concerning the vice president's cheating behaviour to the police. I was aware it would mean more expense, and no action would be taken against the dominant caste men. I suffered it all within. Ever since I decided to enter the panchayat, I am fighting against injustice and atrocities... Be it a Dalit or a non-Dalit woman, our participation in the panchayat administration is never appreciated in this patriarchal country. Then what is the

value of social justice here?" Pushpa had the strong support of
her family and was determined to persevere in her panchayat
activities, but she felt that they lost so much joy as well as money
and property in the process.

Around a quarter of the responses from state actors involved
further obstructions to the women's efforts: they were chased
away, no action was taken, assistance was refused, or bribes were
demanded of them (36 obstructions). Pressure or advice not to
file a complaint or pressure to compromise made up 26 responses
from state actors. Finally, 22 of the women's complaints were
registered, but the police refused to either investigate the matter
or file a charge sheet. This highlights areas of serious concern
regarding state accountability in fulfilling responsibilities to ensure
the effective functioning of panchayats.

GOVERNMENT OFFICIALS

As mentioned above, it was government officials overseeing
development and panchayat governance who Dalit women most
often approached for redressal. These officials were more likely to
render support for the implementation of development works than
redress obstructions, exclusions or discrimination. In fact, some
government officials suggested that their sole jurisdiction was over
issues of panchayat administration, development schemes and
funds. An assistant director for panchayats in Tamil Nadu put it
this way,

> There could have been caste discrimination or violence [in the
> panchayat]. But what we see in the panchayat representatives is
> that they give more importance to administrative problems and
> not to any discriminatory practices. We cannot go and force them
> to talk about such problems. And that is none of our business
> either. It is not our duty or responsibility at all to respond to caste
> problems. If any such problem was brought to our notice, I would
> make it clear that it is none of my business. We monitor only
> Dalit women's administration.

A BDO from the same state similarly pointed out that officials
had no duty to act on complaints of caste or gender discrimination.

Even where officials like a TDO in Gujarat recognised that Dalit women elected representatives faced caste and gender discrimination, they still insisted that they could not intervene in these "very sensitive and emotional issues for the community". The situation of husbands undertaking panchayat duties for elected women representatives evoked a similar response from the TDO: "Government officials cannot do anything in relation to this as it is the social rule that women are controlled by their husbands." Furthermore, these perceptions coloured the functioning of the Social Justice Committees in Gujarat. While acknowledging that important issues like atrocities are discussed by these committees, a TDO admitted that the decisions taken by these committees are rarely implemented in the panchayats.

Thus, while constitutional provisions prohibit caste and gender discrimination, and reservations in the panchayats aim to correct historical and structural discrimination against Dalits and women, government officials leave it to those affected by discrimination to deal with such problems. No monitoring system is in place to ensure the proper and effective functioning of women elected to the panchayats or panchayat committees. This is despite the obvious, negative impacts of such discrimination on Dalit women's ability to effectively undertake their panchayat responsibilities, and on democratic panchayat governance in general. It can be argued that government officials are thus being negligent in the execution of their mandated supervisory roles over the panchayats.

Effective responses from government officials were more likely due to Dalit women's persistence, the cultivation of long-term relationships, effective development work and strong allies. Strategic relationships with higher government officials and the women's assertion of their authority also proved effective in spurring officials into action. In some cases, however, the officials' submission to dominant caste power and complicity in reinforcing this power were also clear. Kamachi, a village panchayat president in Coimbatore district in Tamil Nadu, sought out allies in the administrative system to help her achieve her objectives. She shared the following:

As I realised at an earlier stage that I was being discriminated against because of my caste and gender by [government] officers and others in charge of panchayat related works, I approached the district collector directly for all matters. Upon his orders, the officers had no choice but respond to me. Not all the officers cooperated, however. They went on the instructions of the [dominant caste] vice president to deny my requests... After meeting the collector and getting his advice, I met the other officials. I tried my best to resolve the problems I faced in my panchayat and get explanations about politics and panchayat works by consulting with the collector and other officials when they came for the meetings.

Kamachi noted that other Dalit and women leaders were not respected in the government offices. However, "despite this treatment from government officials, I did not lose heart. I went ahead boldly without minding all these petty problems. Even before the officials offered me a seat, as soon as I entered the office I would take the chair and sit down." As Kamachi indicates, the norm was for government officials to disregard and disrespect Dalit women. General discriminatory practices were prolific in the panchayats. For instance, when Hiraben, a village panchayat president in Surendranagar district in Gujarat, visited the TDO in his office she was told to send her husband, and that she need not speak to him herself. During her term in office, the TDO would visit her house and speak directly to her husband on panchayat matters.

In addition to government officials discriminating against Dalit women, they also reinforced dominant caste power over the panchayats and existing social inequalities. Thilagam, a benami panchayat president from Coimbatore district in Tamil Nadu, was permitted to attend panchayat meetings only if government officials were visiting. Officials would merely greet her and then proceed to discuss panchayat matters with the dominant caste vice president and clerk. She recognised that this was a breach of state duties, but did not know how to change the situation. Shardaben, a village panchayat president in Vadodara district in Gujarat was removed from her post shortly after she began efforts to function a little more independently. On learning that the dominant caste panchayat members and talati had falsified her resignation letter, she approached the TDO with her complaint. She narrated, "He told me that I couldn't continue as president because I was not attending the panchayat meetings and had not been able to do anything in the panchayat. He said that all other members were against me, and there was no need to inquire further into this matter. I finally lost hope and stopped inquiring".

Annammal's negative experience was with a tahsildar. The police and BDO acted on her complaint following a member of her panchayat council occupying land meant for public drainage. However, "before the drainage could be built, [the panchayat council member] occupied the place again. I then made a complaint to the tahsildar. He was bribed and, therefore, spoke in favour of [the member] and questioned me, 'Whose land is that? Is it your father's property?' I had to leave the place in tears." Active and vocal panchayat members like Reshmaben from Ahmedabad district in Gujarat shared similar experiences. In her case, she faced persistent obstructions from actors within and outside of the panchayat council because she was a Dalit woman. She visited the dominant caste TDO and DDO to get justice against caste discrimination and atrocities in the panchayat and to move development work forward, but never received any support. They thus reinforced the status quo and further violated Reshmaben's right to political participation.

Existing socio-political networks and patronage were part of the reason why some government officials supported dominant caste power. For instance, Jasodaben, a village panchayat president from Surendranagar district in Gujarat, was removed through a no confidence motion after she took independent action for Dalit development for the first time. She contacted the TDO, but he took no action and eventually told her nothing could be done. The dominant caste man who engineered her removal replaced her as president. He had contacts in government offices higher than the taluka level. In Jasodaben's words, "No official gives priority to poor people. And among the poor, who cares for the Dalit poor?" These networks were particularly relevant at the local level, where the most accessible state actors are the talatis/clerks, who frequently work closely with the vice presidents to serve the interests of their caste and themselves.

Overall, the prevailing patriarchal caste culture makes it extremely difficult for Dalit women to approach government actors, most of whom are dominant caste men. In accepting others assuming the women's responsibilities and being discouraging when the women do approach them, the response of government officials only serves to entrench a lack of accountability in enabling Dalit women's political participation. These officials serve as an interface for women moving into public affairs and decision-making, and can play a key role in supporting or resisting a cultural shift to increase the social and political space for Dalit women representatives to exercise their powers in local governance. Their responsibilities, therefore, must be a central feature of targeted efforts to enable Dalit women's access to and effective participation in Panchayati Raj institutions.

POLICE

The police demonstrated a gross neglect of their duties on many occasions. While some women's complaints resulted in a registered FIR, investigation and a court hearing, this often required great persistence on the part of the women, and support from other actors such as NGOs. In other cases, the police simply operated as another obstruction, rather than a force of law. They often seemed submissive to dominant caste influences or were complicit in reinforcing dominant caste power through their action or inaction. The women's lack of faith in and fear of the police, as well as their own lack of confidence in engaging with them, were clear.

Police inaction following the women's complaints was a common occurrence. Kamachi, a village panchayat president in Coimbatore district in Tamil Nadu, approached the police to complain about the persistent threats and abuse she faced from various political party members, both in public and in front of her home. The police sought to appease her without filing any complaint or investigating it. Rajakumari also failed in her attempts to have the police consider her complaint. Dominant castes physically prevented her from entering the government office to file a nomination for the post of union panchayat member in Madurai district in Tamil Nadu. They also assaulted her and damaged her property. Despite one attack on her home resulting in visits from officials and police protection, the police refused to act once she filed a complaint. According to Rajakumari, "No further action was taken and the police seemed to have accepted a bribe from the dominant caste men. When I inquired about their progress (on the case), the police simply told me to be quiet and wait." Likewise, the case of Sunitaben detailed at the outset of the chapter provides another example of police negligence. It was only when civil society pressure was forthcoming that the police agreed to file Sunitaben's complaint in an FIR.

Situations also arose where the police ostensibly succumbed to powerful local elites due to patronage or corruption. Leela's experience as a village panchayat president in Madurai district in Tamil Nadu highlights the entrenched power and domination of dominant castes, and the impunity that they enjoy from the state. As noted in a previous chapter, dominant caste villagers tried to secretly auction off Leela's panchayat powers while also holding her house deeds as a guarantee for her cooperation. Once news of the auction appeared in a state newspaper, the district collector immediately issued a warning to the dominant castes against obstructing Leela's political participation. The local police initiated an inquiry into the incident. Consequently, an FIR was filed against 21 people, including the seven landlords taking part in the auction and a local AIADMK district councillor. They were arrested and then released on bail. However, no further action was taken against the accused.

In addition to being subject to dominant caste forces, the police also colluded with dominant caste co-options of power. This was the situation that Vijaya faced. She was a semi-bonded labourer and benami village panchayat president for her employer in Madurai district in Tamil Nadu. Along with her husband and her children, she was completely subject to the control of her landlord, prohibited from leaving the premises without his permission or from receiving visitors. He put her up as a candidate for the SC reserved panchayat president's post. She was elected, but had no role except affixing her signature as directed by her employer.

Four months after I was elected, a panchayat member lodged a complaint with the police saying that I did not attend panchayat meetings regularly. When Arumugam (landlord) learnt of this complaint, he instructed me to tell the police that I was fully involved and that all duties were in my hands. One day as I was working in the fields, a policeman came and took me to the police station for an inquiry. As per the instructions given, I told the police that all panchayat powers and responsibilities are in my hands. At that time the police officer said, 'what you have said now should be told not only to the police, but also to anyone who happens to inquire about this'. They then got my signature on a piece of paper. That is the reason why I do not talk to anybody about anything without my landlord's permission.

Vijaya's situation reflects Dalit women's fear, which prevents them from raising their voices against clear violations of the law and their human rights. Many Dalit women and their families were afraid of raising complaints against the conduct of the dominant castes through the formal state system. Behind this was their fear of the dominant castes and their lack of faith in the state system to respond impartially. However, other women showed some willingness to approach the police concerning disputes within the Dalit community. It is also these cases to which the police seemed more responsive, as Thilagam's experience as a benami panchayat president for the dominant castes in Coimbatore district in Tamil Nadu illustrates. Due to her inability to bring development and other panchayat services for Dalits, the Dalit community took issue with her.

"Tensions built up between me and them, and finally ended in physical assault. They used to come drunk, stand in front of my house and scold me by hurling abusive words at me, saying that I, together with my husband, had made big money by holding the panchayat position and that I didn't do anything good for the Dalits." On one occasion, Thilagam was slapped and pushed down, and her husband beaten. When complaining to a dominant caste village elder did not achieve anything, Thilagam and her husband went to the police with a complaint. "The police intervened and told the Dalits to make peace with me. The Dalits who created the problem then asked pardon from me. Thus, without making any written complaint, the problem was resolved." In contrast, she stated that, "regarding problems created by the dominant castes, I could never think of approaching the police with any complaint... I simply could not do anything against the dominant castes."

COURTS

Thirteen women demonstrated a willingness to seek judicial remedies for violations of their right to political participation by dominant castes. Of the six cases completed at the time of the research, five resulted in a verdict in favour of the Dalit woman. This was the case for Lakshmiben, a village panchayat president in Vadodara district in Gujarat who successfully faced two no confidence motions brought by the dominant caste vice president and panchayat members. She was an active SHG leader who never accepted discrimination and sought to claim her rights. The vice president brought a no confidence motion against her alleging irregular attendance in panchayat meetings and involvement in corruption, all because she refused to support his own corruption. The TDO and DDO conducted an enquiry and found these allegations to be untrue and reinstated Lakshmiben. The same people then instigated all the panchayat members to bring a second no confidence motion against her. She approached the TDO and DDO again for justice, but they said that they could not help her because all the panchayat members had voted against her. Lakshmiben, unsatisfied with this response, approached the Ahmedabad High Court. The high court found all allegations against Lakshmiben to be baseless and ordered her reinstatement as president.

For most Dalit women, however, the court process is expensive and inaccessible. Lakshmiben is the exception, not the norm. She noted her stable economic situation: both her husband and brother-in-law were ONGC labour contractors, and she had previously been an anganwadi worker. She stressed the expense of her struggle for reinstatement, including ₹50,000 for engaging a lawyer and other court costs: "We could face these challenges, but what about the mostly uneducated Dalits? ... It was easier for me because I had the money and contacts, but it is not the same with all women. That is why Dalit women need to be educated about Panchayati Raj and why it is necessary for them to participate in the panchayats. They should have legal knowledge and support to encourage their participation." Thus, judicial successes such as hers should not be underestimated as they provide precedents for shifting the underlying culture in the panchayats. However, their minimal utility for rural Dalit women facing obstructions is an issue.

Seven other cases were pending hearing in court at the time of these interviews. The women who chose to pursue these court cases likewise alluded to an array of factors – especially political allies and knowledge, some prior public experience, education, a reasonably sound economic base, the support of husbands – enabling them to pursue legal remedies. Vanitaben from Ahmedabad district in Gujarat was committed to formal action. "I want to teach them a lesson," she stated. She withstood pressure from the dominant caste villagers to withdraw her nomination for the post of village panchayat president and accept their 'consensus' candidate. However, she later discovered that a dominant caste person withdrew her nomination without her consent. Vanitaben pursued redress through several avenues, each without success. The police refused to file her complaint because it concerned the elections, and therefore did not fall within their jurisdiction. The district collector told her to complain to the mamlatdar in the Election Commission. An election officer and mamlatdar told her to approach the court. Her other appeals, including to the State Election Commission, were also to no avail. Based on these negative responses dismissing her serious complaint, she hired a lawyer to file a legal case regarding both the fraudulent withdrawal notice and the conduct of the officials she had approached. Two other Dalit women who faced a comparable situation filed a joint case with her. The case was brought for hearing in the Ahmedabad High Court twice, with no action resulting. The high court returned the case to the district court to be heard there first, with the hearing scheduled at the time of the interview.

For Jayalaskhmi, vice president of a union panchayat in Thirunelveli district in Tamil Nadu, her background as an active political party member gave her the confidence and knowledge to fight for justice through the judicial system. She acquired knowledge about panchayat administration through her political party, and knew of legal remedies for misconduct in the panchayat process from government trainings. She filed her complaint concerning the president blocking the implementation of a road construction project sanctioned in her area with a non-responsive BDO and then the deputy superintendent of police (DSP). Finally, she brought this matter before the court. Likewise, Reshmaben, a village panchayat member from Ahmedabad district in Gujarat, had an economic base strong enough to be able to pursue legal action through the judicial system. She filed a complaint under the *SC/ST (PA) Act* following the violence instigated against her and other Dalits by dominant castes on the announcement of the election results in her panchayat.

The judicial process, however, is vulnerable to manipulation by the dominant castes. This was the experience of Sareekaben, an elected village panchayat president in Surendranagar district in Gujarat. Her case demonstrates the extent of the control dominant castes can exercise, including over government and judicial institutions.

Sareekaben lives in an area dominated by an aggressive and controlling dominant caste community that acts without regard for the law. Both she and her husband had prior panchayat experience, owned some land and were relatively economically stable. She was removed through a no confidence motion instigated by this dominant caste on allegations of a misappropriation of funds. She met with a host of government officials and the local MLA to oppose the motion, but they sided with the dominant castes and insisted they could not help. She then hired a lawyer to fight her case for two years. The power of the dominant castes, however, proved too strong. Stay orders she acquired were overturned through the efforts of the dominant castes and other Dalit panchayat members, once involving a bribe to the court. After this, Sareekaben went to the high court to seek reinstatement. At the time of the interview, the court case had not been finalised. She stated, "The dominant castes have money and contacts within the police station, bank, taluka and district panchayat, right up to the State Legislative Assembly. In such a situation, any person – no matter how courageous/determined – becomes tired of fighting and loses hope … the dominant castes' influence is everywhere. Laws remain only for namesake. If any incident takes place, their phone call reaches the police before the case itself does."

Her case reinforces the pervasiveness of dominant caste power in local governance and law enforcement mechanisms today. At the same time, it also highlights the possibilities for judicial redress when coupled with other factors like community and family support, finances, self-confidence, knowledge and awareness.

Engagement in judicial processes left some women feeling empowered when they had victory, and they were insistent about the need to stand strong against dominant caste oppression and power. However, the impact that the successful pursuit of judicial redress had on the women has to be balanced against the enormous time and financial resources required to take their cases through the court system. Long delays, court costs and lost income while pursuing the case negatively affected the family's economic base. There were also emotional and psychological consequences. Some of the women emerged with further psychological damage, were disillusioned by the process, increasingly fearful and had lowered self-confidence leading to their withdrawal from the public domain. This largely mirrors the findings of other research, and exposes Dalit women's limited access to judicial redress mechanisms.[3]

OTHER PANCHAYAT REPRESENTATIVES

Dalit women rarely approached other panchayat members for redress. This was because it was most commonly the vice president or president – where women were panchayat members – who were instigating problems for the women. The perspective of a dominant caste vice president in Kheda district in Gujarat embodies a view on Dalit women commonly held by dominant caste panchayat members. He said there's "no need to ask [the

Dalit women president] anything because she doesn't have any knowledge about the panchayat. She doesn't have any new ideas; she has only the skills of using a spade the whole day. They (Dalits) don't know anything about their development and the panchayat administration except working in the agricultural field the whole day." Kalaimani, a village panchayat president in Nagapattinam district in Tamil Nadu, reported similar experiences with union and district panchayat members. These members did not respond to her requests; rather, they refused to release funds for her panchayat, ignored and disrespected her. The plight of union and district level panchayat representatives was highlighted by a head constable at the SC/ST cell in the office of the DSP in Gujarat. He discussed the dilemmas the police face in maintaining order and administering the law: "Politically, there is a lot of pressure – pressure from political parties and MLAs of the ruling party – and yet the police have to maintain law and order. Also, there is less neutrality in investigations. In Gujarat, even the DSP is afraid of the taluka panchayat president (normally a political party member). Hence, what to do in this situation? What is the remedy?"

In sum, the responses of state actors to Dalit women facing obstructions in the panchayats evidence how those employed to maintain law and order, and monitor the panchayats and their administration, instead seem to reinforce unequal caste-class-gender power relations. By their actions, including further obstructions to the women's functioning in the panchayats, government officials, police and political representatives disregarded their responsibility to ensure the implementation of decentralised governance without discrimination and with accountability. Instead, they discriminated against Dalit women through their negligence and a narrow interpretation of their duties, state policies and systems. In doing so, they were often complicit in reinforcing dominant caste male power. Some succumbed to forces of patronage, corruption and entrenched dominant caste power, as seen in the statement given by the head constable at the SC/ST cell in Gujarat, quoted above. In addition, their direct actions, including silencing women and refusing to hear their claims, denied the women access to justice for violations of their right to political participation.

This is a charged context, with traditional forms of gender and caste-based power hierarchies taking precedence and imposing significant limits on the extent to which Dalit women are able to enjoy formal posts of leadership. All actors see the women's social identity, first and foremost, as Dalit women, and not as elected representatives. Yet despite the negative impact systemic obstructions have on Dalit women's political participation, and the way they undermine the integrity of the local governance system, state efforts towards reform are weak. The failure of state mechanisms to respect and protect Dalit women's right to political participation in Panchayati Raj falsely sets Dalit women up to believe there is a space for them in decision-making, and also reinforces a sense of their own incapacity and weakness when they fail to enjoy that space. The lack of effective access to remedies for violations of their right further reinforces the message that while Dalit women may now have access to political seats, it does not mean they can actually wield power. In this sense, dominant forces, both state and non-state actors, continue to collude with and maintain the structural discrimination against, and exclusion of, Dalit women.

Responses by Non-State Actors to Complaints of Obstructions

Of the few Dalit women who approached non-state actors for remedies, in 58 cases non-state actors advised or pressurised the women not to file a complaint or to reach a 'compromise'. For a further 23 obstructions, the non-state actors approached did not respond at all or provided no useful response. Together this shows that just over two-thirds of the responses received from non-state actors did not support Dalit women in achieving effective redress for obstructions. Non-state actors helped women reach a compromise or solution for only 25 obstructions. Finally, for 11 obstructions, non-state actors encouraged the women to persevere in their efforts to access or participate in the panchayats. Essentially, then, only just over one-fifth of non-state actors took positive action to aid Dalit women in confronting and overcoming obstructions. The vast majority, however, undermined or ignored the women's pleas for support and advice.

DALIT ELDERS AND LEADERS

The support extended to Dalit women elected representatives by internal community mechanisms seems weak. Only rarely did Dalit women approach Dalit elders for support in dealing with panchayat related obstructions. Dalit elders supported Preetikaben, a village panchayat president from Anand district in Gujarat, in her mobilisation of the community to demand support from the TDO and DDO for village reconstruction following heavy rains. By contrast, due to the social ostracisation of her family, Sunitaben, another village panchayat president from the same district, received no support from Dalit elders in her attempts to overcome opposition to Dalit development initiatives in the panchayat council.

For a number of Dalit women, their community elders simply reinforced dominant caste instructions and pressurised the women to concede to their demands. Pressure lay on Dalit village elders to conform to dominant caste interests through fear, often given their own dependence on dominant castes for their livelihoods, or for reasons of self-interest or manipulation by dominant castes. Kamachi, a village panchayat president in Coimbatore district in Tamil Nadu, recognised that her family or Dalit leaders would not help her overcome the obstructions she faced. On the contrary, "They only tried to tell me that I should be submissive to the enemies ... they wished me to be a dummy in the hands of the dominant castes." She further explained, "When I broke away from the control of the dominant caste panchayat members, my family asked me to accept the demands of dominant caste leaders." A similar situation existed for Jasodaben, a benami village panchayat president in Surendranagar district in Gujarat. She was removed by a no confidence motion after taking her first active steps for Dalit development.

> I expected that if I told the elders and my kin, then they would
> do something. But they replied that this problem had been

created by the panchayat council and that I should approach the panchayat [for a solution]. When I approached the panchayat vice president, he told me to ask for forgiveness and that I should prostrate myself at his feet. When he said this, I decided that it was better to resign now instead of asking for forgiveness and lying at their feet. All the [Dalit] elders asked why I didn't ask for forgiveness. But I wouldn't do that.

FAMILY MEMBERS

Support from family members, however, was a different story. Many women reiterated the enormous support they received from their husbands and families, allowing them to withstand obstructions and participate more effectively in the panchayats. Reshmaben, a village panchayat member in Ahmedabad district in Gujarat, noted, "My husband has always helped me understand my role and responsibilities as a panchayat member… I was able to face the challenges because of my [sub-caste] community's support and my husband."

On the other hand, some Dalit women did not recognise the need to take action against obstructions when their husbands and male relatives used them as benamis, or they were reluctant to make negative comments against their husbands. The reinforcement of gender roles relegating the women to domestic duties and allowing their husbands to participate in panchayat governance in their place was evident in a number of cases. Their vulnerability in the family meant that it was all the more difficult for women to fulfil their role as panchayat leaders. Family members extended their control over the women in this new public domain, and in doing so failed to support the women's emergence as independent actors.

POLITICAL ACTORS

Political actors such as local MLAs and district political party presidents gave mixed responses to Dalit women's appeals for help in overcoming obstructions. For some women, they provided political guidance or directed the obstructers to recognise and support the women in their roles. Generally, however, even where political actors expressed an intention to take remedial action to support the women, action did not follow. Sunitaben's experience, recounted at the outset of the chapter, is one illustration. The MLA was sympathetic but not able, or not prepared, to stand against the dominant castes obstructing her. Similarly, Reshmaben, a village panchayat member from Ahmedabad district in Gujarat, found political actors largely unhelpful. She met the MLA, district Congress party president and BJP district delegate on a variety of issues including dominant caste encroachment on community land and an atrocity case she filed following an attack on Dalits after her election to office. While these political actors indicated that they would speak to others on her behalf, no action resulted.

Nonetheless, a few women showed a strong aptitude for using the political system to overcome obstructions to their effective participation. Ramilaben, a taluka panchayat president from Vadodara district in Gujarat, responded to opposition from the dominant caste vice president through her persistence and active participation in the panchayat council. She also appealed to different political institutions and individuals, and built her networks. Political actors helped her further develop her knowledge of panchayat politics and form political strategies to overcome problems. They lacked the authority and political will, however, to take stronger action and demand respect for her and her authority. They also only supported her because she was so active and strong, and had a solid understanding of politics and a strategic approach. In terms of support, Ramilaben recounted, "Generally, if a woman approached the party with difficulties, for guidance or to discuss development works, she was not given any attention. But the higher ups in Congress helped me, giving advice and sending an All India Congress Committee (AICC) member to help me. This was because I am an active woman and understand some politics, knowing who to approach at what time... The lower level [Congress] party members in the panchayat council never supported me. They never respected women in meetings." An incident that backs up her statement is her discovery of a plot to remove her from her post, and her complaint about it to the taluka-level Congress president. He helped her develop a political strategy to ensure the motion failed. Incentives were given to Congress members to be absent when the no confidence motion was planned to ensure a quorum was not present to pass the motion.

In a second incident concerning false allegations of corruption made by a Dalit panchayat member, Ramilaben wrote to the Congress party national president Sonia Gandhi, saying something along the lines of 'the 33 per cent reservation policy was given to women by Rajiv Gandhi's government, so why is it that women were given no space in the Congress party?' In response, an AICC member instructed the district Congress president to go to the panchayat to resolve the problem and to tell the other Congress panchayat members to cooperate with Ramilaben. The district Congress president did so. However, obstructions from other panchayat members continued until the end of her term. Ramilaben believed the Congress higher-ups also knew this, but they wanted her to remain a face of the party and not become an active party worker since she was a Dalit woman. She said, "That is why they supported me, but only in a superficial way – they didn't make things change for me within the panchayat council."

NON-GOVERNMENTAL ORGANISATIONS

NGOs played a small but positive role for Dalit women. They supported the women in writing appeals to government officials, accompanied them to police stations to take legal action, provided lawyers and offered moral support. Village panchayat president Annammal from Madurai district in Tamil Nadu, for example, believed that much of her success and ability to counter opposition from both dominant castes and other Dalits was due to the support she received from her husband, the local youth movement and an Arunthathiyar women's movement. However, Ramilaben, referred to in the previous subsection, was disappointed by the lack of support she received from women's organisations. Despite daily information in the newspapers about the expected no confidence motion against her, she said that not a single women's organisation helped her. This raises questions around an NGO's role in aiding Dalit women through knowledge development, confidence and leadership building, and direct action to redress violations against the women participating in Panchayati Raj institutions. Many NGOs claim to support marginalised groups – women, Dalits – in enjoying their civil and political rights, yet Dalit women often fall through the gaps. There is insufficient recognition of their specific needs and priorities, and a lack of strategies to effectively respond to the obstructions they face through formal and informal mechanisms.

OTHERS

Rajakumari from Madurai district in Tamil Nadu went to Chennai to meet a representative of the National Commission for Scheduled Castes and Scheduled Tribes (NCSCST) to seek urgent redress when dominant castes prevented her from filing her nomination for the post of union panchayat member, damaged her property and committed other crimes. This was after the police failed to take adequate action. She said, "They asked me what had happened. However, no step has been taken so far to bring the culprits to justice ... Despite approaching so many people, I received no justice."

Very few Dalit women resorted to approaching institutions such as the State or National Human Rights Commissions, the NCSCST, or the National Women's Commission, to redress discrimination and other obstructions to their political participation. This is not surprising given the institutions' advisory nature, and their distance from local level governance. However, there is scope for these institutions to play a stronger role in hearing and redressing Dalit women's complaints and monitoring government implementation of the reservation policy. Their reach to the panchayats is crucial given the number of Dalit women, Dalits and women for whom reservations have meant they now have a stake in the equitable functioning of local governance. Concurrently, a greater awareness of these institutions and their roles, processes and remedies is required for women at the local level.

In sum, very few non-state actors – in the community, the non-governmental sector or the political realm – have stood by Dalit women as they seize opportunities to take on greater public responsibilities in the political sphere, an endeavour proved to have a major learning curve. Political actors have not stepped up and used their power to redress obstructions and confirm Dalit women's place as equal panchayat representatives. Dalit elders have not stood in solidarity with their women representatives, helped to cultivate their leadership or break through the traditional tools of exclusion used by dominant castes. NGOs have not developed a visible and active presence to facilitate Dalit women exercising their authority in panchayats, or their access to information, advice and support with regard to accessing redressal mechanisms.

The power of both caste and patriarchy are again prevalent here. Dalit elders and politicians often seemed unable to stand against caste forces. Economic vulnerability or dependence may play a role in dictating the position of elders, while politicians seem to have succumbed to forces of patronage and political survival, courting support from the most powerful lobbies in the panchayat constituencies. Informal power structures, premised on caste, class and gender, ultimately hold sway. For those within the Dalit community, patriarchal resistance to supporting the women's independent functioning also remains strong. Women thus encounter men both obstructing them and reinforcing obstructions when women turn to them for help. The result is to isolate and demoralise the women further. The refusal to remedy wrongs sends a message to the women that they are operating outside their rightful boundaries and should retreat to the domestic realm.

Still, Dalit women viewed support from non-state actors as a prerequisite to their effective participation in the political sphere. A group of Dalit women elected representatives in Cuddalore district in Tamil Nadu said the following: "A separate forum for Dalit women elected representatives is needed to enable better participation in Panchayat Raj, but it must be a forum of different groups – groups comprising Dalit elders, Dalit panchayat members, husbands and relatives of the Dalit woman president – with experience and knowledge to guide us on how to approach panchayat matters. Their support is necessary, and we must plan some schemes in order to get their support." Therefore, in the larger patriarchal caste context where dominant caste power operates, the women viewed solidarity and support from Dalit men as necessary in enabling the space and possibility to function in the panchayats.

In Conclusion: Impunity and Gaps in the State System

Overall, the majority of Dalit women remained silent in the face of obstructions, including discrimination and other violations of their rights. The predominant reasons for this silence were the fear of dominant castes, a lack of faith in state or non-state actors to provide legal redress, and social conditioning to the effect that there was no way to remedy the situation. Generally, remedies for violations of the right to political participation and associated rights were not available, accessible or effective for the women. Nonetheless, driving the actions of several women were the need for justice and a determination to succeed in the panchayats. They exposed themselves to significant risks and equipped themselves with the political skills and knowledge to take charge of their posts and drive development. Personal characteristics combined with economic resources and a supportive family proved critical to Dalit women's readiness to seek redress for obstructions and their success in doing so.

The Dalit women who did seek remedy for obstructions to their political participation exhibited a greater willingness to approach local government officials and the police than non-government and community actors. An increasing readiness to use the formal state system indicates a growing awareness of the state system and its mechanisms. It also points to a corresponding interest in transferring power from the informal to the formal sphere. A state response that only reinforces the old informal power hierarchies then becomes even more disillusioning. The responses that women received showed that dominant caste male power remains intrinsic to state governance and law enforcement institutions at the local level. The pervasiveness of this power was evident in the extent of the obstructions from dominant caste individuals, and even more so through their effectiveness in preventing Dalit women from seeking remedies. The collusion between state and non-state actors then underlay the impunity with which Dalit women's right to political participation was violated.

IMPUNITY

The Indian state is accountable to its citizens for the effective administration of laws and policies to protect and fulfil their fundamental rights. Access to justice, therefore, is central. Dalit women must be able to access remedies for violations of their rights before a court of law or the appropriate administrative mechanism. This research, however, showed state actors consistently and persistently refusing to monitor the panchayats to eradicate benami representation and prevent caste-class-gender discrimination. This refusal extended, in some cases, to a persistent denial of the very existence of the problem itself. As an assistant director of panchayats in Tamil Nadu said, "In our country and in the Panchayati Raj system, there is no caste or gender discrimination. Only when there is discrimination or trouble, we will have to look for a solution. When there is equality in our country, where is the need for monitoring?" Others recognised the issues, but attributed the problem to the weak capacity of Dalit women or to social norms over which the state has no control. This is yet another instance of state actors, to whom Dalit women turned for assistance, violating their rights directly.

All these responses of state actors promote impunity. Impunity refers to "the impossibility, *de jure* or *de facto*, of bringing the perpetrators of violations to account – whether in criminal, civil, administrative or disciplinary proceedings – since they are not subject to any inquiry that might lead to their being accused, arrested, tried and, if found guilty, sentenced to appropriate penalties, and to making reparations to their victims."[4] Impunity arises from a state's failure to meet its obligations to investigate violations, take measures to bring perpetrators to justice and provide victims with effective remedies, and take other necessary steps to prevent the recurrence of violations. Over half of the responses by state actors following Dalit women's appeals to them to redress panchayat-related violations suggest state failure in these areas. There is ostensibly a lack of political will to meet their state duties concerning Dalit women. Both the actions of state actors as well as their inaction point to the systemic nature of caste-class-gender discrimination at the local level and within the state system.

Impunity exists because of gaps at several levels in the state system that preclude Dalit women's effective political participation and access to effective remedies for obstructions. National and international laws provide clear human rights standards; gaps, however, occur at the implementation level. The legal and institutional structures through which human rights get interpreted and implemented limit the extent to which Dalit women can effectively make claims and have them realised. The law concerns the operation of power and authority, and extends beyond legislation and the judiciary to informal codes of conduct and corollary mechanisms for dispute resolution. Institutional structures, namely government administration and law enforcement agencies, interpret laws and policies for implementation. However, people enter into political processes through which they claim rights using both formal and informal channels. Formal channels include legal cases to push for the interpretation and enforcement of the law. Informal channels include people's knowledge and political skills applied through collective action to claim rights.

LEGAL STRUCTURES

The formal legal framework for understanding the right to political participation was outlined in the introduction to this book. Informal laws that exclude Dalits from society and from political institutions of power, however, continue to exist. This creates a conflict whereby formal laws are interpreted and applied in contradiction of informal social codes based on caste and gender. Informal codes regulate community conduct and define the boundaries of responses appropriate to women and men of different castes in different situations. Dalit women and other local actors frequently spoke of the social norms that dictate what Dalit women can and cannot do. For example, Dalit elders and male villagers from Surendranagar district in Gujarat shared, "Whether our woman president is working, or is in a meeting at the taluka or district levels, she is always in fear ... The dominant castes don't like a Dalit woman to be elected. Women, especially Dalit women, face lots of obstacles like their husbands not allowing them to leave the house and their lack of speaking skills. If a woman opposes anything, then it becomes a big issue and all the men raise allegations against her that she is going outside the social rules and traditions." These norms are enforced by their families, their Dalit community, the dominant castes and state actors through their interactions with the women. The women also seemingly 'accept' and self-enforce informal norms out of fear of the negative social consequences of challenging these norms.

Hence, while Dalit women increasingly see state actors as the relevant and appropriate channel for redress, this does not necessarily mean that they are free from the informal codes that underlie dispute adjudication. In fact, the strong resistance to Dalit women's participation evident in this research highlights that these norms have readily transferred to formal state structures and underlie much of the decision-making regarding the women's complaints. This also reflects the tendency for the distribution of power and authority in political relations at the local level to be more hierarchical and embedded in local social structures and norms. The problem thus starts with the informal codes that govern the interpretation of laws and policies, which then penetrate institutional structures of implementation.

INSTITUTIONAL STRUCTURES

At the level of the interpretation and implementation of the law, on which political authority in the panchayats is built, institutional responses are predominantly based on caste, class and gender discrimination. Powerful, particularly dominant caste, men's agenda to maintain their stranglehold on power and resources is furthered by other institutional obstacles such as corruption, patronage and prejudice. "Petty corruption by officials works in tandem with patronage systems. Patronage blends with exclusive personal networks and clan or ethnic allegiances, which proliferate within power-broking institutions in many, if not most societies, to the exclusion and detriment of those without access to them."[5] The consequence of this web of patronage relations is that state actors breach their core legal obligations to the Dalit women who approach them for redress. They do so by reducing the protection and services that they are obliged to provide for Dalit women citizens. Deeply embedded social attitudes that belittle and demoralise Dalits and women serve to reinforce the connections between officials and the powerful, mostly dominant caste, men seeking to influence state processes, and ultimately reinforce traditional patterns of exclusion and rights violations.

The political will of government officials to implement institutional reforms that advance the right to political participation for Dalit women thus appears weak. While making appearances of compliance with new laws, policies and mechanisms, state actors do little to push forward substantive change or reinforce new policies by adjusting acceptable practices. Rather, police and government officials enforce traditional social codes, whether out of fear of dominant caste forces, prejudice, their own caste affiliations, or corruption and self-interest. Officials often come to view the law as a means of protecting their own power rather than protecting citizen rights, particularly in relation to Dalits where the law has served as an instrument of control and social engineering. This is arguably evident in this research where officials acted on behalf of dominant caste elites and were indifferent or even hostile to the rights of the most marginalised and excluded social groups. As one author asserts, "[w]here a climate of impunity becomes established, authority not only fails to protect the excluded, but comes to abuse them."[6]

POLITICAL PROCESSES

Dalit women have a key role to play in ensuring the effective enforcement of the law to enable and protect their access to the right to political participation. Given the aforementioned structural impediments, the realisation of their rights will necessarily require Dalit women to stand against violations and assert their rights as equal panchayat representatives. Currently, there is but a small percentage of women who feel empowered enough to recognise and act against violations of their right to political participation. As one report on enhancing access to human rights for the excluded highlighted, "[w]here exclusion is historically entrenched, groups may internalise the prejudices of the dominant groups regarding their 'inferiority' as a way of rationalising their status. Internalisation of inferiority is a barrier to contemplating remedial action of any sort."[7] Compounding this situation are the financial resources and livelihood insecurities limiting women's responses to discrimination and other obstructions. These areas require holistic redress.

Nevertheless, some Dalit women are claiming their rights through other means. They are building their own skills and political networks, participating in Dalit organisations, women's federations and SHGs, filing legal complaints and starting to seize the power inherent to their political posts. In doing so, they are pushing open spaces within the local public realm for other women. Political parties and NGOs, in particular women and Dalit organisations, have a far greater role to play in this process. Efforts to support dialogue, knowledge and skill building, mobilisation and solidarity are essential in helping Dalit women increase the space for their effective political participation. Further concerted efforts are required to weaken and eliminate the impunity surrounding the violations of their right to political participation. The state must invest in the comprehensive training of its personnel regarding their obligations under international and Indian law. Intermediary institutions such as national human rights institutions also can play strong monitoring, capacity development and advisory roles to state institutions in ensuring the effective political participation of disadvantaged groups, including Dalit women. A shift within state institutions must occur, in the process ensuring that legal disciplinary action is taken against perpetrators in the state system. This includes civil complaint procedures to redress administrative complaints regarding misconduct in the panchayats or by the government officials responsible for their effective operation.

There is also a need to explore and prioritise methods that increase the number of Dalit women seeking redress for obstructions to their political participation. Where the majority currently opt against engaging with both state institutions and non-state redressal mechanisms, the factors underlying their decisions need to be addressed. Collectives of Dalit women panchayat representatives could provide a great source of strength. Enlightened state actors could champion their participation and engineer a change in the dominant culture. Ultimately, through long-term action on multiple fronts, political, legal and institutional elements can coalesce in creating a supportive and enabling environment for Dalit women. These women elected panchayat representatives could then exercise their rights and fulfil their responsibilities, working with state actors to obtain equal and fair access to justice and development. At the same time, democratic processes and spaces, alongside a culture of human rights, would be enhanced to the benefit of all Indians.

Notes

1.   Article 26, *International Covenant on Civil and Political Rights 1966.*
2.   International Council on Human Rights Policy, *Enhancing Access to Human Rights: Summary* (Versoix: ICHRP, 2004), p. 51.
3.   See Irudayam, A. et al, *Dalit Women Speak Out: Caste, Class and Gender Violence in India* (New Delhi: Zubaan, 2011); Haan, M., *An Analysis of 112 Judgements of Special Courts for SCs and STs (PoA) Act Cases* (Hyderabad: Sakshi Human Rights Watch, 2005).
4.   Orentlicher, D., *Addendum, Updated Set of Principles for the Protection and Promotion of Human Rights Through Action to Combat Impunity*, UN Doc. E/CN.4/2005/102/Add.1 (2005), p. 6.
5.   International Council on Human Rights Policy, supra note 2, p. 39.
6.   *Ibid*, p. 2.
7.   *Ibid*, p. 3.

9

CONCLUSION

More and more Dalit women should contest the elections and become elected to the panchayat, and help the Dalit community become liberated from their bondage. Like the dominant castes, all the Dalit sub-castes should join hands and stand together against the dominant castes. They should be able to work independently in the panchayat and stop being benamis in the hands of the dominant castes. We Dalits need to focus on our progress, throwing off our subordination.

– Annammal, village panchayat president in
Madurai district, Tamil Nadu

Reservation has made little difference other than formal elections: it has not meant any real change for women other than their ability to move outside the home.

– Dalit women elected representatives,
Ahmedabad district, Gujarat

Annammal's appeal, seen above, highlights the need to persevere with the 'social revolution' that the panchayat system and reservations therein have started in India. The Gujarati panchayat representatives' more tempered assessment, however, pinpoints the current challenge: formal political authority does not equate to political power. While Dalit women are contesting and assuming positions in the panchayats, severe caste-class-gender obstructions operate to deny them the opportunity to exercise political authority. This debilitating context compromises Dalit women's ability to deliver more gender and caste responsive development outcomes, and circumscribes the space in which they can reshape underlying socio-economic inequalities. In fact, the caste-class-gender nexus precludes most women from asserting their right to political participation in the first place. More broadly, it limits these women's ability to fulfil the panchayats' core objectives: that is, equitable development and, ultimately, social justice.

This research study aimed to generate data on Dalit women's experiences of accessing and enjoying their right to political participation in Panchayati Raj through reserved seats. This included looking at the women's responsiveness to Dalit and women's development needs, and the steps they took to transform inequitable social relations. Particular attention was paid to the enabling and disabling factors that facilitated or hindered the 200 Dalit women's access to, participation in and impact on rural panchayats in Gujarat and Tamil Nadu. These were largely women who had to juggle household responsibilities with remunerative work in addition to their panchayat duties. The women and their families had little to no political knowledge or experience in the panchayats, and had relatively low levels of education and socio-political networks. The analysis also focused on the role of state institutions in both preventing and responding to cases of obstructions against these women, including discrimination and violence.

A narrative thread that runs through this book is that Dalit women faced tremendous struggles in accessing the panchayats and, if they were successful, in asserting their right to active, free and meaningful participation in local governance. Power often remained steadfastly in the hands of dominant caste men and, to a lesser degree, Dalit men. The former were intent on advancing their socio-economic and political authority and interests through the panchayats and, more broadly, maintaining the power inequalities embedded in the patriarchal caste-based social structure. The latter worked to reinforce the male-dominated 'public sphere' and traditional patriarchal order, as well as advancing their own political interests. Both groups of men appropriated the women's role and authority in the panchayats. They used Dalit women benami representatives and a diverse range of obstructions to undermine the ability of the reservation system to empower Dalit women and enable their equal participation in governance, thus reinforcing the patriarchal caste system, which the panchayat system sought to weaken.

Being a participatory governance structure, Panchayati Raj has the potential to transform political institutions and development programmes and make them more inclusive, accountable and responsive. This structure could also contribute to the eradication of age-old structural discrimination and injustice. Spaces are opening "for women to come to occupy different categories [wherein they are] expected to enact roles that make them agents in influencing the developmental and democratic outcomes".[1] However, legal, political, social and economic structures continue to be driven by informal power hierarchies that reinforce caste, class and gender inequalities. Discrimination, exclusion and violence against Dalits are built into these structures to protect dominant castes' economic and political interests. State impunity, manifested in denying Dalit women access to justice, further reinforces this situation. As Mohanty stated, "[s]ituations of chronic poverty together with rigid caste hierarchies, entrenched patriarchy and an apathetic bureaucracy have given rise to a situation where women have failed to participate in a meaningful way."[2] The underlying causes for the exclusion of Dalit women remain unaddressed, thus precluding the political system's progression towards its goals, including enabling Dalit women to assert their human rights.

Examples of individual change occurring amidst this constraining context, however, speak of the potential for further political and social reform, for Dalit women show tremendous strength, passion and a readiness to seize opportunities and carve out spaces to impact development outcomes and their social landscape.

Phases of Political Participation Process

ACCESS

The election process continues to be marked by strong, caste-based patriarchal control. As Mohanty points out, "who will stand for election is a matter rarely decided by the women. The 'politics' of representation in these invited spaces is a combination of local dominance, cultural codes of patriarchy and working of the local administrative bureaucracy."[3] Caste-based patriarchy heavily influenced Dalit women's decisions to contest panchayat elections. Most of the women were unable to freely decide whether to access the political sphere. Instead, their husbands and dominant caste men made this decision for them. Dominant castes also sought to engineer elections by consensus, thereby making the reservation policy redundant. The primary tool for this, and one generally used to control access to reserved panchayat seats, was benami or proxy politics – primarily played by the dominant castes. Dalit men were less likely to participate in benami politics, and were themselves occasionally acting at the behest of the dominant castes. Political parties also played a small role in benami politics, often in combination with dominant caste villagers, especially in the higher panchayat tiers where party politics were more pronounced. The effective use of benami candidature provided legitimised political space for dominant caste leaders to exploit Dalit women and reinforce their own interests, thereby adding to the suppression of these women. Dalit women thus provided a vehicle for traditional elites to maintain their control over panchayat authority and resources.

Benami politics aside, control over Dalit women was also achieved through the means of preventing or discouraging them from filing a nomination, or forcing or coercing them to withdraw their nomination. On the one hand, direct pressure was applied through personal attacks, both physical and verbal, reinforcing their low caste and gender status and undermining their capacity to govern. On the other hand, social norms – demanding women fulfil household roles and responsibilities, for example, or curtailing their freedom of movement in public – restricted the women's freedom to operate outside the private sphere of the home. Furthermore, obstructions arose from Dalit caste or sub-caste assertions against women candidates who were benamis for dominant castes. Identity politics, both within the Dalit community and those engineered by external (dominant caste) forces, thus influenced the electoral process. On the whole, Dalit men sought to ensure the women yielded to their authority in both the domestic and public domains. In contrast, dominant castes sought to retain control over panchayat authority and resources to protect their economic and political interests, alongside preserving hierarchical caste and gender relations. It is unsurprising then that most of the 17 per cent of women who failed to secure a panchayat post were independent candidates, and were educated, critical-minded, socially active and/or had a reputation for defending Dalit interests.

Only a minority of the women, approximately one-third, could independently and freely contest the elections. The election process evidenced a clear drive for authority by socially aware, motivated Dalit women. They sought to invest panchayat resources in the development of their community and others. Both personal factors, such as education, experience on social issues, prior good performance in the panchayats and political negotiation skills, and external factors including family support, good relationships with other villagers, economic stability and their family's political contacts, enabled the women to access panchayat positions. At the same time, their low social, educational, economic and gender status rendered them vulnerable. Panchayat electoral campaigning drained many Dalit women's meagre income and resources. Multiple obstructions throughout the electoral process also wore on the women's resolve, including blatant breaches of the rule of law and democratic electoral process both on the election day, and following the announcement of the election results.

PARTICIPATION

Dominant caste male control over panchayat resources and ingrained caste-class-gender discriminatory attitudes continued to largely govern the experiences of Dalit women elected representatives in the panchayats. Three categories of political participation were evident in the Dalit women who participated in this research: benami participation; participation hindered by several obstructions impacting the women's responsiveness to their panchayat constituencies; and participation in which women could overcome obstructions to a great extent. Around one-third of the elected Dalit women representatives could exercise their right to political participation in panchayat meetings and decision-making through speaking, raising issues and/or deciding on these issues. Two-thirds, however, were unable to freely and independently discharge their official responsibilities. The authority that presidents, in particular, were expected to have and wield was instead appropriated and used by others. Thus, just as men determined who had access to representation, they also dictated what representation meant in practice – dominant caste men and, to a lesser extent, Dalit men and political parties controlled by dominant castes were the real sources of authority in many Dalit women headed panchayats. When dependent on others, women mainly turned to their husbands or other male relatives; this included asking for advice, making decisions and capacity development. However, it should be remembered that dominant castes often worked through the women's husbands, using Dalit men to direct their wives' decisions on panchayat matters. Ultimately, it was clear that a dominant caste-gender nexus exercised control over elected Dalit women representatives and, through them, the panchayats.

The role and influence of political parties on Dalit women's political participation clearly intensified from the village to district level, as did power struggles for political visibility, status and access to resources. Women elected representatives at the union/ taluka and district panchayats were required to participate within the agenda of the party whose ticket on which they were elected or on whose support they relied. The ability to function actively and effectively within this framework relied on various factors, including the women's knowledge about public affairs and socio-political networks. Several women readily used both their own and their husbands' political connections when exercising their political authority, while also seeking to maintain their independence from political influence. Regardless of these strengths, however, political actors played an equivocal role in supporting women elected representatives to overcome obstructions: they often made a pretence of support but either did not rock the caste-power boat, or did not enforce their own order to cooperate with the Dalit women elected representatives when they took action against lower level political party actors.

Dalit organisations and movements worked to support Dalit women through strengthening their organisational, negotiation and public speaking skills, and advised them on decisions in order to support their effective functioning and strengthen development outcomes for Dalits. SHGs, mahila sanghas, NGOs and youth associations also played a role, albeit a minor one. The findings of this research call for civil society groups to step up their support in advancing the objectives of local governance and, in particular, to increase their efforts to ensure an enabling environment for Dalit women's political empowerment.

Like in struggles to access panchayat institutions, gender, caste and class inequalities were also behind impingements on Dalit women's free and meaningful political participation. On the one hand, one saw the complete appropriation of benami representatives' political authority. On the other hand, the restrictions on and Dalit women's exclusions from active participation in panchayat council meetings, as well as obstructions to the completion of their statutory duties in panchayat administration reinforced the gender and caste norms that circumscribed their political participation in the first place. Caste-based dominance over panchayat activities was often achieved through a combination of socio-economic and political power; for example, dominant castes refusing to share information that would enhance the women's administrative capabilities. The most powerful tools used to obstruct Dalit women elected representatives, however, were the no confidence motions which dominant castes used to threaten, attempted to pass or actually passed against panchayat presidents. These motions aimed to instil fear in Dalit women elected representatives in order to curb their independent decision-making. They sent a clear message that political participation did not change the women's 'low' caste-class-gender status and power. Mohanty observed the following while exploring the problems that women come up against when they ignore or infuriate their families and society by efforts to actively participate in panchayat governance: "the choices that women might exercise in fulfilling their ambition are hijacked by the state and the larger society to keep women confined to what the culture demands of them."[4]

Not surprising then, nearly 90 per cent of the Dalit women elected representatives felt they were treated differently than other elected representatives in their panchayats. They attributed this discrimination and abuse primarily to their status as women and Dalits. The complex methods of segregation and discriminatory practices prevalent in the panchayat offices largely mirrored practices of 'untouchability' prevailing in the villages. Identities imbued with additional negative connotations, such as widows or separated women, exacerbated discriminatory practices. So too did the women's poor economic status, illiteracy, benami status, lack of knowledge about panchayat administration or outspokenness on social issues. It was through such discrimination that the formal panchayat system was made subservient to local community power structures, effectively reinforcing rather than transforming unequal power relations. In fact, discrimination operated as a form of justification when subverting democratic politics to fulfil one's own caste and gender interests. The backlashes against Dalit women for exercising their right to political participation in contradiction of gender and caste norms also sought to replicate and preserve the unequal social power relations that exist both within and outside the panchayats. This protected dominant caste interests and ensured the continuance of their socio-economic control.

IMPACT

Many Dalit women elected representatives could not exert a substantial enough influence in the panchayats to ensure development benefits for their communities, though many did put forward Dalit interests. Caste and political party pressures dominated development decisions at all levels of the panchayats. Consequently, most resources and development benefits continued to be channelled to dominant caste communities, and Dalit women elected representatives' responsiveness to their constituencies was limited by the co-option of their powers by others, alongside the lack of effective accountability mechanisms. Similarly, in terms of social impact, a few assertive Dalit women leaders did generate some shifts in their own self-perception, their status in their families, and sometimes in the Dalit or dominant caste communities. However, these shifts generally did not result in broader transformations of caste or gender prejudices, or a reduction in discriminatory practices. This reality contrasts sharply with the statement of the then prime minister Manmohan Singh on the impact of reservations for women in local governance, where he claimed that the reservation policy "has brought about a significant shift in public policy and in social attitudes towards women."[5]

The generation of more caste and gender-responsive development outcomes and social change through local panchayat posts requires Dalit women elected representatives to take up both women's *practical and strategic gender needs*, and Dalits' *practical and strategic caste-class needs*. Of the three levels of outcomes observed, the first was Dalit women elected representatives enabling some positive development benefits for individual Dalits and women through their participation in panchayat meetings and monitoring the implementation of development schemes. Their actions addressed more practical needs such as housing, health and road services. However, less commonly were they able to alter underlying power inequalities through, for example, enabling access to land or employment for Dalits and women.

A second level of outcomes relates more to how practical and strategic needs are realised in terms of changing institutional rules and resource allocations in favour of Dalits and women. On this front, there was little success. The women's ability to generate development outcomes remains significantly limited by the implementation of the Panchayati Raj system, including the lack of a full devolution of functions, powers and resources to the local level. Within this limited context, there was little evidence to suggest that the Dalit women panchayat representatives could significantly increase attention and resources to address the critical livelihood needs of Dalits and women. Most women did not have decision-making power over the use of panchayat revenue, development and welfare funds. Dominant caste male monopolisation of panchayat resources and benefits instead continued through the channelling of development benefits to their communities, and securing personal commissions and contracts for the same. Most women were also restricted in their ability to ensure the equitable distribution of panchayat funds, participate in gram sabhas, and monitor the use of panchayat funds or implementation of development works.

The third level of change would see the restructuring of gender and caste social relations with a view to social equality and justice. This research evidenced little structural change as an outcome of Dalit women's political participation. Entrenched caste interests, linked to dominant caste exercises of socio-political power and control over resources, prevented strategic caste-class needs from being realised through the panchayats. Thus, there was little change in the women's ability to participate in decision-making processes at the village level or higher. Changes in support patterns, respect and the attitudes of dominant castes and men towards some Dalit women panchayat representatives appeared to be more transitional, for they were based on 'positional' respect – that is, respect attached to the post and not necessarily to the person occupying said post – and efforts to secure personal interests. This respect did not include the recognition of Dalit women's power and authority, especially as panchayat heads. Moreover, a negative effect of Dalit women's political participation was increased factionalism among the Dalit community because of dominant caste instigated divisions. Similarly, Dalit women's presence as local panchayat representatives did not have any significant impact on structural relations at the family and community levels. The small number of women who experienced changes at the personal and family level – including increased self-confidence, social contacts and freedom of movement and higher status within the family – were counter-balanced by women who were benamis for their husbands, and whose increased dependency on male family members reinforced gender norms. Caste and gender hierarchies were similarly reinforced when women experienced socio-economic losses, including the extreme vulnerability caused by harassment, threats and violence.

This research nevertheless suggests some important positive developments. Greater freedom of speech in both family and public spaces emerged as one of the most significant outcomes of Dalit women's active political participation. Women who were assertive, independent and able to use their political authority to bring about some development impact also noted positive changes in the social attitudes and respect they were accorded. These developments resulted in further benefits that facilitated other rights, such as greater freedom of expression, movement and public participation. These developments did not, however, lead to any similar gains for Dalits or women as a whole. Some multiplier effect was noted, whereby other Dalit women increasingly recognised their own capacities for leadership and the potential for contributing to change. While this may be attributed in part to the 'positional' respect and economic benefits gained through the panchayats, the mobilisation of women for political and social activism beyond panchayat elections (such as for SHGs, women's groups, gram sabhas or social work) suggests a deeper shift. Similarly, where women freely and independently participated in the panchayats and created some development impact for their community, some women noted a greater confidence exhibited by Dalits as well as increased unity among them.

Enabling and Disabling Factors for Effective Political Participation

What the above analysis suggests is that a host of factors aid or hinder Dalit women's political participation through each stage of involvement in Panchayati Raj institutions. Enabling factors need to be further strengthened and institutionalised, while disabling factors require rectification if grassroots democracy promoting social and economic justice is to become a reality in India.

DISABLING FACTORS

The extent of benami politics in the panchayats conceal the real holders of political power, and these politics are the central cause of Dalit women elected panchayat representatives' inability to access and exercise political power for better development and social justice outcomes. Benami control and negative reactions to Dalit women's independent assertions of political power tightly restricted the space for these women's participation. This in turn ensured the perpetuation of a dominant caste male culture in the panchayats and prohibited many women from using their political participation to raise and address strategic caste-class-gender needs. Dominant caste actors also sought to reinforce social norms of submissiveness, stifle political voice and control 'low' caste women. They sought to set up a formal political power structure that replicated and further consolidated their social and informal political power, acting in contradiction of the very purpose of decentralised governance. Some Dalit male family members and panchayat members also played a destructive role, seeking to advance their own interests through Dalit women elected representatives by appropriating their authority and reinforcing the idea that a women's place is within the private sphere of the family. Government refusal to recognise, monitor and oppose benami representation, as well as conduct that supports and reinforces the use of benamis, further entrenches this form of politics.

Benami politics combined with other external inhibiting factors, such as isolation from political or social associations, a lack of support from state institutions, families and community, and caste-class-gender based obstructions, prevent Dalit women elected representatives from exercising their authority for the development of their community. For many women, the obstructions they were forced to confront at all stages of the process were disempowering and debilitating, particularly when the obstructions came from dominant caste employers or other powerful figures, as well as the women's own communities.

These external factors proved even more detrimental to the women's efforts at political participation when they were reinforced by internal factors. A lack of education, often combined with insufficient access to information on panchayat administration and a lack of self-confidence, were major negative influences on political participation. This draws attention to the state's responsibility to provide information and capacity-building programmes for Dalit women representatives. Further hindrances included a lack of prior political experience and limited social and political contacts, militating against the women's attempts to find information and support to strengthen their political participation. Economic insecurity and dependence on dominant castes, low status in the caste-class-gender hierarchy and internalised discriminatory gender and caste norms were also critical barriers.

ENABLING FACTORS

On the bright side, a number of Dalit women who participated in this research demonstrated enormous tenacity and possessed the strength to overcome the debilitating context they faced and seize opportunities to access panchayat posts, actively participate in panchayat governance, and institute changes addressing practical and strategic gender-caste-class needs. Facilitating their responsiveness, effectiveness, efficiency and accountability in political life were a range of internal and external factors, the accumulation of which facilitated Dalit women's exercise of their substantive right to political participation. These internal and external factors must therefore be seen as determinants for Dalit women's effective access, participation and impact in Panchayati Raj.

Education and knowledge about the Panchayati Raj system gave some Dalit women elected representatives the requisite confidence to freely and actively engage in their panchayat responsibilities. The ability to comprehend panchayat documents, keep records and review panchayat accounts are obvious benefits, but education also affects social status to some degree, in terms of circumventing the social biases illiterate women face from other panchayat members and government officials. Education was thus a central enabling factor. So too was the knowledge provided through trainings by NGOs and the state, alongside the supportive information and guidance given by some husbands and family members.

Other internal factors, including self-confidence, political know-how, the ability to speak in public, articulate issues and negotiate, and to mobilise and influence others, proved highly valuable in gaining electoral support, holding political authority and fulfilling panchayat duties. The desire to serve their community and the drive for change that motivated many Dalit women also seemed very important to their perseverance despite obstructions. These factors are closely linked to the women's sense of 'power within' and to leadership skills which must be further cultivated and harnessed for Dalit women's effective political participation.

A series of external factors were also important enablers of Dalit women's political participation. A few women with previous panchayat experience, either personal or through a family member, benefited from the additional political knowledge, skills, confidence, support and political contacts necessary for effective participation. Previous engagement with social issues in the village, including as SHG leaders or engagement with NGOs, also provided similar benefits. In the same way, active political party membership for either the women or their families helped develop their knowledge and build allies for political participation. Two other prominent external enabling factors were the women's relative economic security and independence, and the support they received from various external actors. Women made more significant inroads into effective political participation through building good working relationships with and receiving support from their husbands and family members, the Dalit community, political parties and members of higher panchayat tiers, NGOs and support groups like SHGs, and government officials and the police.

These were also the factors behind Dalit women having the courage and wherewithal to seek redress for the obstructions they faced in the panchayats. Not all these factors needed to be present, but their accumulative presence made it easier for the women to exercise their political rights and overcome any obstacles encountered in the panchayats.

Responsiveness of the State

Considering the violations of a Dalit women's right to political participation and the associated rights detailed in this research, the Indian state appears to have failed to respect, protect and fulfil these women's human rights. Law enforcement machinery and the district administration repeatedly failed to prevent and adequately respond to the obstructions Dalit women elected representatives faced when carrying out their panchayat duties, thereby denying the women the right to an effective remedy. State actors repeatedly failed to properly administer the rule of law through implementing protective laws and ensuring access to formal channels of justice for legal violations of the women's political participation. In a complex society structured along highly unequal caste-class-gender lines, to make Dalit women entirely responsible for their right to political participation and the free and independent exercise of political power thereafter clearly points to an abdication of state duty.

Dominant caste power remained entrenched within systems of state governance and law enforcement, as well as society as a whole, thereby reinforcing the caste-class-gender norms driving obstructions in the first place. Dalit women's experiences in this inequitable social and political context, as well as their social conditioning, directed many to remain silent in the face of obstructions. Moreover, in the approximately one-quarter of cases where women sought redress for obstructions, there was often no justice. It is unsurprisingly that most women received unsupportive responses: most non-state actors approached were largely driven by dominant caste power in the locality and refused to support Dalit women in seeking effective redress for obstructions. Just over half of the responses from state actors, including the police, government officials and others, also suggest a breach of duties. This involved inaction, chasing the woman away, demanding a bribe, pressurising her not to file a complaint or refusing to investigate the matter. Dalit women most commonly approached government officials for recourse, and these officials were more likely to mobilise around the implementation of development works than redress the obstructions, exclusions and discrimination that Dalit women faced. Even for the former, effective responses were more likely when Dalit women persisted in the face of bureaucratic delays in granting development requests. Government officials were also often complicit in reinforcing dominant caste male power by their discriminatory treatment towards Dalit women, and ignoring or supporting the gender and caste-based discrimination they witnessed. Thus, experiences of state officials being responsive, aiding women in filing complaints, advising them or acting to resolve obstructions were far from the norm.

Major gaps in the process of Dalit women asserting their right to political participation arguably lie in the state's interpretation and implementation of law and policy. The state's lack of accountability includes restricting the scope of a government official's duties concerning panchayat functioning, such that the officials neither monitor nor act to ensure the equitable implementation of the reservation policy, and fail to be proactive in preventing a recurrence of policy breaches that marginalise Dalit women. The police also failed to enforce the law when it went against the interests of dominant castes. A lack of accountability was further demonstrated in the police and government officials' failure to investigate or recognise violations of the rights of Dalit women, take measures to bring perpetrators to justice and provide Dalit women with effective remedies.

Police and government officials continue to interpret and apply policies and laws on the basis of caste and gender. Steeped in a context of power hierarchies and structural discrimination, state agents may use their positions to project their (male, dominant caste) power rather than protecting citizen rights. The result is that instead of supporting the realisation of the goals of an equitable distribution of resources and reduction of social inequalities, the system of decentralised governance continues to reinforce dominant caste patriarchal power and authority. A dominant construction of caste and gendered participation manipulates state institutions and shapes participation. This has a significant impact in terms of state responsibility and what is needed to truly actualise the Panchayati Raj system and reservations therein. As Mohanty discusses in relation to women and their access to meaningful political spaces through panchayats:

> Stereotyped understandings of women's public roles restrict their participation in invited [state-created] spaces, so long as the state – in its role as space-maker – acts as a putatively neutral facilitator of this participation. The state sides with the dominant social

forces, groups and individuals to avoid conflicts. The process take[s] place in such a manner that women are excluded from its sphere. A dominant construction of gendered participation manipulates the state institutions and shapes participation, and is [premised] upon four critical aspects of participation: wisdom, space, power and voice.[6]

State actors are not 'neutral facilitators' in this process. They have human rights obligations to actively monitor, implement and enforce the reservations system in letter and in spirit. This issue lies at the core of the responsiveness required to give greater substance to the reservation system and thereby support Dalit women's meaningful political participation.

Instances where government officials worked alongside Dalit women presidents, by contrast, demonstrated great potential for the effective participation of Dalit women in the panchayats when provided sufficient space, capacity development and support. Some women showed a strong aptitude for using the political system itself to overcome obstructions to their effective participation, including persistent activism, a strong presence in the panchayat council, appeals to different political institutions and individuals, and network-building. Several Dalit women were driven by the need for justice and change, exposing themselves to significant risks and equipping themselves with the political skills and knowledge required to take charge of their panchayat posts and drive Dalit development programmes. These women cannot carry this burden alone. Adequate support and institutional reforms are needed to assist the restructuring of power they are working towards.

Emerging Issues

There is no doubt that the system of local governance, with mandated quotas for socially marginalised groups, has enabled Dalit women across the country to take up *en masse* political posts that directly influence economic, political and social developments. The legal and policy changes that have enabled this situation are not in question. There are, however, some major myths or assumptions about the reservations system, particularly about the political participation of Dalits and women, that need to be recognised and exposed in order to develop more realistic strategies for sustainable political, social and economic change.

POLITICAL EMPOWERMENT AND SOCIAL TRANSFORMATION

A common myth is that *the election of large numbers of Dalit women to panchayats posts through reservations leads or equates to the political empowerment of these women.* As an assistant director of panchayats in Tamil Nadu said, "the reservation system helps the policy of social justice. Only through reservations can equality come. We strongly believe that only through reservations will the marginalised and women get the power due to them." Dalit women expressed an almost unanimous support for the reservation system. They saw reservations as the key means to equal political participation. As a group of Dalit women elected representatives from Cuddalore district, Tamil Nadu shared, "Only through reservations, equality will be realised and women and the oppressed can be empowered." Dissent only came from those disillusioned with benami politics and the obstructions entrenched in the reservations system that work to reinforce women's subordination.

This research demonstrates that a Dalit woman's election to a panchayat post does not guarantee her access to and free use of the institutional power and resources implied by said post. For most Dalit women elected representatives, their political power was usurped by dominant caste males both inside and outside the panchayat and, to a lesser extent, by Dalit men. This also addresses another common myth that prevails: *that Dalit women are mostly benamis for their husbands, as in the case of other caste women.* Caste's stranglehold on political power in the panchayats is made abundantly clear throughout this research: 59 per cent of all the women interviewed were benamis, and of them, less than one-fifth were benamis for their husbands. Coercion to act as benamis aside, dominant castes also restricted other women's efforts towards independent functioning through persistent obstructions and by manipulating caste-class-gender norms to maintain and perpetuate their own socio-political power and control. This extended into the state system where the bureaucracy and police also proved to be major hurdles for Dalit women to overcome.

Another unfounded assumption exposed by this research concerns the idea that *elected Dalit women representatives can ensure that Dalit and women's development needs are met through the panchayats*. In reality, caste-class-gender discrimination means that few Dalit women elected representatives were able to exert any substantial influence in the panchayats to enhance social justice or facilitate the fulfilment of Dalit women's, Dalits' or women's development needs. There remains a gross underestimation of the obstructions that Dalit women face in claiming their place as equal representatives in panchayat governance. These struggles cut across all actors – state and non-state – and all levels – personal, familial and societal – including social norms which effectively keep Dalit women under dominant caste patriarchal control. The caste-class-gender nexus must be recognised and appreciated in order to institute adequate measures to counter it. This in itself is a fundamental prerequisite to creating space for Dalit women to claim and exercise political authority.

The insufficient recognition given to the pervasiveness of the barriers confronting Dalit women is clear from another common myth concerning social change, that *the social transformation of power relations between Dalit women, Dalit men and dominant caste men can occur through political and legislative acts like reservations in the panchayats*. Legal and policy measures fail without concomitant measures that address the root causes of Dalit women's political exclusion; that is, measures that address power inequalities. This is particularly the case where informal, traditional power structures hold sway. Equally relevant is the assumption that *Dalit women's presence in the panchayats instigates more inclusive government policy and results in a positive evolution of social attitudes towards them*. It is evident in this research that there is currently neither a political space nor a supportive environment that enables Dalit women's assertions of their own needs or those of their community, let alone one that allows them to influence and shift the structural hierarchies upon which their exclusion is built.

All these myths and assumptions relate to an inadequate recognition of and responsiveness to the needs and dynamics of any transformation of power relations, particularly one that contends with the historic suppression and exclusion of a social group like Dalit women. This is at the core of the reason why the potential of the Panchayati Raj system has not yet been fully realised. Over two decades after the *73rd Constitutional Amendment Act 1993* was passed, gaps prohibiting its full execution continue to require further attention.

It has been asserted that "empowerment cannot transcend power relations; it is enmeshed in relations of power at all levels of society."[7] Processes of empowerment engage with the different aspects of power: self-perception as an active citizen, or power *within*; the collective ability to take action, or power *with*; and the enhancing power *to* initiate change. Power should be used in positive and transformative ways to reconstruct and renegotiate the power hierarchies between social groups and the structures underlying them. At the same time, empowerment is dependent on the very structural constraints and traditional practices it seeks to reshape.[8]

Thus, policy and technical solutions for change that leave the underlying power inequalities untouched are not enough. Empowerment with a view to social transformation demands more than a formal space for decision-making, or even a space for the renegotiation of power. It requires holistic strategies that, on the one hand, help marginalised Dalit women to understand the forces of subordination and inequality in their own lives; redress their educational, social and economic disabilities; develop goals and plans of action; and build movements expressing their collective identity in order to strengthen their bargaining position and challenge injustice. On the other hand, these strategies must engage with prevalent structures of power to *enable* the desired change. Redress of broader political and economic structures, social and cultural prejudices, and legal and political institutions are then necessary. Without adopting, implementing, monitoring and enforcing legal, policy, administrative, social and educational measures to deal with caste-based patriarchal practices, little sustained change is feasible. In fact, the potential for abuse of reservations to reinforce existing power inequalities makes them limited and even dangerous without actions to address the root causes of Dalit women's exclusion and building an enabling environment to permit a substantive transfer of power to these women.

ENABLING ENVIRONMENT FOR POLITICAL PARTICIPATION

The Indian state engineered the system of reservations in Panchayati Raj as part of its responsibility to govern its people through participatory democracy. Yet, the state prevalently views itself as a neutral facilitator. This myth, that *government officials in charge of monitoring the implementation of the Panchayati Raj system have no responsibility to deal with issues of caste-class-gender discrimination and violence*, must be challenged. So, too, must the broader misconception that *the state's responsibility to ensure that Dalits and Dalit women have access to the panchayats ends with providing reserved quotas for them and setting up instruments for the implementation of local governance* be challenged. What must be recognised are the caste-class-gender prejudices that exist within state structures. Police and government officials persist in interpreting and applying policies and laws that draw on caste and gender biases. This leads to a situation in which state action tends to reinforce rather than overturn traditional inequalities and injustices. The dominant belief that *caste-class-gender discriminatory norms exist solely in Indian society, and are not reinforced by the state*, is false. State implementers and enforcers cannot continue to act as idle bystanders. The Indian state must reconstruct its own role, moving away from being a neutral facilitator and becoming a proactive implementer and enforcer, thus ensuring accountability for the protection of Dalit women's right to political participation.

The state's legal obligation to respect, protect and fulfil Dalit women's right to political participation requires substantive, rather than merely formal, implementation.[9] It demands more than legislative and policy measures. The state is obliged to provide an enabling environment to ensure that Dalit women can realise this right. To do so it must, on the one hand, move to fully devolve functions, funds and functionaries to the panchayats so that they have effective political power and are able to discharge their duties and functions as local institutions of self-governance. On the other hand, the state's obligation extends to the fulfilment of other fundamental human rights which contribute to overcoming the barriers to equal political participation. These include the right to an effective remedy, to equality and non-discrimination, to information, and to a decent standard of living. There is a particular need to improve the economic conditions and socio-economic independence of Dalits in rural areas, both of which are necessary to facilitate their political participation. To do so, the state must set short and long-term goals for the development of Dalit women and their communities, alongside providing some financial support to Dalit women contesting panchayat elections.

Given that the reservation system is justified on the grounds of the historical discrimination and exclusion that marginalised social groups such as Dalit women have faced, further attention is required in three key areas: regular monitoring of the panchayats and the implementation of laws and development schemes; strengthening Dalit women's capacities; and instituting remedial measures to counter obstructions in the panchayats. Specific measures must be devised, including policy reforms or additional legal penalties to eliminate incentives for (forced) consensus panchayats, benami politics and the misuse of no confidence motions. Alongside training sessions targeted at strengthening the women's political, legal, financial and leadership capacities, there is a need for all government officials concerned with the panchayats, including election officers and the police, to understand and respond to issues of caste and gender discrimination and violence in the panchayats. The state should consider creating specific mechanisms at the state and district levels to oversee and ensure that support in the aforementioned three key areas reaches marginalised social groups participating in the panchayats. It might go further, as recommended by the National Commission for Scheduled Castes and Scheduled Tribes, and institute a mandatory process requiring that all three panchayati tiers prepare an SC development plan with a clear gender component. This plan should become a charter to work towards regarding the economic development of Dalits in the panchayats. Moreover, disaggregated data should be periodically provided on the functioning of Dalit women and other socially marginalised groups in the panchayats overall, and in reserved seats in particular. All this requires a strong political will.

As a formal state-structured space, it is inevitable that Panchayati Raj becomes a contested political space. Its potential threat to traditional caste structures and the interests of powerful dominant castes means its implementation will occasion opposition, manipulation and violations from those fearing a loss of their dominant position. Thus, those responsible for the implementation of Panchayati Raj must be prepared to struggle to enforce the system. State actors must critically analyse and test its implementation at each level. They must protect the Dalit women who access and participate in the panchayats, while simultaneously taking comprehensive measures to ensure an enabling environment for Dalit women to seize the opportunities the system provides. They must institute broad ranging awareness and education campaigns as well as economic and social programmes to support cultural shifts towards participatory and equitable democracy. And the state must be bold enough to impose strict legal sanctions against its own officials if they neglect to respond to complaints by persons for obstructions faced while accessing or participating in reserved panchayats. Direct intervention by local government officials, particularly those in higher echelons, in order to recognise women's legitimate interests can be a key enabler for women's agency in the political system.[10] In particular, officials must challenge the traditional social stereotypes that to date govern their own and societal interpretations of the reservation systems in local political participation. Any such process is long-term, but structures and processes that enable and monitor Dalit women's political participation must be put in place now to provide Dalit women a space in which they can create the change they need.

Conclusion

Panchayati Raj – with all its aims and ambitions – must be institutionalised, but must also be revisited with a view to the core concerns raised by this research. Structural factors of caste, class and gender that underlie the political, economic and social exclusion of Dalit women largely preclude them from taking up opportunities for political leadership, development and social change. While reservations have allowed the transfer of formal power in the panchayats to Dalit women, they are yet to endow these women with the actual power to drive development and social change. Further efforts are required on the policy level, but more so in creating and strengthening mechanisms and processes of implementation. To see a realisation of the vision of local governance engendered by the Indian Constitution, the government must continue to build on the reservation policy and enact comprehensive structural reforms to equalise caste-class-gender power bases. Essentially, the government must start within its own ranks, to ensure a political will to monitor and implement the Panchayati Raj system and reservations therein. Civil society also has key responsibilities here. Civil society organisations should build on the collective strength of Dalit women through various Dalit, women's, youth and social associations to mobilise and organise these women to participate in greater numbers in public issues. Alongside building their political knowledge of the panchayats and capacity for leadership and public decision-making, civil society organisations should provide direct support to women as they engage in the panchayats, including fostering collectives of Dalit women elected representatives.

There is no doubt that power has shifted in the past two decades. The space for Dalit women to assert their voice and agency as panchayat leaders has increased. However, it is fundamentally important to build an environment that is more supportive of these women's assertions and more responsive to their needs. Sustained systemic change requires that multiple state and non-state actors at the state and national levels work together to influence formal and informal local institutions of power and strengthen Dalit women's capabilities and leadership. Creative ways must be explored, foremost with Dalit women, but also with Dalit men and non-Dalits, to capitalise on the success stories of Dalit women's political leadership, and cultivate their growth.

Ultimately, these efforts must lead to a transformation in Dalit women's access to and control over key resources to ensure their equitable development. Concurrently, a societal culture of human rights that demands accountable governance and equality for all must emerge.

Notes

1. Mohanty, R., "Gendered Subjects, the State and Participatory Spaces: The Politics of Domesticating Participation in Rural India", in Cornwall, A. and Coelho, V.S.P. (eds.), *Spaces for Change: The Politics of Citizen Participation in New Democratic Arenas* (London: Zed Books, 2007), p. 80.
2. *Ibid*, p. 81.
3. *Ibid*, p. 85.
4. *Ibid*, p. 87.
5. Prime minister Manmohan Singh's speech at the East Asia Gender Quality Ministerial Meeting (New Delhi, 06.12.2007), reported in "We are Committed to Providing Quotas for Women in Governance", *The Hindu*, 07.12.2007.
6. Mohanty, supra note 1, p. 90.
7. Parpart, J., Rai, S. and Staudt, K., "Rethinking Em(power)ment: An Introduction" in Parpart, J., Rai, S. and Staudt, K. (eds.), *Rethinking Empowerment: Gender and Development in a Global/Local World* (London: Routledge, 2002), p. 4.
8. *Ibid*; Miller, V. et al, *Making Change Happen: Power: Concepts for Revisioning Power for Justice, Equality and Peace* (Washington DC: Just Associates, 2006).
9. CEDAW Committee, *General Recommendation No. 23: Political and Public Life*, UN Doc. HRI/GEN/1/Rev.5, para 8.
10. Mohanty, supra note 1, p. 93.

ACKNOWLEDGEMENTS

Gujarat State Team

STATE COORDINATOR
Manjula Pradeep, Executive Director, Navsarjan Trust, Sanand

RESEARCH ASSOCIATE
Satyendra Kumar, Young Professional on deputation from Dalit
    Foundation

GUJARAT JUNIOR RESEARCHERS
Madhu Vaghela
Ramila Parmar

GUJARAT FIELD INVESTIGATORS
Ashok Rathod
Chandrika Kristi
Dina Vankar
Gita Makwana
Hansa Makwana
Jaya Parmar
Kailash Parmar
Kanta Parmar
Madhu Koradiya
Mili Parmar
Natu Chauhan
Saroj Makwana

Tamil Nadu State Team

STATE COORDINATOR
R. Thilagam, Programme Director, Evidence, Madurai

TAMIL NADU JUNIOR RESEARCHERS
S. Kalaivani
I. Malarvizhi

TAMIL NADU FIELD INVESTIGATORS
R. Anandhavalli
K. Andichamy
G. Gajendran
S. Kausalya
S. Kribakaran
P. Lakshmi
S. Maharasi
S. Muthulakshmi
C. Panchavarnam
T. Alaghu Rani
L. Shyamala
A. Vincent Raj (Kathir)

State-level

GUJARAT OFFICE SUPPORT
Naresh Parmar, Navsarjan Trust

GUJARATI TRANSLATORS
Rajesh Parmar
Satyendra Kumar

TAMIL NADU FIELDWORK LOGISTICAL SUPPORT

M. Azhagesan, Programme Coordinator, Village Educational Service Association, Nagapattinam

S. Balasundaram, Thamaraipulam Panchayat President, Nagapattinam

M.A. Britto, Director, Vaan Muhil, Palayamkottai

T.A. Edison, Activist and Consultant, Virudhachalam

S. Janaki, Avinasi

R. Kanagaraj, Programme Coordinator, Kudisai Social Service Society, Thirunelveli

R. Karuppusamy, Director, Padi, Erode

C. Nambi, Director, Centre for Social Education and Development, Thiruppur

I. Pinaygash, Programme Associate, Vaan Muhil, Palayamkottai

TAMIL TRANSLATORS

Eugine Sebastine Rosario SJ

Freddie Xavier Joseph SJ

National Level

RESEARCH CONSULTANT

Christie Maria Joseph SJ, Director, Loyola Institute of Business Administration, Chennai

DATA ANALYSIS CONSULTANT

Prof. Shanmuga Vadivelu, Statistics Department, St Joseph's College, Trichy

PRINTING COORDINATOR (INDIA)

Cyril SJ, Director, Vaigarai Publishing House, Dindigul

DATA ENTRY

V. Nirmal Kumar, S. Ram Kumar, E. Suresh Kumar, Madurai

SECONDARY DATA CONTRIBUTION

Human Rights Research and Advocacy Foundation, Chennai

TYPING & OFFICE SUPPORT

L. Jenova Mary, A. Sahaya Sathya, IDEAS, Madurai

With special thanks to

Jebamalai Raja SJ, Director, IDEAS, Madurai

Tony Fernandes, Programme Coordinator, Dalit Research Programme, Justitia et Pax, The Netherlands for their encouragement and support in undertaking this research

Justitia et Pax, The Netherlands for sponsoring the research.